The Teacher's Grammar Book

James D. Williams
California State Polytechnic University, Pomona

LAWRENCE ERLBAUM ASSOCIATES, PUBLISHERS
1999   Mahwah, New Jersey   London

Illustrations by Margo Witkowsky, Communications Services, Governor's State University.

Lawrence Erlbaum Associates, Inc., Publishers
10 Industrial Avenue
Mahwah, NJ 07430

Cover design by Kathryn Houghtaling Lacey

Library of Congress Cataloging-in-Publication Data

Williams, James D. (James Dale), 1949–
The teacher's grammar book / James D. Williams.
p. cm.
Includes bibliographical references and indexes.
ISBN 0-8058-2272-0 (alk. Paper)
1. Englich language—Grammar. 2. English language—Grammar—Study and teaching. I. Title.
PE1112.W46 1999
428'.007—dc21   98–35223
                                                          CIP

Books published by Lawrence Erlbaum Associates are printed on
acid-free paper, and their bindings are chosen for strength and durability.

Printed in the United States of America
10 9 8 7 6 5 4 3 2 1

The Teacher's Grammar Book

Contents

Preface

The Teacher's Grammar Book is intended for students preparing to become teachers, for those who already have their teaching credentials, and for general readers who find language fascinating. It emerged out of my work in linguistics but was most influenced by the education students I have taught since 1981, when I offered my first grammar class for teachers at UCLA. *The Teacher's Grammar Book* has several goals, but one of the more important is to present an overview and exploration of the grammars that dominate language study. Chapter 1 therefore examines traditional grammar; Chapter 2 phrase-structure grammar; Chapter 3 transformational-generative grammar; and Chapter 4 cognitive grammar.

At the beginning of each chapter, a summary of historical factors contextualizes the individual grammars. Taken together, these summaries explain why we have different approaches to the study of language and how the approaches are related. Chapter 5 examines dialects, focusing on Black English Vernacular and Chicano English. One overarching goal of this book is to help readers have fun with language and grammar. Toward that end, the example sentences and those in the many activities loosely construct a comical story about several characters who are mutually embarked on life's journey.

A reality of teacher preparation today is that most students in credential programs know very little about grammar. Even though grammar instruction commonly begins in third grade, the methodology used ensures almost no retention. In recognition of this fact, *The Teacher's Grammar Book* takes as given that most readers must start at the beginning. The discussion of traditional grammar in Chapter 1 provides a review of terms and ideas that form the groundwork for sentence analyses. It starts with basic concepts, such as nouns and verbs, subjects and predicates, and the difference between form and function.

This chapter also sets the tone for the entire text. *The Teacher's Grammar Book* is not just about grammar—it also is about teaching grammar. Developed from a linguistic perspective, it takes the position that traditional grammar has little value aside from its terminology for sentence analysis because it is prescriptive rather than descriptive and because, being Latin-based, it is not particularly accurate when applied to English. In addition, *The Teacher's Grammar Book* recognizes that grammar instruction in our schools is largely intended to help students become better writers and speakers. There is little evidence, however, that studying grammar per se accomplishes this goal, in part because those features of language that we most readily attribute to poor speaking and writing are almost entirely in the realm of usage, not grammar. Consequently, this text devotes considerable space to analyzing and discussing common errors in usage, and it offers advice on a wide range of usage conventions that are congruent with formal Standard English.

Chapter 2 builds on Chapter 1 by showing how to use the groundwork of terminology for sentence analysis. It begins with quite simple sentences, such as *Dogs bark*, but moves on fairly quickly to more complex constructions. This chapter has several aims, one obviously being to immerse readers in the analytical techniques of phrase-structure grammar. An equally important aim is to help readers understand that there is no single approach for looking at language. As sentences become more complex, we must enhance our analytical tools to examine them. By the end of the chapter, students have the ability to analyze quite challenging sentences.

Chapter 3 introduces transformational-generative grammar and explores some of the factors that led to its development. The goal is not to present a detailed discussion of the grammar as an analytical tool but rather to familiarize readers with its general features through application of a few transformation rules. Deemed more important are the theoretical characteristics of the grammar, such as its reliance on a rule-governed model of mind, the language acquisition device, the distinction between deep structure and surface structure, and the competence/performance construct. Many texts neglect any consideration of the problems inherent in transformational-generative grammar, but *The Teacher's Grammar Book* examines them in some detail, suggesting that the generative component creates difficulties that are so difficult to overcome that it seriously weakens this entire approach to language study.

These difficulties are at the heart of cognitive grammar, which is the topic of Chapter 4. Although cognitive grammar emerged during the mid-1980s, it is not nearly as well-known as phrase-structure or transformational grammars. In most respects, cognitive grammar is not a "grammar" at all; rather, it is an attempt to develop a model of how the mind operates that includes language and grammar as important components. It rejects the assumption in transformational-generative grammar that grammar can provide a theory of language and mind. The grammar portion of this approach actually is phrase-structure grammar. Phrase-structure grammar, because it emphasizes description rather than theory, provides the most appropriate tool for talking about the intricacies of language. The theoretical portion is grounded in cognitive science and a perspective on mental operations known as *connectionism*.

Together, these four chapters provide a comprehensive overview of grammar, language, and usage that has been tailored to the needs of teachers and credential candidates. They are complemented by Chapter 5, which introduces dialects and focuses on Black English Vernacular and Chicano English. Everyone speaks a dialect, but our schools implicitly or explicitly attempt to move students toward the dialect we know as formal Standard English, the dialect of writing and the educated elite. For most students, this effort is fraught with difficulties because instruction must attempt to modify language patterns acquired from birth, patterns that are very resistant to change. The challenge is exacerbated by the fact that, increasingly, students who speak nonstandard dialects lack the motivation to adopt Standard English. Among African- and Mexican-Americans, the lack of motivation is particularly strong, for the shift toward bidialectalism is often viewed as a loss of personal and cultural identity. This chapter explores these issues, and it also looks briefly as some of the characteristic features of Black English and Chicano English grammars.

ACKNOWLEDGMENTS

Many people have figured significantly in the writing of this book, and it would be impossible to acknowledge all of them. I am very grateful to all the fine students who have shared my enthusiasm for grammar over the years and who have willingly followed me down often twisting paths of syntactic analysis. I appreciate a great deal the many helpful suggestions of the reviewers of the manuscript for this book, Irene Brosnahan, Illinois State University; Larry Andrews, University of Nebraska - Lincoln; and several anonymous reviewers. I am grateful to my linguistics professors at the University of Southern California—Jack Hawkins, Steve Krashen, and Sue Foster Cohen—who were inspiring teachers. I am ever grateful to my friend and editor at Lawrence Erlbaum, Naomi Silverman, who did not complain when I fell behind schedule. But most of all, I am grateful to my wife, Ako, and my son, Austin, just because being with them brings me so much joy.

—*James D. Williams*
Chicago, Illinois

1

Traditional Grammar

THE ORIGINS OF GRAMMAR

Like so many other elements of our lives, the formal study of grammar began in ancient Greece, probably around the 6th century B.C. The Greeks loved language, and they loved classifying the world into its components. They also were concerned that their language was degenerating from the Greek of Homer's Golden Age. These factors combined with the rise of democracy and the need

1

for a better-educated citizenry to make reading and writing instruction key parts of Greek education. Young students were taught by a *grammatistes,* who provided instruction in the alphabet (*grammata*), reading, writing, and grammar. A *grammatistes* also gave instruction in other subjects, such as music and mathematics. When students were proficient readers and writers, they were deemed *grammatikos*, or literate.

An important part of this early instruction was the study of Homer, not only because of the moral messages in his work but also because it represented the ideal form of language that students were expected to mimic. The goal was to preserve the "purity" of Homeric Greek. Thus, Greek education developed a prescriptive stance with respect to language and grammar, defining notions of "correct" and "incorrect" language use in terms of adherence to literary norms that, at best, characterized Greek 600 or 700 years in the past. The ancient Greeks assumed that the structure of their language embodied universals of human thought and language. The most influential grammar books of the Greek period were produced by Dionysius Thrax in the 2nd century B.C. and Apollonius Dyscolous in the 2nd century A.D.

The attempt to preserve Homeric Greek was predestined to failure because change is an inherent characteristic of language; the only languages that don't change are dead. Moreover, there is no way to reverse changes once they occur, so the efforts of the teachers were futile in that respect. In time, Greek divided into two forms; classical Greek, which was used in writing; and Demotic Greek, which was used in speech. When, in 1958, the great modern Greek author Nikos Kazantzakis published a sequel to Homer's *Odyssey*, the work was strongly criticized by politicians and academics because it was in Demotic.

The prescriptive focus of Greek grammar was maintained in Rome because the Romans imported nearly all of the Greek educational system. Sicily and much of southern Italy had been colonized by Greeks when Rome was just another tribal village where education was provided to sons by their fathers.[1] As Rome started to emerge as a center of power, the Romans had to develop a more formalized system of education. They naturally turned to the Greeks, their more experienced neighbors. Grammar, therefore, was also a central part of Roman education, and students studied both Greek and Latin poets as models, following the Greek tradition of basing grammar study on literary texts. The most influential grammars of the Roman period were written by Donatus in the 4th

---

[1]Although the example of Sappho (perhaps the most famous lyric poet in ancient Greece, and a female) suggests that women could attain high degrees of literacy in the ancient world, she was an exception. Girls were educated at home in the responsibilities of household duties. Only boys had the opportunity to receive formal schooling.

century A.D. and Priscian in the 6th century A.D. Their works were so popular that they were used throughout the Middle Ages.

It is important to stress that the educational system we have today is very much a product of Greco-Roman tradition. Even though educational reforms have modified certain features of formal education, and even though in the United States we attempt to educate everyone through a compulsory system, the core of what our schools are about is linked to the distant past. At best, American education represents the evolution of the Greco-Roman model to fit our society. Children begin their education by learning the alphabet just as their counterparts did in the ancient world. American students study literature, history, and math—the liberal arts—with the goal of becoming well-rounded people. Ancient formal education had little place for vocational training, and neither does ours.

The significance of the Greco-Roman education system with respect to grammar was at least twofold. First, as the Empire expanded, it provided schools or modified curricula in existing schools to meet Roman standards. Grammar instruction throughout Europe therefore had a coherent orientation that emphasized adherence to a literary norm. Second, after the Empire collapsed, the fragmented European societies had a new Golden Age—the time of the Empire—and Latin was their bridge to a more civilized and sophisticated past. Thus, even as the Latin language was changing rapidly into Spanish, Italian, French, and Portuguese, the schools continued to use Latin as the basis of instruction and continued to teach Latin grammar. Eventually, Latin ceased being the language of instruction, but Latin grammar was applied to the vernacular languages. It was even applied to English, which is not a Latin-based language but instead is Teutonic.

Throughout the Greek and Roman periods, grammar and logic were distinct areas of study. But during the Middle Ages, this distinction disappeared as language scholars connected the two areas in an attempt to make language as orderly as logic. Initially, Latin was viewed as the logically normal form of speech, but the rapid development of mathematics during the medieval period led to more formal logical structures that increasingly became the norm by which to measure language. Scholars began comparing the natural language of speech to the artificial languages of math and logic and asserted that natural language should conform accordingly. We see the outcome of this effort in the argument that double negatives, such as *He don't do nothing*, are incorrect because two negatives make a positive (which is certainly true in math).

The appeal of order may have been the result of fundamental changes in the way Europeans viewed the world. Before 1250 A.D., people viewed reality in qualitative terms. For example, the cardinal directions were not viewed merely as points on a map—they had a more profound signification. As Crosby (1997) noted:

> South signified warmth and was associated with charity and the Passion of Jesus. East, toward the location of the terrestrial paradise, Eden, was especially potent, and that is why churches were oriented east–west with the business end, the altar, at the east. World maps were drawn with east at the top. "True north" was due east, a principle to which we pay respect every time we "orient" ourselves. (p. 38)

The shift to a quantitative world view may well have altered reactions to language that deviated from both the literary norm and assumed connections between speech and logic. We know that during this same period scholars produced a variety of general grammars that were different from their predecessors in that they attempted to show how linguistic structure was based on logical principles. What emerged was the view that people who spoke "incorrectly" were not only violating the rules of the grammar but also were being *illogical*. In a world increasingly dominated by logic rather than faith, the label of "illogical" was damning—and still is.

During the 18th century, two other factors influenced work in grammar: prestige and socioeconomic status. The spread of education and industrialization created greater socioeconomic mobility, which in turn led to a mingling of people from different backgrounds that had not been possible for more than 1,000 years. Increasing numbers of people from the growing middle class started having regular contact with the upper class. Although in England both upper-class and middle-class people spoke the same language, there were noticeable differences in pronunciation, structure, and vocabulary—what we term *dialect*—much like the differences we notice in the United States between speakers from Mississippi and California. Because the upper-class dialects identified one with prestige and success, mastering the upper-class speech patterns became very desirable, and notions of grammar became more normative than ever.

Language scholars during this time suffered from a fundamental confusion that had its roots in the notion of linguistic decay first formulated by the Greeks. They noted that well-educated people wrote and spoke good Latin; those who were not so well educated, on the other hand, made mistakes. These scholars did not recognize that reproducing a dead language is an academic exercise, and they applied their observation to modern languages, concluding that languages are preserved by the usage of educated people. In this view, those without education and culture corrupt the language with their deviations from the established norm. Accordingly, the discourse forms of books and upper-class conversation represented an older and purer level of language from which the speech of the common people had degenerated.

It is this legacy that teachers bring into today's classrooms whenever they embrace the prescriptive notions of school grammar. Out of this background emerged strong views regarding what we term *nonstandard* and *formal standard* language. We discuss these terms in more detail on pages 6–7, but for now it is sufficient to note that they do not describe two different forms of language use by two different groups of people. At their simplest, formal Standard English is the language of published texts and a relatively small group of speakers, whereas nonstandard is the language of poorly educated persons, people of low socioeconomic status (SES), and speakers of certain dialects. A more sophisticated analysis, however, indicates that language use is best characterized as a continuum, with nonstandard on one end and formal standard on the other. People commonly change positions along this continuum as a result of changed circumstances, and there is a great deal of overlap, such that we often see standard features appearing in the language of nonstandard speakers, and vice versa.

PRESCRIPTIVE GRAMMAR IN OUR SCHOOLS

In nearly every instance, school grammar is traditional grammar. It is concerned primarily with correctness and with the categorical names for the words that make up sentences. Thus, students study grammatical terms and certain "rules" that are supposed to be associated with correctness. Grammar instruction is justified on the assumption that students who speak or write expressions such as *He don't do nothin'* will modify their language to produce *He doesn't do anything* if only they learn a bit more about grammar. Consequently, like their ancient Greek counterparts, our grammar schools—as the name implies—give much attention to grammar, usually beginning instruction in the second or third grade. Regardless of the grade level of students, the instruction follows the same routine, with students using workbooks or handouts to complete exercises that ask them to identify nouns, verbs, adjectives, adverbs, and so forth, much in the same way that students in ancient Athens and Rome did.

We say that traditional grammar is prescriptive because it focuses on the distinction between what some people do with language and what they *ought* to do with it, according to a preestablished standard. For example, students who utter or write *He don't do nothin'* are told that they ought to use *He doesn't do anything*. The chief goal of traditional grammar, therefore, is perpetuating a historical model of what supposedly constitutes proper language. Those who teach traditional grammar have implicitly embraced this goal without recognizing that many of the assumptions that underlie school grammar are false. For example, both experience and research show that learning grammatical terms and completing grammar exercises have little effect on the way students use language.

In addition to its foundation on flawed assumptions, there are two fairly serious problems with adopting a prescriptive grammar. First, prescription demands a high degree of knowledge to prevent inconsistency, and few people have the necessary degree of knowledge. That is, when teachers make prescriptive statements concerning language, they must be certain that their own speech and writing does not violate the prescription. This seldom is the case. Even a casual observation of how people use language illustrates that deviations from the prescribed standard are common. We can observe teachers correcting students who use a construction such as *Fred and me went fishing* (the problem involves case relations, which we discuss on pages 16–18). The formal standard is *Fred and I went fishing*. But if these same teachers knock on a friend's door and are asked *Who is it?*, they will say *It's me*—even though this response violates the same convention. The formal standard is *It's I*.

This reality is related to the second problem, which is that everyone *acquires* language as an infant, and what we call the *home language* rarely matches the formal standard used in prescriptive grammar, which generally is *learned* in school. The illustration in Fig. 1.1 suggests how one's home language and the formal standard overlap in some areas, but not all. In addition, the two forms commonly compete with each other, as in the case of someone whose home language accepts *Fred and me went fishing* but who has learned that *Fred and I*

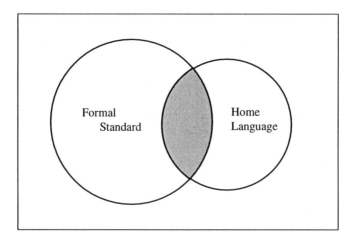

FIG. 1.1. Formal standard and home language. Some features of home language and formal Standard English overlap, but many do not.

went fishing is "correct." The gap between acquired language and the formal standard is normally narrowed through classroom instruction, reading, writing, and association with people who speak the formal standard. Unfortunately, such learning is slow and difficult. The home language acquired in infancy is so strong that in many situations—perhaps most—it dominates. As a result, one may have learned that *Fred and I went fishing* is preferable in most situations, but when it comes time to write or utter that statement, the home language wins the competition and one utters or writes *Fred and me went fishing*.

Although most teachers in our public schools continue to prescribe language, linguists dropped prescription long ago, replacing it with the concept of *appropriateness conditions*. This expression signifies that language use is situation specific and that there is no absolute standard of correctness that applies to all situations. People modify their language on the basis of circumstances and dominant conventions, which means that in some instances—as in the case of *It's me*—the preferred form of expression is technically nonstandard. Generally, what is appropriate (and acceptable) in one situation may not be appropriate (and acceptable) in another. However, this principal is not as clear-cut as we might wish because the issue of appropriateness is almost always unidirectional. Standard usage is acceptable under most conditions, but nonstandard is not. With the exception of a few nonstandard expressions that have become preferable to the standard, nonstandard usage is deemed appropriate only in informal conversations or notes among friends and family. It usually is deemed inappropriate for school work, the workplace, or any other public venue. Since the 1960s, some people have argued that students have a right to their own language and have urged schools to allow them to use nonstandard English for speaking and writing. For the most part our schools have rejected this argument, implicitly recognizing that it would hopelessly confound the blurred lines that separate public and private discourse.

An important goal of modern language study is to understand the conventions that govern appropriateness and public language. The largely unidirectional nature of appropriateness means that achieving this goal involves close attention to usage, to what differentiates standard from nonstandard. A central assumption is that formal language study must begin with the features of public discourse rather than private. As a result, much of what this text has to say about appropriateness and acceptability is tied to mastering standard usage conventions.

Traditional grammar is not well suited to such mastery. It does not meet the real need of teachers or students for a means of talking about, analyzing, and understanding language, and there are a number of reasons why it should be replaced in our schools today, just as it was replaced many years ago among scholars as a tool for analyzing language. Nevertheless, the classification system that traditional grammar developed has been incorporated into all newer grammars. Traditional grammar, on this account, always will play a role—albeit a limited one—in the study of language. Learning the names of the various constituents that make up sentences therefore remains an important part of language study, and the rest of this chapter takes up this task, setting the groundwork for more interesting analyses in the other chapters.

In addition, there is no denying that people judge one another on the basis of language. We do have a prestige dialect that to one degree or another accepts certain conventions and rejects others. These conventions usually don't involve grammar, but they do involve usage. We may wish that language prejudice were not so intense, but denying that it *is* does not provide a solution. For this reason, regular discussions of usage conventions appear throughout this text. They are designed to examine the nuances of usage rather than to be prescriptive, but it goes without saying that any notion of a standard presupposes some level of prescription. To reduce the inconsistency inherent in developing a text that focuses on description rather than prescription, discussions of standard usage conventions should be understood in terms of appropriateness. In situations that call for more formal language—such as school, certain jobs, writing, and so forth—standard conventions are more appropriate than nonstandard because they are more acceptable to a wider range of people. This admittedly controversial topic forms the basis for Chapter 5.

FORM AND FUNCTION IN GRAMMAR

Grammar deals with the structure and analysis of sentences. Any discussion of grammar, therefore, must address language on two levels, which we may think of as *form* and *function*. Sentences are made up of individual words, and these words fall into certain grammatical categories. This is their form. A word like *Macarena*, for example, is a *noun*—this is its form. A word like *jump* is a *verb*, a word like *red* is an *adjective*, and so on.

The form of a word is generally independent of a sentence.[2] Dictionaries are an exploration not only of meaning but also of form because they describe the grammatical category or categories of each entry. But language exists primarily as sentences, not individual words, and as soon as we put words into sentences they work together in various ways—this is function. For example, nouns can

---

[2]It is important to be a bit cautious here because many words change their classification on the basis of their function in a sentence. For example, *running* is a verb in some sentences (*Fred is running in the race*), but it has all the characteristics of a noun in others (*Running is good exercise*). The ability of words to change classification in this way enhances the richness of language—it also causes great confusion among students.

function as *subjects*, adjectives *modify* (supply information to) nouns, and verbs establish *predicates*.

Form and function are related in several ways. For example, on a simple level, the terms we use to describe grammatical form and function come from the Greco-Roman tradition. *Noun* comes from the Latin word, *nomen*, for name; *verb* comes from the Latin word, *verbum*, for *word*; *predicate* comes from the Latin word, *praedicare, to proclaim*. On a deeper level, the form of a given word often determines its function in a sentence—and vice versa. Traditional grammar usually describes form in terms of the *eight parts of speech*: *nouns, verbs, adjectives, adverbs, conjunctions, particles, prepositions*, and *articles*. This is a useful starting point. Likewise, traditional grammar identifies six functions that words may perform in sentences: *subject, predicate, object,*

TABLE 1.1

Form and function: Nouns and verbs can function in several ways, whereas function words, including adjectives and adverbs, generally cannot.

Example	Form	Function	Sentence
Candy	Noun	Subject, object	Subject: Candy can rot your teeth. Object: We ate the candy.
Evening	Noun	Subject, object, adjectival	Subject: The evening was warm. Object: In the evening, we went walking. Adjectival: She wore an evening gown.
Jump	Verb, noun	Subject, object, adjectival, predicate	Subject: The jump was the longest in history. Object: We made the jump without fear. Adjectival: The jump ball decided the game. Predicate: He must jump higher than ever.
On	Preposition, particle	Preposition, particle	Preposition: The pan was on the stove. Particle: Maria put on her sweater.
Sleepy	Adjective	Adjective	Adjective: The child was sleepy.
Because	Subordinating conjunction	Subordinating conjunction	Subordinating conjunction: Macarena went to the market because she needed milk.

complement, modifier, and *function word.* The words that have the broadest range of function are nouns and verbs. Form and function usually are the same for adjectives, adverbs, conjunctions, particles, and prepositions. Table 1.1 may help you conceptualize the distinction between form and function.

In this chapter, we examine what these various terms mean so as to lay the groundwork for grammatical analysis. The goal is to introduce or provide a review of terminology and concepts. This review makes no attempt to be comprehensive; thus those readers desiring a more in-depth presentation should turn to a handbook.

SUBJECTS AND PREDICATES

Although sentences can be infinitely rich and complex, they are based on nouns and verbs. Nearly everything else provides information about the nouns and verbs in some way. We will examine nouns and verbs in more detail later, but at this point we can say that nouns tend to be the names of things, whereas verbs tend to be words that describe actions and states of being. Moreover, sentences generally express relations, most often between nouns and verbs (between *agents* and *actions*), or they express an *existential* relation.[3] Sentences 1 and 2 illustrate the two types.

1. Dogs bark.
2. The tree was tall.

The word *dogs* is the agent of Sentence 1. It performs the action conveyed in the word *bark.* Agents function as *subjects* of a sentence. Thus, *subject* is our first function category. The word *bark* supplies information about *dogs*, stating or describing what they do. Words that state an action of this sort and that supply information about the nature of subjects or what they are doing are referred to a *predicates.* Thus, *predicate* is our second function category. Although in Sentence 2 *the tree* is not an agent, the sentence expresses a fact about the tree's existence—it was tall. *The tree,* therefore is the subject, and *was tall* is the predicate. Understanding subject and predicate is important because these are the two central functional parts of all sentences. If one is missing, we don't have a sentence. Functionally, everything else in a sentence is related to its subject and predicate in some way.

---

[3]These relations often are described as *propositions.* The most fundamental definition of a proposition is that it is a claim about reality. Understanding propositions is an important part of expository writing, which is largely about a writer's claims regarding the nature of reality.

Clauses

All sentences in English can be divided into the two constituents of subject and predicate, even when, as sometimes occurs, the subject isn't an explicit part of a given sentence. Almost everything else that one may see in a sentence will be part of either the subject or the predicate. In addition, a subject/predicate combination constitutes what is referred to as a *clause*. This means that every sentence is a clause.

Independent and Dependent Clauses. There are two major types of clauses: *independent* and *dependent*. One way to differentiate the two types is to understand that dependent clauses always supply information to an independent clause. Another way is to understand that dependent clauses begin with a word (sometimes two words) that links them to an independent clause. A clause that begins with one of these words cannot function as a sentence. *Only independent clauses can function as sentences.* Listed in the following table are some of these words:

because	if	as
until	since	whereas
although	though	while
unless	so that	once
after	before	when
whenever	who	whom

Consider Sentence 3:

3. Fred went to the market *because he needed milk.*

This sentence has two major parts. The first part, *Fred went to the market*, contains the subject *Fred* and the predicate *went to the market*, so it is a clause. The second part, *he needed milk*, also has a subject, *he*, and a predicate, *needed milk,* so it is another clause. Note, however, that the second clause begins with the word *because* and that it also explains why Fred went to the market. Thus, we have two criteria with which to label *because he needed milk* as a dependent clause.

PHRASES

Although the two major categories of nouns and verbs provide an adequate classification system for simple grammatical analyses, they do not sufficiently account for the fact that sentences are made up of groups of words (and not just subjects and predicates) that function together. Subjects, for example, are not always composed of a single noun; more often than not they are made up of a noun and one or more other words working in conjunction with it. For this reason, the discussions that follow use the term *phrase* regularly. *A phrase can be defined as one or more words functioning together as a unit.* On this account, the subject and predicate of *Dogs bark* are made up of a noun phrase (NP) and a verb phrase (VP), respectively, and the subject of *The tree was tall* is also a noun phrase.

We generally identify a phrase on the basis of a key word at its beginning, such as a noun or a verb. Consider these examples:

- *flowers* in her hair
- *running* with the bulls

In the first case, the phrase begins with *flowers*, which is a noun. In the second case, however, the phrase begins with *running*, which is a verb. We also refer to these words as *head words* because they are at the head of the phrase and the other words in the phrase are attached to them.

OBJECTS

As it turns out, sentences like *Dogs bark* are not the most common type in English. Far more common are sentences that have an agent, an action, and a recipient of the action, as in Sentence 4:

4. Fritz hit the ball.

In this sentence, *the ball* was what was hit, so it received the action of Fritz's hitting. Constructions that receive the action of the sentence are referred to as *objects*. Thus, *object* is our third function category. Nevertheless, because of the two-part division noted previously, *objects are part of the predicate.* In Sentence 4, *Fritz* is the subject, and *hit the ball* is the predicate; the predicate then can be further analyzed as consisting of the verb *hit* and the object *the ball,* which also is a noun phrase.

COMPLEMENTS

Sentence 2, *The tree was tall,* is different from sentences 1 and 4 in an interesting way: The word *tall* does not receive the action conveyed in *was*; in fact, as noted earlier, *was* conveys existence or state of being, not action, so it is not like *bark* or *hit.* Nevertheless, *tall* has something in common with *the ball*: It serves to complete the predicate. Just as *Fritz hit* does not sound complete (and isn't), *the tree was* does not sound complete (and isn't). Because *tall* completes the predicate in Sentence 2, it is referred to as a *complement*. A *complement* is our fourth major function category. *The ball* and *tall* both complete the predicate, but we assign them different function categories because they are classified as different forms. This difference is explained later.

APPLYING KEY IDEAS

Part 1

Directions: Examine the following sentences and use lines to separate the functional constituents of subject, verb phrase, and object. Then label each part.

Example: The gangster / owned / a casino.

1. Fred rented a truck.
2. Fritz felt very tired.
3. Macarena bought a new dress.
4. Buggsy was fairly short.
5. Fred borrowed $100.

Part 2

Directions: In the sentences below, use brackets to identify the independent clauses. Underline the dependent clauses and circle the word that marks the construction as dependent.

Examples: (When) Macarena woke up, [she heard Fred cooking breakfast.]
            [Fritz knocked on Macarena's door] (until) his knuckles were sore.

1. Before he drove to Las Vegas, Fred had lunch with Buggsy.
2. Macarena wore a long evening gown, as though she were going to a party.
3. Fritz loved to bet on the races, whereas Fred loved to bet on the fights.
4. Buggsy kept in very close contact with "the boys," although officially he had retired.
5. The car that Fritz wanted to buy had once belonged to a famous movie star.
6. Macarena seldom returned anyone's phone call, which kept Fred and Fritz in a constant state of anxiety.
7. Fred had not slept well since he saw Macarena at Buggsy's party.
8. Fritz loved Los Angeles because it was such a seedy place.
9. He decided he would live in Venice Beach until he could find a better place.
10. His landlady was Ophelia DiMarco, who also owned a pool hall, a pawn shop, and a taxi-dance club.

NOUNS

As noted earlier, subjects and predicates are related to nouns and verbs. Traditional grammar defines a noun as a person, place, or thing. However, this definition is not the best because it isn't sufficiently inclusive. The word *Monday*, for example, is a noun, but it is not a thing, nor is *freedom* or any number of other words. For this reason, it is tempting to define a noun in terms of function: A noun is any word that can function as a subject.

Although this definition is better than the traditional one, it is not completely accurate. A word like *running* can function as a subject, and when it does it has the characteristics of a noun, but some people argue that the underlying nature of the word—its form as a verb—doesn't change. To better describe the complexity and nuances of this situation, linguists call words like "running" *nominals*. This term can be applied to any word that has a classification other than noun that can be made to function as a noun. (By the same token, nouns can function as modifiers—e.g., as adjectives—which we discuss later. It follows that nouns functioning as adjectives are called *adjectivals*.)

If the situation seems complicated, it is. In fact, defining the term *noun* is such a problem that many grammar books do not even try to do it. Accepting the idea that the concept of *noun* is fairly abstract, however, can point us in the right direction, toward a reasonably acceptable definition. From this perspective, *nouns are the labels we use to classify the world and our experiences in it.*

As suggested earlier, nouns function as the head words for noun phrases. Thus, even complex noun phrases are dominated by the single noun that serves as head word.

Common Nouns And Proper Nouns

There are two major types of nouns. *Common nouns*, as the name suggests, are the largest variety. Common nouns signify a general class of words used in naming and include such words as those in the following list:

Typical Common Nouns

car	wood	computer
baby	disk	pad
elephant	book	star
speaker	politician	movie
picture	telephone	jacket
ring	banana	flower

Proper nouns, on the other hand, are specific names, such as *Mr. Spock, The Empire State Building, Ford Escort*, and the *Chicago Bulls*.

PRONOUNS

English, like other languages, resists the duplication of nouns in sentences, so it replaces duplicated nouns with what are called *pronouns* (No one is sure why languages resist such duplication.) The nouns that get replaced are called *antecedents*. Consider Sentence 5:

    5. ?Fred liked Macarena, so Fred took Macarena to a movie.[4]

The duplication of the proper nouns *Fred* and *Macarena* just does not sound right to most people, and that is because English generally does not allow it. The duplicated nouns are replaced, as in Sentence 5a:

    5a. Fred liked Macarena, so *he* took *her* to a movie.

Notice that Sentence 5b also is acceptable:

    5b. *He* liked *her*, so Fred took Macarena to a movie.

In this instance, however, Sentence 5b is not quite as appropriate as 5a because the sentence lacks a context. Real sentences, as opposed to those that appear in books like this one, are part of a context that includes the complexities of human relationships; prior knowledge related to past, present, and future events; and, of course, prior conversations. The pronouns in Sentence 5b suggest that *Fred* and *Macarena* already have been identified or are known. This suggestion is contrary to fact. In Sentence 5a, on the other hand, *Fred* and *Macarena* appear in the first part of the sentence, so the pronouns are linked to these antecedents without any doubt or confusion about which nouns the pronouns have replaced. At work is an important principle for pronouns: They should appear as close to their antecedents as possible to avoid potential confusion.

Personal Pronouns

Pronouns that replace a duplicated noun are referred to as *personal* or *common* pronouns. The common pronouns are:

---

[4]This sentence illsutrates a convention in linguistics of putting a question mark in front of questionable sentences. Another convention consists of putting an asterisk in front of ungrammatical sentences. This book uses both conventions throughout.

Singular: I, me, you, he, him, she, her, it

Plural: we, us, you, they, them

In addition, there are several other types of pronouns: *demonstrative, reciprocal, possessive, indefinite, reflexive,* and *relative.* Possessive and relative pronouns are examined in detail later in the book, with special attention paid to relatives because they are part of an interesting construction called a *relative clause.* The discussion of these types here, therefore, is brief.

Case.   Before going forward with this discussion of pronouns, we need to pause and explore *case.* The functional relations in sentences are important in all languages, but not all languages signify those relations in the same way. English relies primarily on word order. On a basic level, we know that subjects normally come before the predicate and that objects normally come after. Other languages, however, do not rely so much on word order but instead alter the forms of the words to signify their relations. Japanese, for example, uses word order *and* form, attaching particles to words to signify their function: *Wa* is used for subjects, and *o* is used for objects. Thus, "I read this book" is expressed as follows:

Watashi-wa kono hon-o yonda.

Translated literally, this sentence reads, "I this book read," because Japanese has a word order different from English. Notice, however, that we also could state:

Kono hon-o watashi-wa yonda.

This shift in word order ("This book I read") would be appropriate if the speaker wanted to emphasize that it was a particular book that he or she had read. The point, of course, is that subjects and objects in Japanese can move fairly freely because the subject and object markers—rather than word order—always signal the proper function.

We use a special term to describe changes in the forms of nouns based on function—*inflections.* Some languages are more inflected than others, with modern English being largely uninflected. At one time, however, English was highly inflected, and it retains a vestige of this past in the various forms of its pronouns, some of which change on the basis of whether they are functioning as a subject or an object.[5] As indicated earlier, the relation of subjects and objects

---

[5]A few English nouns retain inflection for gender. Consider, for example, the two spellings available for people with yellow hair—*blond* and *blonde.* Although pronounced the same, the former is used for males, the latter for females. *Actor* and *actress* are two other words that retain inflection. Over the last several years, however, there have been concerted efforts to eliminate all gender inflections, such that female performers increasingly are referred to as *actors* rather than *actresses.*

to a sentence is determined with respect to their relation to the action conveyed in the predicate. Subjects are agents, whereas objects are recipients of the action. More formally, these relations are expressed in terms of *case*. Thus, when a word is functioning as a subject, it is in the subject or *nominative* case; when a word is functioning as an object, it is in the *objective* case.

Case does not affect nouns in English, but it does affect pronouns. Consider Sentence 6:

    6. *Fred* and *I* went to the movies.

Both *Fred* and the pronoun *I* are part of the subject, so they are in the nominative case. When these words function as objects, *Fred* does not change its form, but *I* does, as in Sentence 7:

    7. Macarena kissed *Fred* and *me*.

Me is the objective case form of the personal pronoun *I*.

Usage Note

Nonstandard usage commonly reverses nominative case and objective case pronouns, resulting in sentences like 8 and 9 below:

    8. ?Fritz and *me* gave the flowers to Macarena.
    9. ?Buggsy asked Fred, Raul, and *I* to drive to Las Vegas.

Formal standard usage reflects the application of different cases, as in sentences 8a and 9a:

    8a. Fritz and *I* gave the flowers to Macarena.
    9a. Buggsy asked Fred, Raul, and *me* to drive to Las Vegas.

School grammarians generally react fairly negatively to the nonstandard treatment of case exemplified in sentences 8 and 9. As we have already seen, however, an equally troublesome problem with case gets little attention. When someone knocks on a door and is asked, "Who is it?" the response nearly always is *It's me*. In formal standard usage, the response would be *It's I* because the verb *is* establishes equality between the subject, *It*, and the noun complement at the end of the predicate. This equality includes case, which means that the noun complement in standard usage would be set in the nominative case. Even so, few people ever use *It's I*, not even people who use standard English fairly consistently.

The question of case in this situation is interesting because it illustrates the influence of Latin on notions of correctness. Latin and Latin-based languages are more inflected than is English, so problems of case rarely arise. For example, we just do not observe native Spanish speakers using an objective-case pronoun in a nominative position. If a speaker is asked, "Who is it?" the response always is *Soy yo*, never *Soy me*. All native Spanish speakers will reject *Soy me* as an appropriate response. In an uninflected language like English, on the other hand, speakers rely on word order not only to determine what is acceptable but also, on a deeper level, to determine what is grammatical. In a word-order-dependent language, case is largely irrelevant. As a result, *Fritz and me gave the flowers to Macarena* is acceptable to a huge number of people because it conforms to the standard word order of English. The pronoun *me* is in the subject position and is understood to be part of the subject regardless of its case. Likewise, *It's me* will be accepted because the pronoun is in what normally is the object position. This analysis explains, in part, why most people think *It's I* sounds strange. More is at work than our infrequent exposure to the formal standard structure; we also expect to see a nominative case pronoun at the end of the predicate. Nevertheless, formal standard usage, influenced by notions of correctness that apply more to inflected languages than to word order languages, places considerable value on matching case and function.

Demonstrative Pronouns

There are four demonstrative pronouns:

this, that, these, those

They serve to single out, highlight, or draw attention to a noun, as in sentences 10, 11, and 12:

10. *That* car is a wreck.
11. *Those* peaches don't look very ripe.
12. *This* book is really interesting.

Usage Note

The demonstrative pronoun *this* does not always work to draw attention to a noun. In certain situations, it replaces an entire sentence, as in the following:

Fritz cleaned his apartment. *This* amazed Macarena.

Here, *this* refers to the fact that Fritz cleaned his apartment, and in this kind of construction it usually is referred to as an *indefinite demonstrative* pronoun because there is no definite antecedent. In this particular instance, with the two sentences side by side, the relation between them is clear. However, inexperienced writers do not always attend to the matters of construction necessary to convey the connection between the antecedent and the indefinite demonstrative pronoun in the best possible way. As a result, they often will have several sentences separating the indefinite demonstrative *this* and the fact or action to which it refers. Readers do not have an easy time figuring out the connection, as in this example:

> The romantic model of teaching that views writing as an independent and isolated process has dominated the classroom for years. The model may be poetic, it may feel good for teachers, but it is not practical. It does not take into account the pragmatic social factors that contribute to successful writing. *This* can present a major problem for teachers seeking to implement new models and strategies in the classroom.

The word *this* in the last sentence should refer to the idea in the previous sentence, but it doesn't; there is no real connection between implementing new models and the fact that the romantic model does not take into account social factors. The last sentence seems most closely linked to the first, but the relation is not clear, and it certainly is not strong, because of the intervening sentences. Using the indefinite demonstrative in this instance is not appropriate because it negatively affects clarity and understanding. The sentence would have to be moved upward to be successful.

The misplacement of sentences that begin with the indefinite demonstrative *this* occurs frequently in the work of inexperienced writers. Often there is no preceding sentence for the pronoun; the reference is to a sentence in the writer's mind that never was put on paper. Moreover, many experienced writers object to any usage of *this* in such a broad way, arguing that an alternative, more precise structure is better. They recommend replacing the indefinite demonstrative pronoun with an appropriate noun. In the previous example, replacing *this* with *the romantic model* would solve the problem.

Reciprocal Pronouns

English has two reciprocal pronouns—*each other* and *one another*—which are used to refer to the individual parts of a plural noun. Consider sentences 13 and 14:

13. The friends gave gifts to *each other.*
14. The dogs looked at *one another.*

Usage Note

Each other and *one another* do not mean the same thing; thus they are not interchangeable. *Each other* signifies two people or things, whereas *one another* signifies more than two. Thus, Sentence 13 refers to two friends; Sentence 14 refers to more than two dogs.

APPLYING KEY IDEAS

Although no strong connection between grammar and writing quality exists, it is easy to find one for usage. Most writing, for example, is improved when writers make certain that their indefinite demonstrative pronouns have clear antecedents. For this activity, examine some of your writing, especially papers you have submitted for classes, and identify any instances of indefinite demonstrative pronouns that lack clear antecedents. In each instance, revise your writing to provide an antecedent or to eliminate the pronoun. Doing so can help you avoid this problem in the future. You also may find it interesting to check your writing to see whether your use of reciprocal pronouns is congruent with the standard convention. If you can, you should share your revision efforts with classmates to compare results, which can give you better insight into revising.

Possessive Pronouns

Possessive pronouns indicate possession, as in sentences 15 and 16:

15. *My* son loves baseball.
16. The books are *mine*.

The possessive pronouns are:

Singular: my, mine, your, yours, her, hers, his, its
Plural: our, ours, your, yours, their, theirs

Indefinite Pronouns

Indefinite pronouns have general rather than specific antecedents, which means that they refer to general entities or concepts, as in Sentence 17:

17. *Everyone* was late.

The indefinite pronoun *everyone* does not refer to any specific individual but rather to the entire group, which gives it its indefinite status.

Indefinite Pronouns in English

all	any	anybody
anything	anyone	another
both	each	every
everybody	everyone	everything
either	few	fewer
many	neither	nobody
no one	none	one
several	some	somebody
something		

Reflexive Pronouns

When subjects perform actions on themselves, we need a special way to signify the reflexive nature of the action. We do so through the use of *reflexive pronouns*. Consider the act of shaving, as in Sentence 18, in which Macarena, the subject, performs a reflexive action:

   18. Macarena shaved Macarena.

This duplication is not allowed, but we cannot use a personal pronoun for the object, *Macarena*. Doing so results in a different meaning, as in Sentence 18a:

   18a. Macarena shaved her.

In Sentence 18a, the pronoun *her* cannot refer to *Macarena* but instead must refer to someone else.

   To avoid this problem, English provides a set of special pronouns that signify a reflexive action:

   Singular: myself, yourself, himself, herself, itself
   Plural: ourselves, yourselves, themselves

Thus, to express the idea that Macarena shaved Macarena, we would have 18b:

   18b. Macarena shaved *herself.*

Usage Note

Sometimes reflexive pronouns work as *intensifiers*, as in sentences 19 and 20:

19. They *themselves* refused to sign the agreement.
20. We *ourselves* can't abide deceit.

On page 17 we saw how nonstandard usage confuses nominative case and objective case pronouns. People will use a nominative case pronoun in the subject position, and vice versa. Many people are aware of this problem in their language, probably as a result of instruction, but they do not know how to fix it. In an attempt to avoid the problem, at least with respect to the pronouns *I* and *me*, they will use a reflexive pronoun in either the subject or object position, as in sentences 21 and 22:

21. *Macarena, Fritz, and *myself* went to Catalina.
22. *Buggsy took Fred, Macarena, and *myself* to Acapulco.

Using a reflexive pronoun to replace a personal pronoun, however, simply creates another problem because there is no reflexive action. Replacing a personal pronoun with a reflexive is a violation of standard usage.

Relative Pronouns

As we saw on page 11, dependent clauses begin with words that link them to independent clauses. We have considered subordinate clauses—one type of dependent clause—but another important type is the *relative clause*. Table 1.2 illustrates the types of clauses we have considered so far. Relative clauses are linked to independent clauses via a *relative pronoun*, as in these sentences:

23. Fritz knew a woman *who had red hair.*
24. The woman *whom Fritz liked* had red hair.
25. The book *that Fritz borrowed* was a first edition.

In these sentences, *who, whom*, and *that* are relative pronouns. These and others are shown in the following list.

Major Relative Pronouns in English:

who	whom	that
which	whose	where
when	why	

TABLE 1.2

Clause Types: At this point, we have considered independent, subordinate, and relative clauses.

Clause Type	Example	Significant Feature
Independent	*Buggsy loved Las Vegas.*	Can be punctuated as a sentence
Subordinate	Macarena danced *until her legs were weak.*	Linked to independent clause via subordinating conjunction
Relative	Macarena, *who loved spicy food,* owned three Mexican cook books.	Linked to independent clause via relative pronoun

VERBS

Verbs are the words we use to signify an action or a state of being. They make up the head of the predicate (they are the head word of the predicate) and are interesting in large part because they convey so much information in sentences. For example, actions can occur in the past, present, or future, and verbs commonly change in relation to the time an action occurred. We call this feature *tense.*

Although three tenses are possible, English has only two: past and present. The future has to be conveyed in a way that does not involve changing the verb. Sometimes, we use the words *will* or *shall* to indicate the future, as in *We will eat soon*, but English is flexible and allows us to signify the future in other ways, like the present, as in *We eat soon*. In fact, English is so flexible that sometimes we also can signify the past by using the present, as in:

So last night he asks me for money. Can you believe it?

Romance languages like Spanish have three tenses, whereas other languages, such as Hopi, have only one. Differences in verb tense across languages played an important role in the shift from traditional grammar to phrase-structure grammar in the early 1900s (a topic that we take up in the next chapter).

Comparing English and Spanish verbs illustrates the nature of tense and how English differs from a Latin-based language. Consider the verb *speak*, which in Spanish is *hablar*:

Past	*Present*	*Future*
spoke	speak	—
hablé	hablo	hablaría

Aspect

In addition to tense, verbs have another interesting characteristic, which is called *aspect*.[6] Aspect provides information about the duration or ongoing nature of an action. In Standard English, it normally is conveyed by two verb constructions, the *progressive verb form* and the *perfect verb form*.

Sentences 26 and 27 show progressive verb forms:

26. Fred *was washing* his car.
27. Fritz *is reading* a book.

The progressive, as 26 and 27 indicate, consists of a tensed form of the verb *be* and a verb that has *-ing* attached (the *-ing* suffix is called the *present participle marker*):

$$be \text{ (marked for tense) } verb + ing$$

Sentences 28 and 29 show perfect verb forms:

28. Macarena has visited Buggsy before.
29. Fred and Fritz had eaten too many tacos.

The perfect, as these sentences indicate, consists of a tensed form of the verb *have* and a verb that has *-ed* or *-en* attached (the *-ed* and *-en* suffixes are called *past participle markers*).

$$have \text{ (marked for tense) } verb + ed/en$$

Transitive and Intransitive Verbs

There are several different kinds of verbs. Although we cannot examine all of them, we can look at some of the more important categories. Sentence 4 on page 12—*Fritz hit the ball*—has a subject, a verb, and an object. Sentence 1—*Dogs bark*—however, has just a subject and a verb. The difference is related to the fact that *hit* and *bark* are different kinds of verbs. Some verbs either require or can work with an object; *hit* is such a verb. We call these verbs *transitive* verbs. Other verbs, such as *bark*, cannot work with an object. We call these verbs *intransitive* verbs. This distinction is straightforward and does not cause confusion, but many verbs can function both transitively and intransitively, and this fact can be confusing:

---

[6]In chapter 5, we examine Black English and see that Standard English and Black English have different ways of dealing with tense and aspect.

30. Fred ate an apple.
31. Fred ate.
32. Macarena stopped the car.
33. Macarena stopped.
34. Fritz cooked the dinner.
35. Fritz cooked.

To repeat:

- Transitive verbs are followed by object.
- Intransitive verbs are not followed by object.

Usage Note

Perhaps one of the more widespread departures from standard usage involves the verbs *lay* and *lie*. *Lay* is a transitive verb, so it requires an object; *lie*, on the other hand, is an intransitive verb and does not. Nevertheless, huge numbers of people use *lay* intransitively, as in Sentence 36:

36. ?I'm going to *lay* down for a nap.

Standard usage is reflected in Sentence 37:

37. I'm going to *lie* down for a nap.

A few teachers try to help students keep these verbs straight by providing them with a memory aid: *Dogs lay down, but people lie down*. This memory aid, of course, is wrong—the verb in both cases should be *lie*.

Some scholars argue that the intransitive use of *lay* has become so ubiquitous that it now is standard. This argument, however, fails to account for the fact that many people in influential positions continue to follow standard usage and judge the nonstandard usage negatively. Being able to apply the difference between *lay* and *lie* therefore has clear advantages because the intransitive *lay* is inappropriate in many situations, especially those that involve writing. Many teachers, for example, cringe whenever they see a student using *lay* intransitively, even though this usage has become so common that they cringe daily.

Incomplete Transitive and Incomplete Intransitive Verbs

A transitive verb requires a noun construction to complete the predicate, but an intransitive verb does not. A subclass of transitive and intransitive verbs, however, requires another kind of construction to be complete. These special verbs are called *incomplete transitives* and *incomplete intransitives*, respectively. They require an additional element, a *prepositional phrase,* which is discussed in detail later. For example, consider the verbs *put* and *deal*, as illustrated in these sentences:

38. Mrs. DiMarco *put* the rent money under her mattress.
39. Buggsy *dealt* with the problem.

Sentence 38 would be incomplete without the construction *under her mattress.* Likewise, Sentence 39 would be incomplete without the construction *with the problem.*

Ditransitive Verbs

On pages 24–25, we saw that transitive verbs require an object. A special category of verbs, called *ditransitives*, usually appears with two objects, as illustrated in sentences 40 and 41:

40. Fred sent *Macarena* a *gift*.
41. Buggsy asked *Fritz* a *question*.

In these sentences, *a gift* and *a question*, respectively, are recipients of the action of their verbs, so we call them *direct objects.* *Macarena* and *Fritz*, on the other hand, accept their direct objects, so we call them *indirect objects.* (Macarena accepted the gift; Fritz accepted the question.)

Ditransitive verbs raise an interesting question. Do these verbs *require* two objects, or are there instances in which they can take only one, which means that they can *accept* two objects? In the case of *ask*, the answer clearly is that the verb can take a single object: *Buggsy asked Fritz a question* can become *Buggsy asked Fritz*; "a question" is implicit in the statement. For other ditransitive verbs, however, the answer is not so clear. In the case of *Fred sent Macarena a gift*, dropping the direct object may be grammatical, but it changes the sentence grammatically and semantically:

Fred sent Macarena.

Dropping *a gift* maintains a grammatical sentence, but suddenly *Macarena* becomes the direct object rather than the indirect object, and the meaning is not even close to the original. An equally troubling example occurs with the ditransitive verb *buy*:

• Fred bought his mother a present.

- ?Fred bought his mother.

From this analysis, it appears that ditransitive verbs *require* two objects in most situations. The fact that there are some ditransitives, such as *ask*, that allows us to drop the direct object without changing the grammatical relations or the meaning of the sentence is sheer coincidence and fairly trivial.

Indirect objects also can be located in a phrase, usually one that begins with the word *to*, as in Sentence 40a:

40a. Fred sent a gift *to Macarena*.

In this instance, *Macarena* is the indirect object, even though it is part of a prepositional phrase. English allows us to express indirect objects either as a simple noun phrase, as in sentences 40 and 41, or as a prepositional phrase, as in Sentence 40a.

Linking Verbs

Earlier, we saw that verbs describe an action or are existential. Sentence 2—*The tree was tall*—illustrates how the verb *was* expresses existence or a state of being. We give such verbs a special classification: *linking verbs*. Linking verbs link a complement to the subject of a sentence. All forms of *be* can function as linking verbs, as can all sensory verbs, such as *taste, smell, feel, look*, and *sound*. Other linking verbs include *seems, prove, grow*, and *become* (*got* also can function as a linking verb when it is used in the sense of *become*, as in *Fred got tired*). Note, however, that some of these verbs, specifically *smell, feel, sound, prove*, and *grow*, also can function as regular verbs, as in *Fred smelled the flowers*.

Gerunds

One of the interesting things about language is its flexibility. Words that we normally think of as existing in a certain category can easily function in another category. Many verbs, for example, can function as nouns, usually just by adding the suffix *-ing*, as in the case of *running, jumping, driving*, and so forth. When such verbs function as nouns, we call them *gerunds*.

An important part of mastering grammar lies in the ability to listen to how people use language and then to compare it to a conventional standard. Listening to how others use language helps one "listen" to one's own language. Spend some time listening to others speak, in the school cafeteria, on TV, on the bus, or some other place where you can be unobtrusive. Focus on two topics that were examined earlier—case and reflexive pronouns—using a notebook to record instances of nonstandard usage. What can you learn from this activity?

MODIFIERS

As noted earlier, we can say that sentences essentially are composed of nouns and verbs and that nearly everything else provides information about those nouns and verbs. The words and constructions that provide such information are classified broadly as *modifiers*. Modifiers are of two major types; those that supply information to nouns and those that supply information to verbs. We call these *adjectival* and *adverbial* modifiers, respectively. These terms describe function, not form. Nouns, for example, can function adjectivally.

The complete picture is more complex than this overview may suggest. Modifiers also may supply information to other modifiers and to sentences or clauses, but their function nevertheless remains adjectival or adverbial.

Adjectival Modifiers

Adjectival modifiers supply information, usually sensory, to noun phrases. The most common type of adjectival modifier is the simple adjective. Consider these sentences:

42. Macarena bought a *red* dress.
43. The *new* book made her career.
44. His *wooden* speech put the crowd to sleep.

Each of these simple adjectives supplies information to its associated noun: The dress was *red*; the book was *new*; the speech was *wooden*.

As indicated earlier, many words can function as modifiers, and when they do they commonly function as adjectivals. Consider Sentence 45:

45. Macarena bought an *evening* gown.

Evening is a noun, but in Sentence 45 it functions as an adjectival. Table 1.3 illustrates the difference between adjective and adjectival.

TABLE 1.3

Adjectives and Adjectivals: Adjectivals are words, like nouns, that are functioning as adjectives.

Simple Adjective	Adjectival	Example Sentences
red	evening (noun functioning as adjective)	1. Macarena bought a *red* dress. 2. Macarena bought an *evening* gown.
wooden	jump (verb functioning as adjective)	1. His *wooden* speech put the crowd to sleep. 2. Fred looked at the *jump* gate

Simple adjectives come before the nouns they modify. However, there are two special adjectives that do not. The first kind is one that we've already seen, in Sentence 2: *The tree was tall*. The word *tall* is an adjective, and it supplies information to *tree*, but it follows the linking verb *was*. As noted on page 13, *tall* in this sentence is a complement. However, because it has a special relation with the linking verb, we give it a specific name: *predicate adjective*. Predicate adjectives always follow linking verbs.

Now we're in a better position to understand the difference between *ball* in *Fritz hit the ball* and *tall* in *The tree was tall*. Both complete the predicate, but *ball* is a noun functioning as an object, whereas *tall* is an adjective functioning as a predicate adjective. Sentences 46 through 48 illustrate additional predicate adjectives:

46. Fritz felt *tired*.
47. The pizza tasted *funny*.
48. Fred was *disgusted*.

The second type of adjective is called an *adjective complement*, which is illustrated in Sentence 49:

49. Macarena painted the town *red*.

Notice that the adjective *red* completes the predicate, but it doesn't immediately follow the verb. Moreover, *painted* is not a linking verb.

Adverbial Modifiers

Adverbial modifiers are versatile. They supply information to verbs, to adjectivals, to other adverbials, to clauses, and to sentences. The information is not sensory but instead deals with the following:

time, place, manner, degree, cause, concession

Like adjectivals, adverbials consist of simple adverbs and words of varying forms and entire constructions that function adverbially. The following examples illustrate each type of modification. Note that adverbials of degree modify adjectivals, or they may modify other adverbials:

Time: They arrived *late*.
Place: We stopped *there* for a rest.
Manner: Fred opened the box *slowly*.
Degree: Macarena felt *very* tired. She opened the box *quite* rapidly.
Cause: We ate *because we were hungry*.
Concession: *Although she didn't like broccoli*, she ate it.

In the last two examples, we see illustrations of longer constructions functioning as adverbials: *Because we were hungry* and *Although she didn't like broccoli* are *subordinate clauses*, which we'll examine shortly (page 37). Another important adverbial construction is the *prepositional phrase*, which we'll examine on pages 39–40. Table 1.4 examines adverbs and adverbials.

Head Words

Modification in English is flexible, particularly with adverbials, which can appear in different places in a sentence. Earlier, we briefly examined an important principle of modification: No matter where a modifier appears, it is linked to one word in the sentence more closely than it is to other words. For example, in *The new book made her career*, the adjective *new* is linked to *book*. In *Fred opened the box slowly*, the adverb *slowly* is linked to the word *opened*. The word to which a modifier is linked is called a *head word*. Head words become important when modifiers are more complex than simple adjectives and adverbs, as in the sentence below from Ernest Hemingway:

TABLE 1.4

Adverbs and Adverbials. Adverbials are constructions, like subordinate clauses, that function adverbially.

Simple Adverb	Adverbial	Example Sentences
slowly	Because we were hungry (subordinate clause)	1. Fred opened the box *slowly*. 2. We ate *because we were hungry*.
very	Although she didn't like broccoli (subordinate clause)	1. Macarena felt *very* tired. 2. *Although she didn't like broccoli,* she ate it.
Suddenly	In the morning (prepositional phrase)	1. *Suddenly,* Macarena became ill. 2. Fred took her home *in the morning*.

Manuel swung with the charge, sweeping the muleta ahead of the bull, feet firm, the sword a point of light under the arcs.

The modifiers here, which we discuss a bit later, are primarily verbal constructions, and their head word is *swung*.

The concept of head words is useful not only because it helps us when we need to talk about modifiers and what they modify but also because of another feature of modification, which sometimes is referred to as the *proximity principle*: Modifiers always should be as close to their head words as possible. Violation of this principle can result is what is termed a *misplaced modifier*, as in this sentence:

?Walking across the window I saw a fly.

We certainly know that the *fly* was doing the walking here, not the subject *I*, but the placement of this modifier suggests the contrary. *Fly* is the head word for the verb construction *walking across the window*, but the two are separated so much that the link is unclear. Misplaced modifiers of this sort are very common in the writing of young students. Fortunately, such students easily understand the notion of head words and the proximity principle after a little instruction.

Usage Note

Large numbers of people have difficulty with the modifiers *good* and *well*. Part of the problem is that *good* always is an adjective, whereas *well* can function as either an adjective or an adverb. In nonstandard usage *good* appears as both an adjective and an adverb, and *well* appears only in limited ways. The example sentences that follow illustrate the most common nonstandard usage of *good*:

50. ?I did *good* on the test.
51. ?You played *good*.

Standard usage is quite clear on this point—*well* is strongly preferred in these instances, as in sentences 50a and 51a:

50a. I did *well* on the test.
51a. You played *well*.

Another situation arises with the verb *feel*. When describing how they are feeling, most people say that they feel *good*, as in Sentence 52:

52. I feel *good*.

However, formal standard usage differentiates between *I feel good* and *I feel well*. *Well* nearly always refers to one's state of health; only in most unusual circumstances would *feel* appear as a regular verb signifying that one has a sense of touch that is working properly. Thus, *I feel well* indicates that one is healthy. More to the point, it indicates that, after some particular illness or disease, one has regained previous health. A person recovered from the flu, for example, might say *I feel well*. *I feel good*, on the other hand, can refer to one's general state of well-being, as in the famous James Brown song, *I Feel Good (Like I Knew that I Would)*. This state of well-being can be either physiological or psychological or both. With respect to one's health, however, *I feel good* does not mean, in formal standard usage, that one has regained previous health; it means that one is feeling better at the moment of the utterance than in the past but that the illness or disease is still present. On this account, one might say, after a few days in bed with the flu, *I feel good today*, meaning that one feels relatively better than the day before.

Equally problematic is the situation associated with the question, *How are you today?* If one responds in a way that signifies general well-being, then the appropriate response is *I am good*, although the inherent ambiguity here is interesting. It could mean that one is virtuous, which certainly is a state of being, but perhaps one more often desired than attained. If, however, one responds in a way that signifies health, the appropriate response is *I am well*. In the United States, such exchanges are nearly always for social recognition rather than for serious inquiry into one's health, so we rarely hear the response *I am well*. In

Britain, the situation is different, and the response, *Very well, thank you*, is common.

The linking verb *feel* is associated with another problem that we observe in the language people use, a problem that can be humorous the first couple of times one thinks about it. When people learn of someone's hardship or accident, it is natural for them to want to express their sadness or remorse, but doing so can be problematic. There are two possibilities:

53. I heard about the accident. I feel *badly*.
53a. I heard about the accident. I feel *bad*.

But look carefully at the construction. *Feel* is a linking verb when referring to one's state of being, so it must be followed by an adjective. *Bad* is an adjective, but *badly* is not—it's an adverb. Consequently, *badly* does not make any sense, really, because it does not refer to a state of being. In fact, if we took Sentence 53 literally, it would mean that the speaker has lost his or her tactile perception: When touching something, the speaker simply cannot *feel* it. This is not a state or condition that people experience very often, and it certainly isn't related to remorse. Thus, *I feel bad* reflects standard usage.

It is interesting to note that we can differentiate those who use *I feel bad* or *I feel badly* by their level of education. However, the results are not what one might expect. Generally, people who have less education will apply standard usage and state *I feel bad*. Those with education, including well-educated Ph.D.s and M.D.s, are much more likely to use *I feel badly*. Reality thus thwarts our expectations.

FUNCTION WORDS

A characteristic of subjects and predicates and most of the words that make up subjects and predicates is that they convey meaning, or what sometimes is referred to as *semantic content*. Indeed, we can say that meaning is a primary characteristic, given that language is by nature full of meaning and signification. For example, the word *ball* has an identifiable meaning, as does the word *tall*. People may disagree on the specific meaning of each word, but the disagreements are not major because everyone accepts their general signification. *Function words*, on the other hand, do not have meaning as a primary characteristic. They commonly connect or mark parts of sentences, and their semantic content is secondary. Function words can be classified into several discrete types, and the sections that follow examine four categories: *determiners, conjunctions, prepositions*, and *particles*.

Determiners

The category of determiners is fairly broad and is made up of several subclasses of words, all of which interact with nouns in some way. In fact, determiners always come before nouns, although not necessarily immediately before. Determiners signal the presence of certain kinds of nouns, which is one reason that in some analyses determiners are designated as adjectives. But as mentioned earlier, the semantic content of determiners is secondary rather than primary; thus, they are sufficiently different from simple adjectives to warrant a separate classification.

At this point, we consider just one type of determiner, *articles*. Later in the text, we examine other types.

Articles. There are two types of articles, *definite* and *indefinite*:

Definite: the
Indefinite: a, an

Nouns are either count nouns or noncount nouns, and all singular count nouns require an article unless it has a number (a quantifier) or a possessive pronoun in front of it. Definite articles signal that a noun is specific, often tangible, or that it is identifiable. Indefinite articles, on the other hand, signal that a noun is nonspecific, often intangible, or that is not uniquely identifiable.[7] Consider these sentences:

54. *The* car was wrecked.
55. We could hear *a* man's voice coming up *the* stairwell.
56. After our ordeal, we had to search for *an* alibi.

Conjunctions

A characteristic of language is that it allows people to take small linguistic units and combine them into larger ones, in an additive fashion. Sometimes the units are equal, in which case they are coordinated; other times they are unequal, in which case some units are subordinated to others. Conjunctions are function words that make many of these combinations possible, and there are two major types: *coordinating* and *subordinating*.

---

[7]An exception occurs whenever we are referring to an entire class of objects or beings. Consider, for example, *The dolphin is a mammal, not a fish.*

Coordinating Conjunctions. Coordinating conjunctions, listed here, join equal linguistic units:

and, but, for, nor, or, yet, so

The following sentences illustrate coordinating conjunctions joining individual words/phrases:

57. Fritz *and* Macarena joined the party.
58. Buggsy drove to the casino *and* bet $100 on the upcoming race.

In Sentence 57, the conjunction joins the two nouns, *Fritz* and *Macarena*. In Sentence 58, the conjunction joins two verb phrases, *drove to the casino* and *bet $100 on the upcoming race.*

Coordinating conjunctions also join equal clauses, as shown in the following list, producing what is referred to as a *compound* sentence:

59. Fred opened the door, *but* Macarena wouldn't come inside.
60. Macarena could feel the ocean breeze against her face, *so* she preferred to stay outside.
61. Fritz asked Macarena to go to Catalina, *and* Fred asked her to go to San Francisco.

Usage Note

Coordinating conjunctions frequently confuse writers who do not know how to punctuate them. For example, when a coordinating conjunction joins two clauses, as in sentences 59 through 61, many writers leave out the comma that comes before the conjunction. It is important to understand that punctuation is a matter of convention, which means that people generally have agreed that it should be done a certain way. In this case, the convention maintains that writers need that comma. Without it, the sentence is called a *run-on.*[8]

Even more problematic, however, is a tendency of many writers, even professional ones, to use a comma to separate two phrases that have been joined with a coordinating conjunction. This tendency manifests itself whenever the conjoined phrases, often verbal, start to get long. Consider this sentence:

---

[8]Writers can connect independent clauses erroneously in three ways: with a coordinating conjunction only, with a comma but no conjunction, or with nothing at all. Composition specialists have different terms to describe these three possibilities. As noted, the first case is a *run-on sentence*; the second case is a *comma splice*; and the third case is a *fused sentence.*

62. ?The governor asked the legislature to reconsider the bill that had failed dur-
     ing the previous session, *and* convened a special task force to evaluate its
     ramifications if passed.

This sentence has a compound verb phrase in the predicate. If we reduce it to
its basic structure, the sentence reads:

62a. The governor asked the legislature [something] and convened a special task
     force.

Clearly, a comma is inappropriate here. In fact, the comma in Sentence 62 is
the equivalent of Sentence 63, which even inexperienced writers do not produce:

63. ?The cat jumped, and played.

The motivation to put a comma in sentences like Sentence 62 may be based
on an unconscious fear that the long, compound predicate will be hard to process, but this fear is unfounded. Moreover, separating the two parts of the predicate with the comma is bound to make some readers think negatively about the
writer because it is such an obvious violation of existing conventions.

Subordinating Conjunctions.   Whereas coordinating conjunctions link
equal elements, *subordinating conjunctions* link unequal elements. More specifically, they link a dependent clause to an independent clause. Because this type of
dependent clause begins with a subordinating conjunction, we refer to it as a *subordinate clause*. A subordinate clause is a dependent clause that begins with a subordinating conjunction.

More Common Subordinating Conjunctions

because	if	as
until	since	whereas
although	though	while
unless	so that	once
after	before	when
whenever	as if	even if
in order that	as soon as	even though
insofar as	as though	inasmuch as
so that		

A list of the more common subordinating conjunctions appeared on page 11, but it is reproduced here for convenience.

The sentences that follow show subordinating conjunctions connecting subordinate clauses to independent clauses:

64. *Since he came home*, Fred hasn't turned off the TV once.
65. Buggsy was thrilled *when Rita de Luna walked into the casino*.
66. One of Buggsy's goons had ushered her to the table *before she could say a word*.
67. *While the band played "Moonlight Serenade,"* Buggsy whispered sweet nothings in Rita's ear.
68. Rita was afraid to move *because she had heard about Buggsy's reputation*.

Subordinate Clauses Are Adverbials. Subordinate clauses always function as adverbial modifiers, and the information they provide usually is related to causality/reason, time, concession, or contrast—a point that was introduced on page 30. Because subordinate clauses are adverbials, they tend to supply information to a verb phrase, but they also can supply information to an entire clause, as in sentences 64 and 67. When they do, we say that they are *sentence-level* modifiers because they are modifying at a level above the phrase.

APPLYING KEY IDEAS

Directions: This activity is designed to help you assess how well you've mastered the information in the previous section related to form and function. Identify the form of each word in the sentences that follow. Next, use parentheses to mark the major constituents and then identify their function.

EXAMPLE: (The surfers) (arrived at the beach just after sunrise).
           subject   predicate

1. Fritz saw the ocean from his apartment in Venice Beach.
2. On the boardwalk, the skaters moved in unnatural rhythms.
3. Macarena made a reservation at China Club for dinner.
4. Fred thought about the hot salsa band and the exotic food.
5. Fred polished his shoes until he could see himself in them.
6. Macarena put on her red dress because it was Fred's favorite.
7. She also put on her pearl choker, even though it was a gift from Fritz.
8. Slowly, Macarena brushed her long hair as she looked in the mirror.
9. Three conga drummers appeared on the boardwalk, and they thumped the skins with taped fingers.
10. Fritz put down his racing form because the drumming was really loud.

Usage Note

Function words have some semantic content, and the semantic content of subordinating conjunctions is related to the type of information they supply to the constructions they modify. For example, in Sentence 64—*Since he came home, Fred hasn't turned off the TV once*—the subordinate clause supplies information of time to the independent clause. In Sentence 68—*Rita was afraid to move because she had heard about Buggsy's reputation*—the subordinate clause supplies information of causality. Standard usage requires a match between the semantic content of the subordinating conjunction and the modification provided by the subordinate clause.

The lack of a match has become very widespread, however. Not only in conversation but also in published texts, it is common to find incongruence with respect to time, causality, and contrast, with a temporal subordinator being used where a causal and/or contrastive subordinator is required. Consider these sentences:

69. ?The President gave the order *since he is commander-in-chief.*
70. ?Rita de Luna wanted to leave, *while Buggsy wanted her to stay.*

In Sentence 69, the relation between the two clauses is one of reason, not time, so standard usage requires the following:

69a. The President gave the order *because* he is commander-in-chief.

In Sentence 70, the relation between the two clauses is contrastive, not temporal, so formal standard usage requires the following:

70a. Rita de Luna wanted to leave, *whereas* Buggsy wanted her to stay.

In addition to these concerns, there is another instance of nonstandard usage that has become remarkably widespread. Consider the following scenario: At a school board meeting, a local principal is explaining why her school needs to have Internet access:

Of course, you want to know why our students need access to the Internet. *The reason is because everyone says that it's important.*

If we look carefully at the italicized sentence, we see that the main part consists of a noun-phrase subject, the linking verb *is*, and a subordinate clause that begins with the subordinating conjunction *because*. However, linking verbs cannot be followed by subordinate clauses. Given the grammar and usage conventions we have outlined here, any use of *The reason is because* would have to be deemed not only nonstandard but also ungrammatical.

Directions: This activity has two parts, both intended to provide an opportunity to apply information from the previous discussion to your own language.

First, listen carefully to the language around you—conversations, class lectures, news reports, and so forth. Over a 2-day period, keep a tally of the number of times you hear someone using one of the nonstandard features discussed previously, such as *I feel badly, I did good,* and *The reason is because.* Discuss your tally with others in your class, perhaps examining the situations in which you observed the nonstandard usage and considering the connection.

For the second part of the activity, examine a paper you wrote recently, focusing on your use of subordinating conjunctions. Does the semantic content of your subordinating conjunctions match the relation you intended to establish between the dependent and independent clauses? If not, change the subordinating conjunction appropriately.

Prepositions

A *preposition* generally works with a noun phrase, and together they compose a prepositional phrase. (When a noun phrase is connected to a preposition, it often is called the *object* of the preposition.) The preposition links its noun phrase to either a verb phrase or another noun phrase, which means that the prepositional phrase functions either *adverbially or adjectivally.* (The adverbial nature of prepositional phrases is important and arises again in chapters 2 and 3.) Sentences 71 through 73 illustrate both types. Note that in Sentence 73 the prepositional phrase functions as a sentence-level modifier:

71. The woman *with the red hair* drove a Porsche.

72. Fritz walked *down the street.*

73. *In the morning*, Fred always has wild hair.

The list of English prepositions is quite long, but some of the more common are shown in the following table, including some multiple-word prepositions.

Common English Prepositions

about	above	across
after	against	along
among	around	as
at	before	behind
below	beneath	beyond
by	concerning	despite
down	during	except
for	from	in
into	like	near
of	off	on
out	outside	over
past	through	to
toward	under	until
up	upon	with
within	without	due to
according to	in spite of	in keeping with

Usage Note

Nearly everyone is told in grade school that they must never end a sentence with a preposition. They aren't told why they must not do this, but they nevertheless are penalized in one way or another if they do. This prohibition is a perfect example of the prescriptive nature of traditional grammar. It also is a perfect example of a prohibition that does not fit the way the English language actually works. Certain types of sentences can quite easily *and quite correctly* end with a preposition.

One of the more obvious examples are questions such as the following:

74. Won't you come *in*?

English grammar allows us to truncate the prepositional phrase in some instances, and this is one of them. There is only one other way to ask this question without ending it with a preposition, and that is to include the noun phrase object that has been dropped, giving us:

74a. Won't you come *in my house*?

A similar situation exists with sentences like 75:

75. Buggsy and his goons walked *in*.

Some might be tempted to argue that the word *in* in these sentences isn't a preposition but rather is an adverb, but that analysis seems off the mark. Prepositions are function words, so unlike adverbs their semantic content is secondary, often subtle. The semantic content of *in* is quite different from the semantic content of words that, although able to function as prepositions, more readily function as adverbs. We always come in *something*; we always walk in *something*. This point becomes clearer if we consider the opposite of being *in something*, which is to be *outside something*, as in Sentence 76:

76. Buggsy and his goons walked *outside*.[9]

Outside is one of those words that can function as either a preposition or an adverb, but in the case of Sentence 76, the semantic content is clear and specific because *outside* means *outdoors*. In Chapter 3, we will look more closely at this question of ending a sentence with a preposition, and we will discuss a grammar rule that produces such sentences.

Usage Note

The word *like* is listed above as a preposition, and in standard usage it introduces a prepositional phrase similar to Sentence 77:

77. There was no one quite *like Macarena*.

Huge numbers of people, however, use *like* as a subordinating conjunction, as in sentences 78 and 79:

78. ?Mrs. DiMarco talked *like she knew something about science*.
79. ?If Fred had taken the money to Buggsy *like he should have*, he wouldn't have to hide from Buggsy's goons.

---

[9]One could argue that *in* means *indoors*, but replacing *in* with *indoors* changes the meaning of sentences 74 and 75, which suggests that this argument isn't sound.

This usage is considered to be nonstandard. In formal standard usage, only a subordinating conjunction is appropriate in such constructions, as in sentences 78a and 79a below:

78a. Mrs. DiMarco talked *as though* she knew something about science.
79a. If Fred had taken the money to Buggsy *as* he should have, he wouldn't have to hide from Buggsy's goons.

It is important to note that the use of *like* as a subordinating conjunction has become so ubiquitous that it appears in the speech of even the most fastidious speakers. As a result, many people now apply the standard usage only when writing or when participating in very formal speaking situations.

Particles

Particles look like prepositions, and they resemble adverbials because they are linked to verbs, as in sentences 80 and 81:

80. Fritz looked *up* the number.
81. Macarena put *on* her shoes.

However, they are different from prepositions and adverbials with respect to how they can move in a sentence. Prepositions, for example, cannot move, but particles can. Sentences 80 and 81 also could be written as:

80a. Fritz looked the number up.
81a. Macarena put her shoes on.

The grammar allows particles to move behind the object noun phrase. Compare these sentences with Sentence 82, which has a true preposition:

82. Mrs. DiMarco stepped into her garden.
82a. *Mrs. DiMarco stepped her garden into.

The question of movement also explains why particles are not true adverbials. Most adverbials can move fairly freely in a sentence, as Sentence 83 illustrates:

83. Macarena walked *slowly* to her car.
83a. Macarena *slowly* walked to her car.
83b. *Slowly*, Macarena walked to her car.

Particles, however, can move only behind the NP object. One possible exception may involve sentences like this:

Fritz picked up the book that Macarena had dropped.

If we move the particle behind the NP object, we have:

Fritz picked the book up that Macarena had dropped.

In Chapter 3, we examine a rule that describes particle movement only to find that it does not work as we would expect. Rather than moving the particle behind the NP object, it moves the particle to the end of the dependent clause, producing:

*Fritz picked the book that Macarena had dropped up.

Therefore, in Chapter 3 we return to this sentence about Macarena's dropped book so we can see how different grammars deal with it.

Usage Note

Sometimes people who assert that ending a sentence with a preposition creates an ungrammatical construction will offer as evidence an ungrammatical sentence that indeed ends with what appears to be a preposition. Such sentences commonly resemble Sentence 84:

84. *Fritz put his shoes and then walked to the Qwikie Mart for a bottle of Wild Turkey on.

There is no question that this sentence is ungrammatical, but the problem is not that it ends in a preposition. *On* here is a particle, not a preposition, and it has been moved incorrectly. If we put the word *on* behind either *put* or *shoes*, the sentence is perfectly correct.

PHRASAL MODIFICATION

On page 31, we looked at a sentence from Ernest Hemingway:

Manuel swung with the charge, sweeping the muleta ahead of the bull, feet firm, the sword a point of light under the arcs.

This sentence is of interest because of the kinds of modifiers it contains. They are known generally as *phrasal modifiers*.

If we analyze this sentence, we see that it contains a dependent clause and three phrasal modifiers:

Dependent Clause: Manuel swung with the charge
Modifier 1: sweeping the muleta ahead of the bull
Modifier 2: feet firm
Modifier 3: the sword a point of light under the arcs

We can say that at least modifiers 1 and 3 have their own head words, *sweeping* and *the sword*, respectively, which define the nature of the constructions. That is, the words that follow *sweeping* and *the sword* merely cluster around these head words. On this basis, we can say further that Modifier 1 is a verb phrase (because *sweeping* is a verb) and that Modifier 3 is a noun phrase (because *the sword* is a noun phrase). Thus, verbs and nouns compose two types of phrasal modifiers.

Modifier 2 is different because it has a noun that is followed by an adjective. In fact, it is representative of a type of phrasal modifier that has two related forms. The first form we see in Modifier 2; the second form we see in the following: "Fred, *his head pounding*, took two aspirin and lay down."

The italics set off the phrasal modifier, which in this case is composed of a noun phrase and a verb. This type of modifier, in its two forms—noun phrase plus adjective and noun phrase plus verb—is call a *nominative absolute*. The verb phrase, the noun phrase, and the nominative absolute are three of the major kinds of phrasal modifiers. The fourth major kind is the prepositional phrase, which is explored in more detail in the next chapter. Note that verb phrases can be either progressive participles (*-ing*) or past participles (*-ed*).

Phrasal modifiers are used primarily in narrative-descriptive writing to provide details and images. In addition, phrasal modifiers can appear in three positions relative to the independent clause: in the initial position, the medial position, and the final position. Medial phrasal modifiers split the independent clause, separating the subject and the predicate, as in *Macarena, her eyes wild, confronted the waiter*. Most phrasal modifiers, however, are in the final position. Consider the sentences below:

- I danced with excitement, *winding myself around my nana's legs, balling my hands in her apron, tugging at her dress, stepping on her toes*, until finally she gave me a swat across the bottom and told me to go play. (Final position)
- The prisoners stumbled forward, *their ankles chained, their hands tied, sweat pouring down their faces and collecting into small pools at the base of the neck.* (Final position)

- The wind blew in from the desert, *a cold, dry wind that smelled faintly of sage and juniper*, as the moon rose overhead, *illuminating the courtyard and the three men talking in the night.* (Final position)
- *With Fred's cologne exuding from her pores in a thick vapor,* Macarena circulated among the cigar smokers in the hope that the stench adhering to her hair and clothes would at least confuse Fritz when she met him later that night. (Initial position)
- Fritz, *confused and somewhat nauseated by the various aromas coming from her skin and clothes,* suggested to Macarena that she shower before dinner. (Medial position)

The phrasal modifiers in the first sentence are all verb phrases; in the second they are all nominative absolutes; in the third sentence, there is a noun phrase and a verb phrase; in the fourth sentence the modifier is a nominative absolute (introduced by a preposition); the last sentence has one verb-phrase modifier.

During the 1970s, phrasal modification was part of an effort to use grammar as a means of improving writing through what was known as *sentence combining*. Although sentence combining does not appear to offer any long-term benefits to writing performance, the technique of phrasal modification is an important one that can give writers a valuable tool in their effort to make their writing more varied and interesting.

GRAMMAR AND WRITING

Most language arts teachers do not have many opportunities to explore the fascinating intricacies of grammar in their classrooms, but nearly all of them have to teach grammar. The most pressing questions they face, therefore, are the following: What role does grammar play in writing performance? And how does one teach grammar effectively?

One might think that these questions were answered long ago. After all, grammar has been taught to students since the days of the ancient Greeks. But reliable evaluations of the connection between studying grammar and writing performance are fairly recent. One of the more important emerged in 1963, when, summarizing existing research, Braddock, Lloyd-Jones, and Schoer stated:

> In view of the widespread agreement of research studies based upon many types of students and teachers, the conclusion can be stated in strong and unqualified terms that the teaching of formal [traditional] grammar has a negligible or, because it usually displaces some instruction and practice in actual composition, even a harmful effect on the improvement of writing. (pp. 37–38)

This assessment was strong, but it did not stop various researchers from investigating grammar instruction and writing performance, in part because the connection was accepted as a given. Whitehead (1966), for example, compared a group of high school students that received no grammar instruction in writing classes with one that received instruction in traditional grammar, with an emphasis on sentence diagramming. The results showed no significant difference in writing performance between the two groups. White (1965) studied three classes of seventh graders. Two of the classes studied grammar, whereas the third used this time reading popular novels. At the end of the study, White found no significant difference in terms of writing performance. The students who had been reading novels wrote just as well as those who had studied grammar.

Gale (1968) studied fifth graders, dividing them into four groups. One group received no grammar instruction, whereas the other three studied one of three different types of grammar. Students in two of the grammar groups, but not the students who studied traditional grammar, ended up being able to write slightly more complex sentences than students in the other two groups, but there were no measurable differences in overall writing ability.

In another investigation, Bateman and Zidonis (1966) conducted a 2-year study that started when the students were in ninth grade. Some of the students received instruction in grammar during this period; the rest received no grammar instruction. Again, there was no significant difference in overall writing performance.

Elley, Barham, Lamb, and Wyllie (1976) began with a relatively large pool of subjects (248), which they studied for 3 years. Some critics of the earlier studies had suggested that the lack of any measurable differences might be the result of different teaching styles, so the researchers were particularly careful to control this variable. The students were divided into three groups. The first group studied grammar, various organizational modes (narration, argumentation, analysis, etc.), and literature. The second group studied the same organizational modes and literature as the first group but not grammar; instead, they practiced creative writing and were given the chance to do additional reading. The third group studied traditional grammar and engaged in reading popular fiction.

At the end of each year of the investigation, students were evaluated on a range of measures to determine comparative growth. These measures included vocabulary, reading comprehension, sentence complexity, usage, spelling, and punctuation. Students also wrote essays at the end of each year that were scored for content, style, organization, and mechanics.

No significant differences on any measures were found among the three groups at the end of the first year. At the end of the second year, the students who had studied traditional grammar produced essays that were judged to have better content than those of the students who had not studied any grammar, but the raters found no significant difference on other factors, such as mechanics and sentence complexity, which were judged similar for all groups.

At the end of the third year, the various factors related to writing were evaluated a final time. A series of standardized measures showed that the students who had studied grammar performed better on the usage test than those who had not, but no significant differences on the other measures were found. After three years of work and effort, the writing of the students who had studied grammar showed no significant differences in overall quality from that of students who had studied no grammar. Frequency of error in spelling, punctuation, sentence structure, and other mechanical measures did not vary from group to group. As far as their writing was concerned, studying grammar or not studying grammar simply made no difference.

Such studies make it clear that grammar instruction has no demonstrated positive effect on the quality of students' writing. This is not to suggest that it has a negative effect, nor should anyone dismiss the possibility that grammar instruction may have some as yet unspecified effect on students' general language skills. But the data do suggest that teaching students grammar has no measurable effect on writing performance.

Why, then, should we teach grammar? One answer lies in the fact that who we are as individuals, as a society, and as a culture is defined by language. Something so central to the human condition merits serious study. The only way to study and talk about language, of course, is to know the appropriate terms and to understand the various relations among the constructions that constitute the language we use. This is where grammar comes in. It provides information of form and function that allows us to study language and how we communicate. Another answer—less palatable, perhaps—is that grammar is interesting and intellectually challenging. It can enhance analytical and critical-thinking skills. In addition, a knowledge of grammar has been deemed a characteristic of well-educated people throughout Western history. As Hirsch (1987) convincingly argued, there are certain things worth knowing.

The real question is not why we teach grammar, but how. Considering the amount of research that shows no effect of grammar study on writing, it seems reasonable to conclude that it is time for another approach. In lieu of teaching grammar as an independent unit for its own sake (highly desirable), the most viable approach is to link grammar with reading. Reading activities lend themselves nicely to discussions of form and function as well as meaning. Furthermore, they lend themselves to indirect pedagogy rather than direct, which seems to work more effectively, especially with younger students. While discussing a text, the teacher can point out to students an interesting adjective or a provocative phrase. No explanation is necessary, really—just a reference to form and function.

APPLYING KEY IDEAS

Something that emerges from the studies cited earlier is the idea that knowledge of grammar appears to exist fairly well outside the domain of writing. It seems easy to teach people grammar but hard for them to apply that knowledge to the act of writing. The following activity is designed to make these notions more understandable. It is based on the idea that learning grammar rules and applying those rules require significantly different abilities. The first part of the activity consists of learning an invented grammar, whereas the second part consists of using the grammar in writing.[10] After completing the activity, most people better understand why teaching students grammar rules does not improve their writing.

A Make-Believe Grammar

Rule 1: All adjectives must follow the nouns they modify.

Example: The car *old* stopped at the light *red*.
Exception: Any adjective that modifies a noun signifying or related to the body of a person will come before the noun, but the noun will take the suffix -o.
Example: The old *man-o* gave the flower to the young *woman-o* because he liked her pretty *face-o*.

Rule 2: The indefinite article is *zot*. (Indefinite articles are *a* and *an*.)

Example: At the circus, the clown tooted *zot* horn.

Exception: Indefinite articles that come before an adjective are *zots*.
Example: We saw *zots* old policeman riding *zots* brown horse.

---

[10]Although initially you may think that learning invented grammar rules is quite different from learning rules for the grammar you've acquired from birth, it really isn't. Those acquired rules are unconscious, and learning them as you've been doing in this text requires raising them to a conscious level. On this account, the cognitive operations of mastering the rules and applying them are similar, regardless of whether they describe rules associated with an acquired language or invented rules like those in this activity.

Rule 3: The progressive verb form consists of *be* + *verb* + *ing*, but tense is marked as follows—*x* for past, *y* for present, *z* for future.

Example: The man *be-y* washing his car.

Exception: All actions involving nonhumans form the progressive with *be* + *verb* + *ing*, but tense in all instances is marked with *k*.

Example: My dog *be-k* running in the yard.

Part 1

Use rules to correct the following "ungrammatical" sentences:

1. The wind blew in over the dark mountains and chilled the young boys.
2. There was a strange look on the woman's face, as though she was thinking deep thoughts.
3. The waves were crashing against the beach, but the hardy surfers were waiting until the foamy crests were higher.
4. Several people strolled down the boardwalk and tossed a handful of bread crumbs at the screeching gulls that were flying overhead.
5. Macarena was getting cold because she had forgotten to bring even a light jacket.
6. Fritz was bundled up snug and warm in a down parka, but he was not going to offer his warm coat to Macarena.
7. Macarena began walking to her old Ford as the noisy gulls were swooping down at her.
8. Fritz was following slowly behind when one of the gulls stole a piece of a derelict's soggy Big Mac.
9. A few more birds distracted the derelict until he dropped the burger, and then a huge gull grabbed it in his yellow beak.
10. Meanwhile, a sullen Macarena slid into the driver's seat and drove off, leaving Fritz standing in the lot with a silly look on his silly face.

Part 2

In about 10 minutes, write a description of the things you did before going to campus today. Be sure to use our make-believe grammar in your writing.

2

Phrase-Structure Grammar

OVERVIEW

- **From the Universal to the Particular**
- **Phrase-Structure Rules**
- **Tree Diagrams**
- **Direct and Indirect Objects**
- **Prepositional Phrases**
- **Coordination**
- **Expanding the Verb Phrase**
- **Possessives**
- **Subordinate Clauses**
- **Complement Clauses**
- **Relative Clauses**
- **Negatives**
- **Nonfinite Verb Forms**
- **Summary of Phrase-Structure Rules**

FROM THE UNIVERSAL TO THE PARTICULAR

Until the 19th century, Latin grammar was deemed universally applicable to all languages, not just to English and related European tongues. Those who were interested in studying grammar devoted a great deal of their attention to what are known as "linguistic universals"—features of grammar and language that transcend individual languages. All languages, for example, have subjects and predicates, and all have some way of referencing the time of actions in sentences. Within the context of modern grammar, the concept of linguistic universals also is concerned with the knowledge that a person has of language in general. This knowledge is deemed to be the result of certain innate characteristics of being human rather than of education or learning.

Linguistic universals were an important part of traditional grammar and served as a rationale for teaching. The study of English was a means to an end. Students studied English grammar in preparation for studying Latin grammar. It was understood that instruction in Latin could proceed more easily when children mastered terminology and concepts in their own language. But the enterprise was not without its problems. We have already looked briefly at the issue of tense. Latin and its associated languages have three tenses: past, present, and future. English, on the other hand, has only two tenses: past and present. Nevertheless, many scholars opted to consider *will* + *verb* as the future tense in English because doing so appeared to be intuitively correct and logical. Indeed, it does not occur to many people that a language might have fewer than three tenses, although the perceived complexities of language cause these same people to shrug their shoulders in resignation at the prospect that a language might have more than three. Other inconsistencies simply were ignored as being irrelevant to the larger goal of preparing students for Latin.

Although American schools have not taught Latin for decades, traditional grammar continues to try to match English grammar to Latin. Virtually all current handbooks, for example, propose that English has at least three tenses. Most take an inexplicable additional step—rather than exploring aspect, they instead treat progressive and perfect forms as tenses. They describe the *past progressive tense*, the *present progressive tense*, the *future progressive tense*, and so on. In these accounts, English has anywhere from 9 to 16 tenses, depending on the text.

Views on traditional grammar began to change toward the end of the 19th century, and much of the motivation for this change was the result of interest in American Indian tribal languages. Native Americans largely had been ignored after the great Indian wars, but they became the focus of much scholarly attention when anthropologists began perceiving that the distinctive characteristics of these indigenous people were vanishing. An intensive preservation program started, and researchers such as Franz Boas began efforts to record the details of the tribal cultures, particularly their languages.

A few early missionaries had produced some records of these languages, but they were not systematic and lacked the rigor necessary to preserve the languages for the future. In addition, these missionaries used traditional grammar in their efforts, with less than satisfactory results. In his introduction to the *Handbook of American Indian Languages*, Boas (1911) lamented the fact that the descriptions were distorted by the attempt to impose traditional grammar on languages for which it was inappropriate. Trying to get these languages to fit traditional grammar was the linguistic equivalent of forcing a round peg into a square hole.

Tense again provides an interesting illustration. Many Indian languages have only one tense, usually the present, yet they were described as though they have three tenses, like Latin. In some cases, to ensure that the description was congruent with the Latin model, those describing the languages would produce a construction that did not naturally occur among native speakers. These were instances in which the grammar drove the language to such an extent that the finished description did not reflect the way people used the language. As more data were collected, the number of such incompatibilities grew, and researchers were at a loss. When confronted with different dialects of the same language, they could not decide which was "correct" because there was no standard by which to make a judgment. There were no texts. Eventually, scholars like Boas concluded that the goal of traditional grammar, prescription based on a literary model, was inadequate.

Now known as *structuralists*, these scholars, led by Boas and later by Leonard Bloomfield (1933), worked for several years to develop a new grammar, one that did not make the same assumptions about linguistic universals that were inherent in traditional grammar. They called this grammar *Immediate Constituent Analysis* (ICA), a term that was so awkward that, in 1957, when Noam Chomsky dubbed ICA "phrase-structure grammar" the name stuck.

The differences between phrase-structure grammar and traditional grammar are many, but for our purposes we only need to focus on a few distinctive features. One of the more important was that the new grammar abandoned many of the notions of universal grammar and opted instead for the idea that every language is unique, with its own structure and its own grammar. This reorientation reflected a fundamental shift in the way American linguists saw the study of grammar, a shift associated with different philosophies and world views. Traditional grammar was based largely on *rationalism*, which proposes that human knowledge is not based on the senses or experience. Rationalism can be traced back to Plato, who argued that the world of experiences is merely a shadow of a transcendental reality that can be known only through the powers of the intellect, guided by philosophy. The senses are incapable of revealing more than a distorted semblance of reality, an idea that Plato developed with memorable effect in *The Republic* through his allegory of the cave.

Transcendentalism can provide a workable model of reality with respect to certain concepts, such as geometric figures and justice. A circle, for example, is defined mathematically as a plane figure composed of a series of points equidistant from a center point. Drawing such a figure, however, is impossible owing to the problems associated with exact measurement. Thus, a perfect circle exists only in the mind. One likewise can propose that true justice exists only in the mind because the mundane reality of our court system is that it readily sacrifices justice for the sake of expediency. Nevertheless, in both cases the transcendental model is sufficiently close to reality to make a comparison possible. Thinking about a perfect circle can lead to the production of a circle that is a very close approximation of the mental model.

This approach does not work with language. The structuralists found that transcendentalism was so far removed from their experiences with actual language that a comparison was *not* possible. Just *thinking* about grammatical forms never would allow someone to develop a correct description of the tense system in Cherokee. Such a description required data collection, analysis, interpretation, and rule formation. It required, in other words, an empirical approach to language. The orientation of the structuralists therefore was the antithesis of their predecessors, for whereas rationalism proposes that all knowledge comes from reflection rather than from the senses, empiricism proposes that all knowledge comes from the senses rather than from reflection.[1]

Linked to this view was an equally important shift in the grammar, away from prescription to description. Matters of correctness were replaced with what Bloomfield (1933) referred to as *acceptability,* which is determined on the basis of context. Thus, an utterance or a written statement might be grammatical but unacceptable.[2] On this account, grammaticality judgments are linked to attested utterances, not to a literary norm. An immediate consequence of this view is that grammaticality becomes largely a matter of word order, not usage conventions. Consider the following sentences:

- ?He don't got no money.
- He doesn't have any money.
- *Doesn't money he any have.

The first two sentences are grammatical in this view because both conform to the SVO word order of English. The third sentence is ungrammatical because it does not conform to that word order. The first sentence is nonstandard, how-

---

[1]Rationalism describes a closed universe. For example, Plato's ideal forms are absolutes: They do not change, nor do they increase. Nothing new is possible in a universe governed by rationalism. The real universe is characterized by change, which suggests that rationalism is not a very good intellectual tool for understanding the world. With respect to language, change occurs all the time. New words and structures, as well as dialectical variations in pronunciation or accent, appear frequently. Language is an open system, not a closed one.

[2]These terms, of course, do not mean that a listener will reject the utterances of a person who uses an "unacceptable" form. It means that the listener will make a judgment about the utterances (and usually about the speaker). A typical judgment is that the speaker doesn't use "proper" language; another is that the speaker isn't well educated.

ever, so in those situations that call for Standard English it will be deemed unacceptable. It is reasonable to assume that the same would apply to the second sentence, that in those situations that call for nonstandard English—for example, a conversation in the home of a nonstandard speaker—this sentence would be unacceptable. There are occasions in which that assumption is correct, but we cannot say that it always is correct. Nonstandard speakers usually are not critical of standard speakers, even in those situations in which nonstandard English is the norm. Standard speakers, on the other hand, generally are critical of nonstandard speakers in all situations and seldom will accept nonstandard English, regardless of the context.

The emphasis on description rather than prescription has led to widespread misunderstanding of the goals and principles of phrase-structure grammar. The popular perception is that the grammar takes an "anything goes" approach to language. The distinction between grammaticality and acceptability, which is the distinction between grammar and usage, clearly does not endorse such an approach. But the long-standing association between grammar and logic, as well as the pejorative connotations of the expression, "ungrammatical," make it hard for many to embrace the idea that nonstandard English is just as grammatical and logical as standard. The message inherent in phrase-structure grammar is that it is quite difficult for native speakers of a language to produce ungrammatical sentences. This message, as we shall see, has significant implications for teaching grammar and writing.

APPLYING KEY IDEAS

Observe how you change your language on the basis of context. Chances are that your language is more formal in the classroom than it is at home or in the school cafeteria. Using a small recorder, tape your conversations in two contrasting settings, and then analyze your speech in a couple of paragraphs that explain how it differs by context. Look at word choice, sentence length and structure, and degree of repetition.

PHRASE-STRUCTURE RULES

The emphasis on description in phrase-structure grammar is important in many ways, but one of the more salient is its effect on the notion of a grammar rule. In traditional grammar, rules are essentially inviolable, and we are asked to force language to conform to the rules. In phrase-structure grammar, the situation is different. The term "rule" is used very loosely to describe the observed grammatical patterns that exist in a given language. Consequently, when we use the term "rule" in phrase-structure grammar, we are not referring to an inviolable statement about language; instead, we are referring to a pattern of constructions that are characteristic of and that describe a given language. Another way of expressing this point is to say that phrase-structure grammar does not have a generative component. The "rules" we use do not produce sentences; they merely *describe* them. As a result, the "rules" change whenever we encounter a real-world utterance that the "rules" do not describe.

A key to understanding phrase-structure grammar therefore lies in being able to look at a string of words and determine how to describe the string using the grammar. That is one of the tasks of this chapter. We have already noted that grammatical analysis focuses on language at the sentence level; in phrase-structure grammar, this focus is made highly explicit through the kinds of questions it tries to answer and through the shorthand notation it uses for sentence analysis. We can begin examining both issues by considering that phrase-structure grammar recognizes that a sentence (S) has two primary components, a noun phrase (NP) and a verb phrase (VP). The level of grammatical analysis, therefore, proceeds on the basis of phrases. The first grammar "rule" in phrase-structure analysis reflects this basic characteristic:

S → NP VP

This expression is read as follows: "S is rewritten as NP VP." This rule is the starting point of all grammatical analyses in phrase-structure grammar. Keep in mind that this statement is not a rule for generating sentences; it simply describes the fact that English sentences that we can observe on a daily basis normally follow this pattern.

Let's examine how this rule can describe a basic sentence, one that we have seen before:

1. Dogs bark.

S → NP VP

Although this rule describes the makeup of the sentence, it is not sufficiently specific because it does not describe the noun phrase or the verb phrase. We can look at the sentence and determine the composition of these phrases, which in turn allows us to write additional rules for NP and VP.

NP → N

VP → V

To complete the description, we need to assign words to N and V, which results in the following:

N → dogs

V → bark

Each line represents a specific assignment of features designed to reveal the structure of the various parts of this particular sentence. The sentence may consist of a noun phrase and a verb phrase, but what are these phrases composed of? Each is composed of an individual word, a noun and a verb, respectively. The final step is to describe the noun and the verb, to list the actual words that make up the sentence. This set of phrase-structure rules is referred to as a *grammar of the sentence*. The process of producing this grammar reflects the procedures that American linguists used in the 19th century. It builds a lexicon—a list of words—while showing how those words fit together to make grammatical sentences.

The sentence grammar for Sentence 1 is pretty simple, but it contains within itself the power to describe quite complex sentences. The key lies in an important feature of phrase-structure grammar: *recursion*. Recursion is an idea borrowed from mathematics. With respect to language, it conveys the fact that complex expressions can be analyzed in terms of their simpler components. In addition, it bases analysis on *knowledge of the expected outcome*. That is, any analysis of a sentence begins with the completed sentence, not with an abstraction, and not with some unknown endpoint. It is like solving a math problem while knowing the answer in advance. *The goal is not to discover the answer but to understand the steps leading to it.*

The advantages these features lend to analysis become clearer if we look at a series of increasingly complex sentences and adjust the initial rule in ways that allow us to describe each of them grammatically:

2. Fred bought a suit.

The analysis begins with the first phrase-structure rule:

S → NP VP

Notice, again, that we are not attempting to show how the sentence ought to fit together but rather how it does. On this account, our phrase-structure analysis must describe the existing sentence while generalizing in ways that also allow us to describe Sentence 1. First, sentences 1 and 2 reflect differences in the verb phrase—one has an object and the other does not. We have to conclude that

NP is an optional element in the verb phrase. Second, sentences 1 and 2 reflect differences in the noun phrase. The object NP in Sentence 2 has a determiner, the indefinite article *a,* whereas there were no determiners in Sentence 1, and, indeed, there is no determiner in the subject NP of Sentence 2. We therefore have to conclude that determiners are optional elements. Phrase-structure grammar uses a convention for optional elements: It places them in parentheses. With these factors in mind, we can adjust the earlier rules so that they describe both sentences, as shown here:

NP → (det) N

VP → V (NP)

det → art

N → Fred, suit

V → bought

art → a

This sentence grammar is more complex than the previous one, not only because the sentence is more complicated but also because we are writing a grammar that is generalizable to both sentences, with the exception of the individual words assigned. Now consider another example:

3. Maria wore an expensive evening gown.

This sentence is interesting because it adds adjectivals to our basic NP VP combination, and one of them is a noun, *evening.* We therefore must adjust the phrase-structure rules so that they will describe all three of our sentences, which means adding a rule for the adjective phrase (AdjP) that describes both types of adjectivals:

S → NP VP

NP → (det) (AdjP) N

VP → V (NP)

det → art

$$AdjP \rightarrow \begin{Bmatrix} adj \\ NP \end{Bmatrix}$$

N → Maria, evening, gown

V → wore

art → an

adj → expensive

The rule for AdjP introduces another convention—brackets. Brackets indicate that one of the elements, adj or NP, must be chosen. (From this point on, we recognize that *det* is rewritten as *art*, but we will not include this step in our analyses because it involves an unrevealing level.)

Let's take this opportunity to generalize a bit. The rule for AdjP describes all adjectivals in a noun phrase, but it does not describe predicate adjectives, which we discussed in Chapter 1. The sentence, *The tree was tall*, illustrated a basic sentence pattern, with *tall* functioning as a predicate adjective. Having discussed adjectivals in the noun phrase, it is a good idea to extend our analysis and adjust our rules here so that they will describe all instances of AdjP. We can do this by making a simple modification to our rule for VP:

VP → V (NP) (AdjP)

Adjusting the rule for the verb phrase raises an interesting issue with respect to verbs—the status of particles. We examined particles in Chapter 1, but now we can look at them more closely. While doing so, let's consider another construction that can appear in both the verb phrase and the noun phrase—the prepositional phrase. Consider these sentences:

4. The goons with bow ties looked up the number for Pizza Hut.
5. Buggsy put the gun on the table.

The set of phrase-structure rules we have developed so far works to describe parts of these sentences, but not all of them. Unlike sentences 1 through 3, Sentence 4 has two prepositional phrases (PP) as parts of two noun phrases, and it has the verb particle *up* (prt). Sentence 5 has a prepositional phrase as part of the verb phrase. These structures were not in the previous example sentences, which means that we must treat them as optional elements. Adjusting the rules is fairly easy at this point: We must provide for optional prepositional phrases in both NP and VP, and we must allow two possibilities for V, one being a *verb + particle* combination. With these adjustments, we can describe sentences 1–5 and many others:

S → NP VP

NP → (det) (AdjP) (PP) N

VP → V (NP) (AdjP) (PP)

$$AdjP \rightarrow \begin{Bmatrix} adj \\ NP \end{Bmatrix}$$

PP → prep NP

$$V \rightarrow \begin{Bmatrix} V \\ V + prt \end{Bmatrix}$$

N → goons, bowties, number, Pizza Hut, Buggsy, gun, table

V → looked + prt, put

det → the

prep → with, for, on

prt → up

These rules have value beyond their ability to describe sentences 1 through 5. They also help us understand that, as sentences become more complex, the grammar must become more flexible if it is to describe a variety of structures. NP and VP, for example, may have several elements, but they are all optional except for the core features, N and V, respectively. Perhaps the larger goal of phrase-structure grammar is becoming clear. Individual sentence grammars are revealing, but the process of producing a new set of rules for all the possible individual sentences in English (an infinite number) is not practical. Moreover, it does not provide a coherent picture of the whole language. The goal, therefore, is to examine a wide range of sentences to develop a set of highly generalizable statements that describe most (but not necessarily all) of the grammatical sentences that speakers of the language normally produce.

Directions: Write separate phrase-structure rules for each of the following sentences:

1. A bug danced across my palm.
2. The cold wind blew from the distant lake.
3. An old man asked for a drink at the bar.
4. Buggsy put on a coat and walked into the desert.
5. Fritz really liked Macarena.

TREE DIAGRAMS

Grammar is about sentences—the form of the words and their functions in sentences. Consequently, analyzing individual sentences is a major part of grammatical study. Such analysis can provide a great deal of information about language. In the 19th century, Alonzo Reed and Brainerd Kellogg developed a way to diagram sentences in an effort to make grammatical analysis more revealing and meaningful. Many schools continue to use Reed-Kellogg diagrams today, more than a hundred years later. As the examples that follow suggest, the Reed-Kellogg approach to diagraming sentences gets very complicated very quickly. These diagrams have no labels for constituents, so it isn't easy to note at a glance what the constituents are. Understanding the structure of any sentence demands understanding the structure of the diagraming procedure, which is arbitrary and often counterintuitive.

Let's consider three fairly simple sentences:

6. Fred is a good friend.
7. Running is good exercise.
8. Buggsy believed that he was a handsome dog of a man.

Sentences 6 and 7 illustrate the counterintuitive nature of Reed-Kellogg diagrams. Any analysis of a sentence must provide information about form as well as function. The lack of labels in the Reed-Kellogg approach is a big handicap in this regard: It forces Reed-Kellogg diagrams to adopt different structures for words that have identical functions but different forms. In Sentence 6 *Fred* is a noun and functions as the subject, whereas in Sentence 7, the subject *Running* is a gerund (a verb functioning as a noun). Large numbers of students over the years have found such distinctions confusing. The Reed-Kellogg diagram for Sentence 8, on the other hand, is seriously complex. The Reed-Kellogg analysis is shown in the diagrams below:

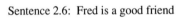
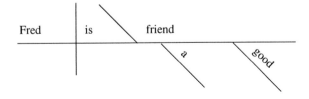

Sentence 2.7: Running is good exercise

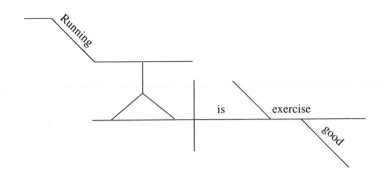

Sentence 2.8: Buggsy believed that he was a handsome dog of a man

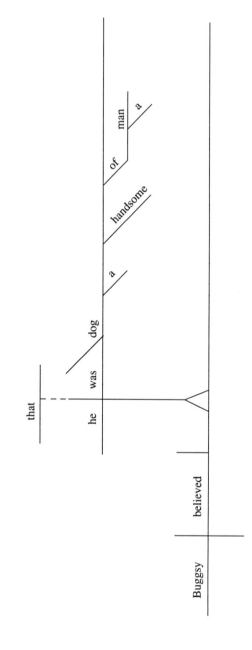

Sentence 2.6: Fred is a good friend

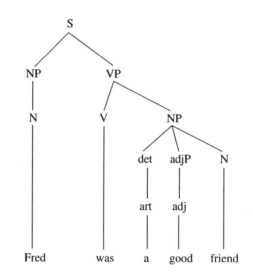

Sentence 2.7: Running is good exercise

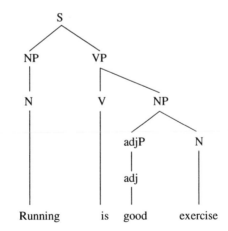

A more revealing and instructional method of analysis is the *tree diagram*, in which all the components are labeled and in which all the relations are easily recognizable. Compare the tree diagrams here with their corresponding Reed-Kellogg diagrams.

Sentence 2.8: Buggsy believed that he was a handsome dog of a man

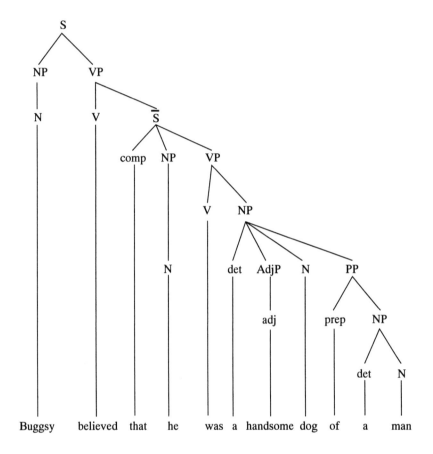

DIRECT AND INDIRECT OBJECTS

We examined direct and indirect objects in Chapter 1 as part of the discussion of transitive and ditransitive verbs. Because the basic sentence pattern in English is SVO, it is important to consider early on how phrase-structure grammar treats objects. We already have a phrase-structure rule that describes objects:

VP → V (NP) (AdjP) (PP)

The only thing we have to keep in mind with these rules is that, for indirect objects that appear as a noun phrase rather than as a prepositional phrase, we add another noun phrase to the analysis. Consider this sentence:

9. Fritz sent his grandmother a gift.

This sentence has a verb phrase of the form V NP NP. Diagraming results in the following analysis:

Sentence 2.9: Fritz sent his grandmother a gift

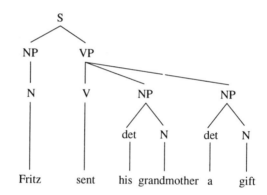

Now consider these additional sentences and their associated diagrams:

10. Buggsy asked a question of the commissioner.
11. Macarena bought her mother a new watch.
12. The police sent the evidence to the crime lab.

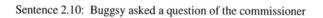

Sentence 2.10: Buggsy asked a question of the commissioner

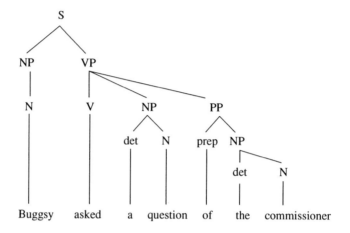

Sentence 2.11: Macarena bought her mother a new watch

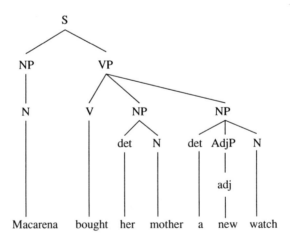

Sentence 2.12: The police sent the evidence to the crime lab

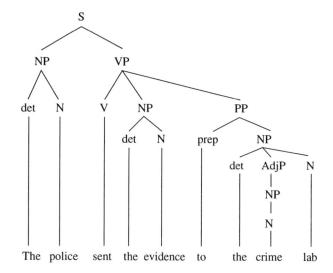

PREPOSITIONAL PHRASES

Prepositional phrases are interesting structures because they are so versatile. They can function as indirect objects, and they also can function as adverbial modifiers and as adjectival modifiers. As adverbials, they can function as sentence-level modifiers, which means that they can modify an entire clause. In Chapter 1, we discussed phrasal modifiers and noted that the prepositional phrase is one of the major types. As indicated in that discussion, prepositional phrases can appear in the initial, medial, or final positions. When they appear in the initial or the medial positions, prepositional phrases are sentence-level modifiers.

13. The goons put yellow flowers on the table. (adverbial)
14. The woman with the red hair drives a Porsche. (adjectival)
15. In the morning, Buggsy went home. (sentence level)
16. Macarena, with a smile, accepted the invitation. (sentence level)

In addition, prepositional phrases can function as complements to certain kinds of verbs, as in Sentence 17:

17. Fred stepped onto the stool. (verb complement)

The tree diagrams below show the various grammatical relations. Note carefully how the prepositional phrases are connected to the constituents they modify. In sentences 15 and 16, the prepositional phrases branch off the S because they are sentence-level modifiers.

Sentence 2.13: The goons put yellow flowers on the table

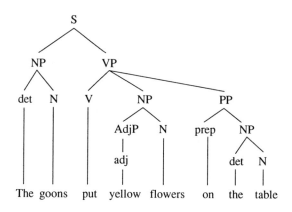

Sentence 2.14: The woman with red hair drives a Porsche

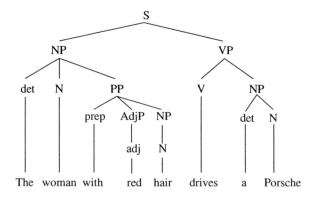

Sentence 2.15: In the morning, Buggsy went home

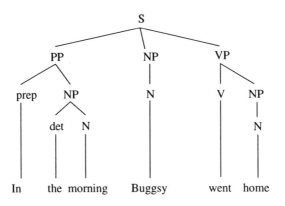

Sentence 2.16: Macarena, with a smile, accepted the invitation

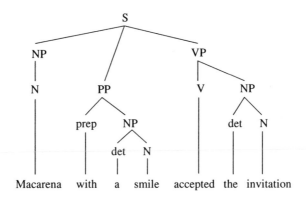

Sentence 2.17: Fred stepped onto the stool

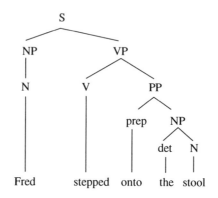

Usage Note

It is interesting to note that, until fairly recently in the history of writing, texts lacked punctuation. Punctuation developed as a result of the spread of literacy and printed texts during the 15th and 16th centuries. Earlier, handwritten books were valued as much as works of art as storehouses of information, but as literacy spread and became more utilitarian, people needed highly readable works. Punctuation helped a great deal, as did a significant reduction in the amount of artwork in books. Paragraphs also became a means of helping readers process texts. Punctuation is therefore largely a matter of convention rather than of rule, and different conventions govern the punctuation of modifying structures at the beginning of sentences, such as the prepositional phrase in Sentence 15. One convention holds that writers should use *length* as the basis for deciding whether to set the modifier off with a comma. In this convention, short structures are not set off, whereas long ones are.

Although this approach is perfectly acceptable, it creates problems for teachers whose students want as much consistency as possible. Another convention holds that *all* modifying structures at the beginning of sentences should be set off with a comma. Many teachers have adopted this convention because it is easier to teach, or at least it is easier for students to accept. They do not have to think about length.

Ambiguity

Language is inherently ambiguous, but certain prepositional phrase constructions are quite obviously so. Under normal circumstances, we use context to disambiguate such constructions, but it is possible to provide a grammatical analysis that also disambiguates. Consider the following sentences:

18. Fred built the bench in the garage.
19. Macarena put the shoes in the box in the closet.

All ambiguous sentences have two possible meanings.[3] In Sentence 18, one meaning could be that the act of building the bench could have taken place in the garage. The second meaning could be that the act of building could have occurred anywhere other than the garage, but the bench is in the garage now. In Sentence 19, the shoes already could be in the box, and Macarena put those particular boxed shoes in the closet. The other meaning could be that the empty box already could be in the closet, and Macarena put the shoes in that box.

Each possibility has a different phrase-structure analysis, which means that each has two trees:

---

[3] Although the possibility exists for more than two meanings, examples are so rare that none could be found for this text.

Sentence 2.18: Fred built the bench in the garage

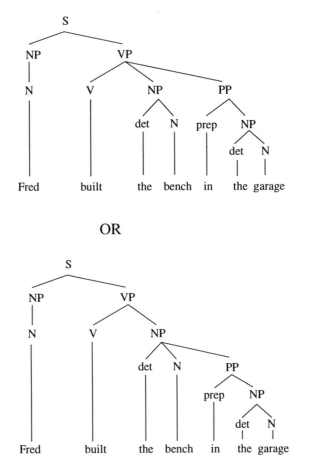

OR

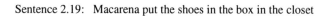

Sentence 2.19: Macarena put the shoes in the box in the closet

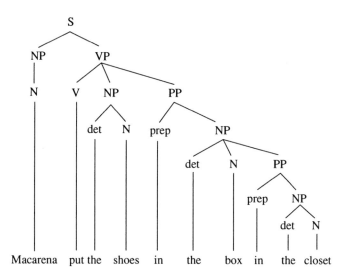

OR

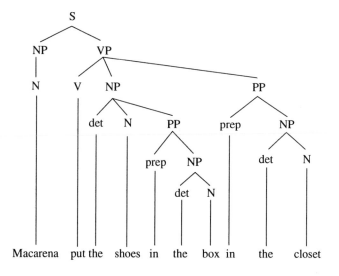

COORDINATION

Coordination is one of the more common features of language, and phrase-structure grammar provides a rule that is generally applicable to coordinated structures. It is called the *Coordinate XP* rule, where X is a variable identifying any element, such as noun or verb, and P is phrase. Coordinating conjunction is designated by CC. This rule supplies two pieces of information. First, any phrase can be conjoined to another phrase of the same form. For example, any two noun phrases can be linked using a coordinating conjunction. Second, the two conjoined phrases function as a single unit that has the character of the individual phrases. In other words, two noun phrases joined by a coordinating conjunction function as a single noun phrase:

XP → XP CC XP

As a result of this second factor, when we diagram a constituent that involves coordination, the outcome is a branch that resembles an equilateral triangle. The diagrams in Fig. 2.1 illustrate this structure.

The sentences that follow offer additional examples of the XP rule at work:

20. Fred and Fritz loved Cheerios.
21. Macarena danced, laughed, and sang at the party.
22. Buggsy glanced over the crowd and into the distance.

Representation of the XP rule for coodination

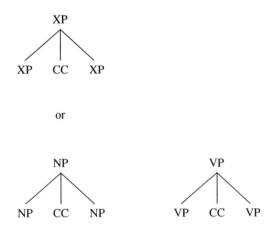

FIG. 2.1. The XP Rule. The XP rule allows us to conjoin any phrasal structure. Although this figure shows two elements conjoined, there is no real limit.

We diagram these sentences as shown in the accompanying diagrams.

Sentence 2.20: Fred and Fritz loved Cheerios

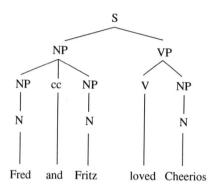

Sentence 2.21: Macarena danced, laughed, and sang at the party

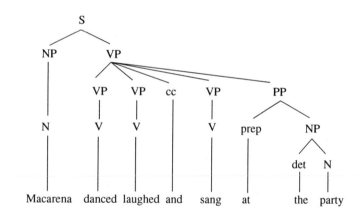

Sentence 2.22: Buggsy glanced over the crowd and into the distance

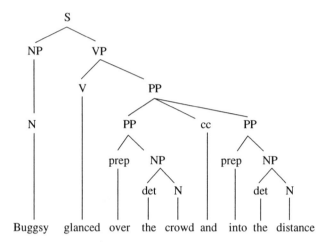

Coordination of Independent Clauses: Compound Sentences

The Coordinate XP rule also applies to entire clauses, which produces a *compound sentence.*[4] A compound sentence is one that has two independent clauses. The analysis proceeds in exactly the same way as we saw earlier, but rather than repeating phrases, the rule repeats sentences, as illustrated in the following sentences. When diagramming sentences with multiple clauses, some linguists number the sentences for each clause. This convention makes it a bit easier to discuss features of each clause.[5]

23. Macarena called Pizza Hut, and she asked for a large deluxe pizza.
24. Buggsy drove to the bank, but the ATM was broken.
25. A goon shot the ATM, so Buggsy made an easy withdrawal.

Before analyzing these sentences, let's summarize the phrase-structure rules we have developed so far:

---

[4]Although it is convenient to differentiate phrases from clauses, phrase-structure grammar (as well as other grammars) generally treats clauses as special types of phrases. Hence there really is no inconsistency in applying the Coordinate XP rule to clauses.

[5]Numbering the clauses (or sentences) when we diagram sentences can aid discussions because they provide a convenient reference. This convention is used throughout the text, but it is important to understand that the numbers do not have any meaning. They do not signify hierarchy or even a sequence; they are simply reference points.

XP → XP CC XP

S → NP VP

NP → (det) (AdjP) (PP) N

VP → V (NP) (AdjP) (PP)

AdjP → $\begin{Bmatrix} \text{adj} \\ \text{NP} \end{Bmatrix}$

PP → prep NP

V → $\begin{Bmatrix} \text{V} \\ \text{V + prt} \end{Bmatrix}$

Sentence 2.23: Macarena called Pizza Hut, and she asked for a large deluxe pizza

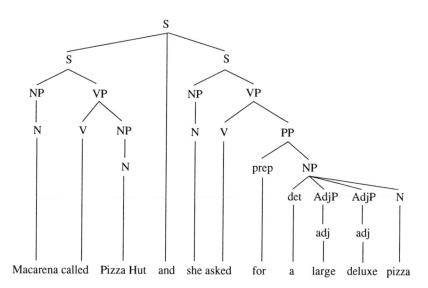

Sentence 2.24: Buggsy drove to the bank, but the ATM was broken

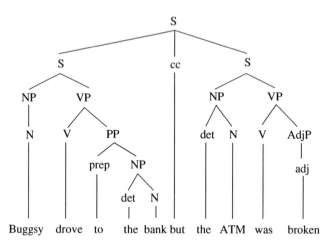

Sentence 2.25: A goon shot the ATM, so Buggsy made an easy withdrawal

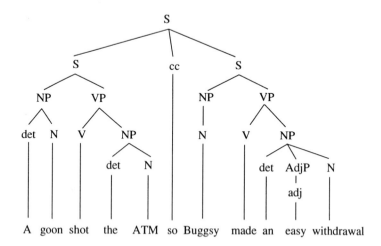

Directions: Draw tree diagrams for the following sentences. In the case of ambiguous sentences, disambiguate with two trees.

1. Macarena put the magazine on the table.
2. Fritz went to the races and bet on Lucky Lady.
3. Fred jogged to the boardwalk and watched the skaters.
4. Ophelia DiMarco and Raul drove to Rodeo Drive.
5. Fritz took the pictures with the camera in the den.
6. Macarena invited Fred for a swim, but he was busy.
7. Fritz sent roses to Macarena, and he bought her a lovely necklace.
8. Mrs. DiMarco baked a pie and a cake.
9. Without guilt or remorse, Buggsy enforced the contract.
10. Buggsy was on the road between Los Angeles and Las Vegas.
11. Raul cleaned the sofa in the living room.
12. Macarena and Fritz danced until dawn at China Club.

EXPANDING THE VERB PHRASE

Our description of verb phrases to this point has been rudimentary. It has not included any specification for tense, nor has it provided any means of describing the future or aspect. To describe these features, we need to expand our analysis of the verb phrase.

We can do this through some minor changes to the phrase-structure rule for verb phrases. Currently, our rule for verb phrases looks like this:

VP → V (NP) (AdjP) (PP)

To describe tense, we can change the rule to include an auxiliary (Aux) constituent that carries tense and other features to be discussed shortly:

VP → Aux V (NP) (AdjP) (PP)

Aux → tense

$$\text{tense} \rightarrow \left\{ \begin{array}{l} \text{past} \\ \text{present} \end{array} \right\}$$

As we noted earlier, the brackets around past/present indicate that one of the two must be chosen.

We also have to account for adverbials that modify the verb phrase, and we can do this by adding an optional adverbial phrase:

VP → Aux V (NP) (AdvP) (AdjP) (PP)

On page 30, we differentiated simple adverbs from adverbials, but at this point we can say that adverb phrases consist of adverbs and adverbials. Whereas simple adverbs are single words, such as *slowly, very, then, often,* and *easily,* adverbials can be phrases and clauses—specifically, prepositional phrases and subordinate clauses. For our purposes here, we consider them to be words only, like nouns, that function as adverbs. Expanding the rule a bit more gives us:

$$\text{AdvP} \rightarrow \begin{Bmatrix} \text{adv} \\ \text{NP} \end{Bmatrix}$$

This rule allows us to describe sentences like 26 and 27:

26. Quickly, she called her bank on the cell phone.
27. Macarena lost her checkbook yesterday.

However, adverbials and adjectivals frequently work together, as in Sentence 28:

28. Buggsy bought his wife a very expensive emerald necklace.

Such sentences lead to another modification of our rules for AdjP and AdvP:

$$\text{AdjP} \rightarrow (\text{AdvP}) \begin{Bmatrix} \text{adv} \\ \text{NP} \end{Bmatrix}$$

Sentence 2.26: Quickly, she called her bank on the cell phone

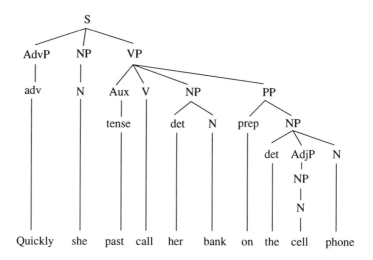

Sentence 2.27: Macarena lost her checkbook yesterday

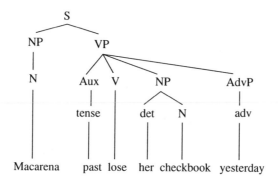

Sentence 2.28: Buggsy bought his wife a very expensive emerald necklace

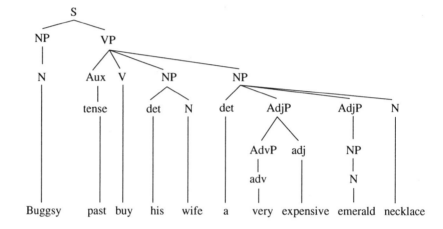

The expanded verb phrase includes a feature of verbs known as mood. Mood is interesting because it indicates the factuality or likelihood of the action or condition expressed by the verb, without our even thinking about these factors. It also can express politeness, a feature that many teachers and scholars find fascinating.

There are three moods in English:

- Indicative—used to state facts
- Imperative—used to express commands
- Subjunctive—used to express conditions contrary to fact, hypothetical permission, and politeness in making requests

The first two moods are fairly concrete, but the subjunctive mood is subtle and sometimes complicated:

- **Indicative**: Buggsy owned the casino.
- **Imperative**: Stop the car!
- **Subjunctive**:
Conditions Contrary to Fact
    1. If the election were held today, the President would lose.
    2. If I were you, I would leave town.

Hypothetical Acts
1. When I lived in Los Angeles, I could drive to the beach every weekend.
2. After the movie, we could have a bite to eat.

Politeness in Requests
1. Would you open the window?
2. Could you close the door?

Usage Note

Linguists have noted a significant change in the use of the subjunctive in contrary-to-fact statements. The example sentences just cited are expressed most commonly as:

- If the election was held today, the President would lose.
- If I was you, I would leave town.

The subjunctive marker is dropped in the verb in the conditional clause, but it is retained in the independent clause. Again, the question of what constitutes standard usage is important. Some people argue that standard usage is whatever the most people use. This argument is off the mark because it fails to take into account the influences of prestige and acceptability that generally govern standard usage. Thus, standard usage is not, and never has been, the form used most widely; it is the form most widely accepted. The subjunctive form is accepted by those who use formal Standard English and by those who do not, whereas the nonsubjunctive form is accepted only by those who use the nonstandard form. Standard usage of the subjunctive, for example, continues to appear in a great deal of writing, with the notable exception of popular journalism.

It is also interesting to recognize that nonstandard usage does not differentiate between *if* and *whether* in contrary-to-fact clauses. As a result, these sentences are deemed equivalent:

- ?I don't know if it's going to snow.
- I don't know whether it's going to snow.

Standard usage, however, does make a distinction. *If* is used to introduce conditional clauses, whereas *whether* is used to introduce clauses that express, implicitly or explicitly, alternative possibilities. Because there clearly are alternative possibilities to snow, the second sentence follows standard usage conventions, but the first one does not.

The subjunctive does not appear to have changed with respect to hypothetical acts, but some observers have suggested that it is disappearing with respect to expressing politeness in making requests. The example requests cited earlier may be more commonly expressed today as commands with a tag question seeking agreement:

- Open the window, ok?
- Close the door, ok?

Identifying the causes of these changes must be a speculative endeavor, but the loss of subjunctive in contrary-to-fact conditions may be related to a principle of behavioral efficiency. Generally, subjects and predicates agree with respect to number. In a wide variety of situations, English follows a pattern of using a singular verb form with singular subjects and a plural verb form with plural subjects, as in *I was tired* and *They were late*. The subjunctive alters this pattern: In contrary-to-fact clauses, there is no such agreement. One therefore could argue that it is more efficient to eliminate the distinction and use the singular pattern of agreement in all situations.

With respect to the disappearance of the subjunctive to express politeness, many contemporary social commentators have remarked on the significant decrease in politeness in American society—or increase in rudeness and outright hostility, depending on one's perspective—which might be a factor in the shift from requests to commands. The decrease in politeness, in turn, is seen as one reaction to the dramatic population increase that the United States has experienced during the last 30 years. As population becomes more dense, there is greater competition for resources and more hostility. The hostility, in turn, appears to be linked to the widely held view—which has erupted like the pox during the last 30 years—that others have no rights and are undeserving of respect or consideration. Social commentators point to a variety of behaviors, seldom observed a generation ago, as evidence for this assessment—the plague of drivers who cut others off in traffic, run red lights, and generally act as though they own the roads; the increase in littering that has piled rubbish ankle deep even in once-pristine cities such as San Francisco; and the general surliness of service providers who have abandoned the traditional motto, "The Customer Is Always Right," for the unsavory alternative, "The Customer Is Always Wrong."

Whatever the causes, these changes manifest themselves primarily in spoken English. The subjunctive continues to be expected in most standard written English, with the possible exception of the subjunctive expressing conditions contrary to fact.

Modals

Some features of mood, such as subjunctive hypothetical permission, are expressed in words that are called modals (M). On this account, our phrase-structure rule for the auxiliary must include two elements, a tense marker for past and present and a modal, which requires another modification. The modals are listed below:

will	shall
may	must
can	

Thus, the phrase-structure rule for Aux would be:

Aux → tense (M)

$$M \rightarrow \left\{ \begin{array}{l} \text{will} \\ \text{shall} \\ \text{can} \\ \text{may} \\ \text{must} \end{array} \right\}$$

The brackets around the modals, remember, indicate that one of the words on the list must be selected.

The tree diagrams for the following sentences show how this new rule affects our description of verb phrases:

29. Macarena attended the opening with Fred.
30. Fritz will visit the psychic tomorrow.
31. Buggsy could buy an expensive gift.

A question that often arises in the analysis of expanded verb phrases is why the tense marker is placed in front of the verb rather than after. The past participle suffix -ed/ -en, after all, comes at the end of a verb, not at the beginning. The answer is that there is no simple way to capture schematically the relations among tense, modals, and verbs. Whenever a verb has a modal, the modal is tensed, not the verb. If our description put tense after the verb, we would solve nothing—we would still have the question of how tense jumps over the verb and attaches to the modal. The placement of tense at the head of the VP is a matter of convention; placing it elsewhere in the VP would not enhance the description. We have to accept the fact that structural analyses are at best an approximate description of the language we actually use. If we wanted to account for the fact that the past participle appears at the end of verbs, we would have to develop a special rule for attachment, which indeed is what linguists have done. We discuss this rule in the next chapter.

When we examine tense closely, it becomes apparent that the relation between tense and verbs is not a simple one. Tense does not merely indicate when an action took place, as evidenced in sentences such as:

Macarena could visit her sick friend in the morning.

The verb *visit* is not tensed in this sentence; instead, the tense marker is attached to the modal. But although the modal is in the past tense, the action is to occur in the future. Many students have a hard time grasping this concept.

Sentence 2.29: Macarena attended the opening with Fred

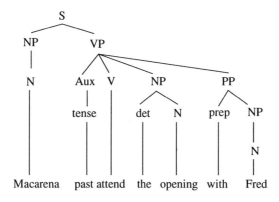

Sentence 2.30: Fritz will visit his psychic tomorrow

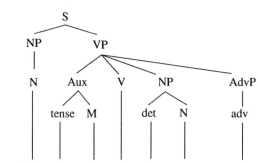

Sentence 2.31: Buggsy could buy an expensive gift

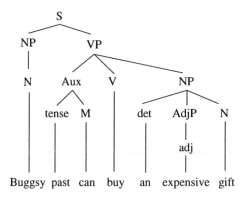

Usage Note

Although modals are function words, they nevertheless have a semantic content. *Can* and *may*, for example, do not mean the same thing. *Can* indicates ability, whereas *may* indicates permission as well as a conditional future. Popular usage has largely eliminated *may* and replaced it with *can*. Formal standard usage, however, continues to differentiate between these words. Consider these sentences:

32. Fritz can play the piano.
33. Fritz may play the piano.

Sentence 32 signifies Fritz's ability to play; Sentence 33, on the other hand, is ambiguous. It can be understood as giving Fritz permission to play, or it can be understood as a comment about Fritz's playing the piano at some time in the future. The condition is uncertain. We easily can imagine this future conditional if we think of Fritz being at a party. Sentence 34 offers another example of *may* as a future conditional:

34. Buggsy may take a trip next week.

It is worth noting that the past-tense form of *may* is *might*. These words differ in that *might* signifies a more uncertain or doubtful future than does *may*. Thus, the likelihood of Buggsy taking a trip is more uncertain in Sentence 35 than it is in Sentence 34:

35. Buggsy might take a trip next week.

Like many other usage distinctions, this one seems to be disappearing. Even speakers and writers of formal Standard English rarely differentiate the two forms.

The difference between *will* and *shall* is far more complicated, and it, too, has essentially disappeared in American usage. The traditional distinction maintains that *shall* is used to indicate the simple future in the first person, as in *I shall go to the movies. Shall* cannot be used in the second and third persons, however, but instead must be replaced by *will*, as in *They will end the strike soon.* The use of *will* in the first person does not express simple future but instead signifies a promised action, as in *I will give you the loan.* The use of *shall* in the second and third persons signifies a command, as in *You shall stop seeing that horrible man immediately.* Currently, the only widespread use of *shall* in American usage, even among standard speakers, is in questions, as in *Shall we go now?*

Do Support

In English, the word *do* is used to emphasize a statement, as in these examples:

36. Fred *does* like the veal.
37. Macarena *did* deposit the check into her account.

When *do* is used for emphasis, it is referred to as *do support*. *Do* is analyzed as part of the auxiliary, as the accompanying diagrams illustrate. In Standard English, *do* cannot appear with another modal, although it can in Black English Vernacular. Note that our rule for writing *Aux* is now:

Aux → tense (M) (do)

Sentence 2.36: Fred does like the veal

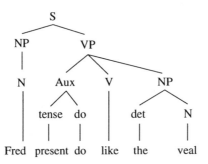

Sentence 2.37: Macarena did deposit the check into her account

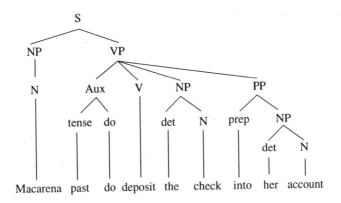

APPLYING KEY IDEAS

Directions: Draw tree diagrams for these sentences.

1. Fred and Macarena drove to the beach.
2. Fritz called Macarena several times.
3. Rita de Luna did return the telephone call.
4. Fritz polished the lenses of the telescope and considered the possibilities.
5. They would be at that special spot near Malibu.
6. Quickly, Fritz made himself a chicken-salad sandwich and poured lemonade into the thermos.
7. Fritz could drive to Malibu in 40 minutes from the apartment in Venice.
8. Buggsy must employ a dozen goons.
9. Buggsy has a mild heart problem, so he should live a quiet life.
10. Mrs. DiMarco does forget things sometimes.
11. Someday, he will regret those poor eating habits.
12. Buggsy could retire completely, but he would miss the action.
13. They might vacation in Acapulco.
14. She can spend money in some remarkable ways.
15. Fred and Fritz do get jealous of each other.

Progressive Verb Forms

The progressive verb form in English indicates the ongoing nature of an action and is considered to be a feature of aspect. Progressives are formed with *be* and a verb to which the suffix *-ing* is attached. Progressive is analyzed as part of the auxiliary, which means that we need to adjust our phrase structure rule from page 89:

Aux → tense (M) (do)

becomes

Aux → tense (M) (do) (prog)

prog → be -ing

where *prog* represents progressive.

This new phrase-structure rule allows us to analyze sentences like the following:

38. Macarena was *dancing* at China Club.
39. The band members were *playing* a hot salsa.
40. They are *thinking* about the next break.

Sentence 2.38: Macarena was dancing at China Club

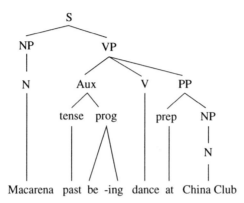

Sentence 2.39: The band members were playing a hot salsa

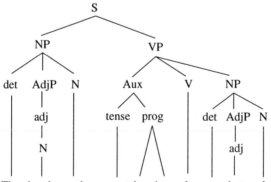

Sentence 2.40: They are thinking about the next break

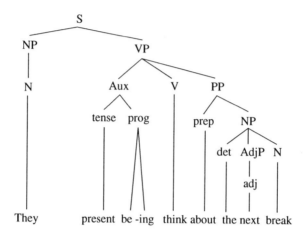

Progressive Verb Forms and Predicate Adjectives.   English presents an analytical problem with sentences like the following:

41. Raul was running.
42. His toe was throbbing.

The structure of these sentences seems to be very similar, and, in fact, it may seem reasonable to analyze them both as having progressive form verb phrases. Such an analysis, however, is not accurate. Sentence 41 indeed has a progressive form verb phrase, but Sentence 42 does not; instead, the VP consists of a linking verb and a predicate adjective. The appropriate analyses are shown in the accompanying diagrams:

Sentence 2.41: Raul was running

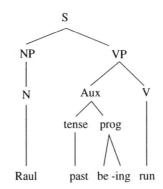

Sentence 2.42: His toe was throbbing

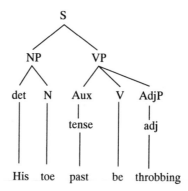

The key to understanding the difference lies in recognizing the distinct roles the two subjects have in these sentences. In Sentence 41, the subject is an agent performing an action. In Sentence 42, the subject is not an agent, so it does not perform an action, which means that *throbbing* cannot describe an action in this case because no action is performed. Instead, *throbbing* provides existential information. On this account, we can say that progressive forms always have an agentive subject.[6] Whenever the subject is not an agent, the verb phrase consists of a linking verb and predicate adjective.

This analysis is supported by the structures of sentences like the following:

- Mrs. DiMarco was boring.
- Mrs. DiMarco was boring Raul.

In the first, Mrs. DiMarco is not an agentive subject, whereas in the second she is. The difference in function not only results in different grammatical analyses but, as we should expect, different meanings. Further support comes from the fact that words like *throbbing* also can function as simple adjectives, as in *She had a throbbing headache.* Following are some additional examples for illustration:

- Macarena *was jogging* along the beach. (progressive verb form)
- The waves *were glistening.* (predicate adjective)
- Buggsy *was watching* from the deck of his beach house. (progressive verb form)
- He found that the sight of all the happy people *was tiring.* (predicate adjective)

Perfect Verb Forms

The perfect verb form in English consists of *have* and a verb to which the past participle suffix -ed/ -en has been attached. It signifies more than one temporal relation. The past perfect, for example, indicates that one event occurred before another event. The present perfect indicates that an event has recurred or that it already has occurred. The future perfect indicates that an event will have occurred by the time that another event will be happening. These three possibilities, respectively, are illustrated in the following sentences:

43. Fred *had eaten* at Spago many times before that fateful day.
44. Macarena *has looked* everywhere for the diskette.
45. Fritz *will have driven* 150 miles before dark.

---

[6]An obvious exception to this generalization is the sentence, *It is raining.* The problem, however, is that this is an idiomatic expression; the subject *it* does not have a referent and appears merely to fill the subject position of the sentence. Not only is *it* not an agentive subject, the word also lacks semantic content. Nevertheless, the predicate clearly contains a progressive verb form. Such idiomatic expressions cause no end of difficulties for grammatical analysis.

Like the progressive, the perfect verb form is analyzed as part of the auxiliary; we abbreviate it here as *perf*. Making the necessary adjustment to the phrase-structure rule results in:

Aux → tense (M) (do) (prog) (perf)

Perf → have -ed/-en

If we use this new rule to analyze Sentences 43 through 45, we have the accompanying diagrams.

Sentence 2.43: Fred had eaten at Spago many times before that fateful day

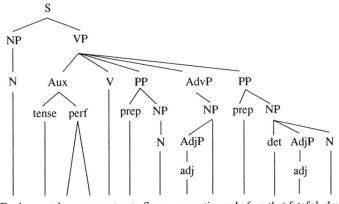

Sentence 2.44: Macarena has looked everywhere for the diskette

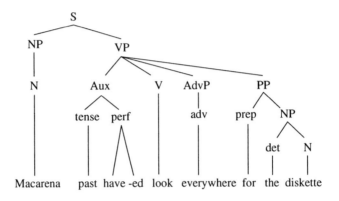

Sentence 2.45: Fritz will have driven 150 miles before dark

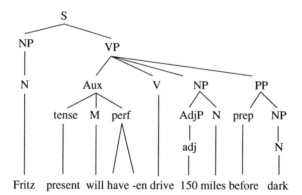

Applying Key Ideas

Directions: Draw tree diagrams for the following sentences.

1. Fritz was carrying a large box.
2. He had surprised Macarena with a mock-rabbit fur coat, and she had looked stunned.
3. She should return it with a cutting comment, but Fritz might be crushed.
4. In Macarena, Fritz had found an ambitious woman.
5. Later, Macarena was driving down the street with Fred in the red Ford.
6. Fred had laughed at the coat.
7. He could afford a real rabbit fur coat for Macarena.
8. In the evening, Fred and Macarena had gone to a party in Malibu.
9. Buggsy was dancing at the party like a wild man.
10. Suddenly, the old heart was doing a hot merengue against the ribs, and the eyes were bulging.
11. One of the goons was calling for paramedics, and another was searching for a stethoscope.
12. Meanwhile, Macarena is wondering about the coat and Fritz, but Fred is drinking champagne.
13. She will return the coat to Fritz in the morning.
14. He can learn about style and taste somehow.
15. He may feel bad about the situation, but it will be good for him in the end.

POSSESSIVES

English forms the possessive using pronouns or a noun and a possessive (poss) marker, as in *her book* or *Maria's book*. Possessives are considered to be in the category of determiners. To this point, our discussion of determiners has included only articles. We might modify the phrase-structure rule, however, to account for possessives by using an expression such as the following:

$$\text{det} \rightarrow \left\{ \begin{matrix} \text{NP} \quad \text{poss} \\ \text{art} \end{matrix} \right\}$$

$$\text{poss} \rightarrow \text{'s}$$

This rule now shows that a determiner is either a noun plus possessive marker or an article.

Now consider these sentences:

46. Macarena wanted Bob's job.

47. Fred's shirt had a hole in it.
48. The bartender's sister's roommate's boyfriend loved China Club.

We would analyze these sentences as shown in the accompanying diagrams.

Sentence 2.46: Macarena wanted Bob's job

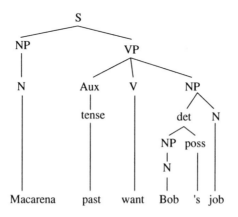

Sentence 2.47: Fred's shirt had a hole in it

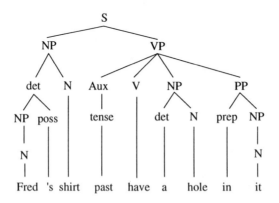

Sentence 2.48: The bartender's sister's roommate's boyfriend loved China Club

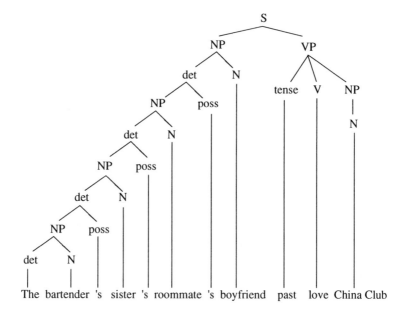

Most grammatical analyses pay little attention to possessive pronouns for good reasons. Initially, one might think that the previous analysis would work fairly well for possessive pronouns, but it doesn't. Designating the possessive *her* as *she + poss* seems counterintuitive because there is no evidence that *her* exists as anything other than an independent pronoun. We form the possessive noun by attaching the possessive marker to the noun. Possessive pronouns, however, exist as independent lexical items and are not formed at all—they already exist in the lexicon. In this analysis, possessive pronouns are much like the indefinite articles *a* and *an*. We do not form *an* by adding *n* to *a*; the two forms exist independently. Consequently, most analyses exclude possessive pronouns from the domain of the NP in the phrase-structure rule, and ours does likewise. The resulting phrase-structure rule looks something like this:

$$\text{det} \rightarrow \left\{ \begin{array}{c} \text{pro} \\ \text{NP poss} \\ \text{art} \end{array} \right\}$$

poss→'s

Pro in this instance always is a possessive pronoun. (As in the case of articles, it is important to recognize how pronouns fit into the grammar, but including them in our analyses does not add anything revealing. Thus we do not apply pro to the diagrams that follow.)

SUBORDINATE CLAUSES

We discussed subordinate clauses on pages 36–38and noted that they always begin with a subordinating conjunction. When a sentence contains a subordinate clause (or any other type of dependent clause) it is called a *complex sentence.* (A sentence with coordinated independent clauses and at least one dependent clause is called a *compound-complex sentence.*) Some of the more common subordinating conjunctions are listed in the following table:

after	although	as
because	beore	if
once	since	though
unless	until	whether
when	whenever	as of
even if	in order that	as soon as
even though	insofar as	as though
inasmuch as		

Subordinate clauses function as adverbials; thus they modify a verb phrase or an entire clause, in which case they are sentence-level modifiers. The difference is related to the restrictive or nonrestrictive nature of the modifier. Let's examine these two possibilities:

49. Fred drove to Las Vegas because he liked the desert air.
50. Macarena exercised until she was exhausted.

51. Although he was uncultivated, Buggsy liked opera.
52. Fritz wore a sweater, even though the evening was warm.
53. Raul, because he was young, felt immortal.

In sentences 49 and 50, the subordinate clause is a restrictive modifier, which means that it supplies necessary or defining information to a verb phrase. In sentences 51 through 53, however, the subordinate clause is a nonrestrictive modifier in the initial, final, and medial positions, respectively. Nonrestrictive subordinate clauses are sentence-level modifiers. An easy way to identify nonrestrictive modifiers is that they are punctuated. Some subordinate clauses at the beginning of a sentence may not be punctuated if the writer is using the length convention for initial modifiers. Such initial subordinate clauses nevertheless are nonrestrictive. They have to be because as adverbials they must modify either a VP or an S. In the initial position, they can modify only an S.

With certain verbs, subordinate clauses can function as complements, as in:

54. We wondered whether the fish were fresh.
55. They could not decide whether the trip was worth the cost.

Ideally, we want a phrase-structure rule that describes all these structures but that also captures the fact that a subordinate clause functions adverbially as part of the verb phrase or as a sentence-level modifier. There is no way to provide such information in the rule, however, so we must be satisfied with a rule that just describes the structure. Several possibilities exist, but the simplest seems to be a rule similar to the XP rule we used for coordination. If we think of a dependent clause as $\bar{S}$ (read bar-S), our rule would be:

$$XP \rightarrow XP \, \bar{S}$$

$$\bar{S} \rightarrow Sconj \, NP \, VP$$

The first expression states that any phrase, XP, can be rewritten as that phrase plus $\bar{S}$. $\bar{S}$, in turn, can be rewritten as a subordinating conjunction (Sconj), a noun phrase, and a verb phrase. Stated another way, any XP may have an $\bar{S}$ attached to it. As in the rule for coordination, XP can represent either a clause or a phrase. We must explain, outside the rule, that when $\bar{S}$ is a subordinate clause, it attaches either to S or VP. We can do this because the grammar is concerned primarily with describing existing sentences. If structuralists had given the grammar a generative component—that is, if it were more concerned with how people generate sentences with subordinate clauses—they might have attempted to develop an expression that addresses the question of placement.

Without this concern, the issue is moot because placement is given in the utterance being described.

We want a rule that is very generalizable, of course, so shortly in this chapter we expand the definition of S̄ to include other types of dependent clauses, which means that S̄ attaches to various types of phrases.

With the phrase-structure rules described previously, we can examine more closely the structure of the earlier example sentences, as shown in the accompanying diagrams.

Sentence 2.49: Fred drove to Las Vegas because he liked the desert air

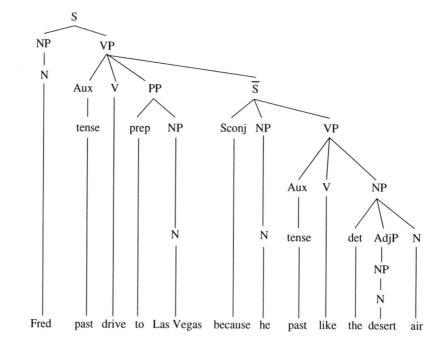

Sentence 2.50: Macarena exercised until she was exhausted

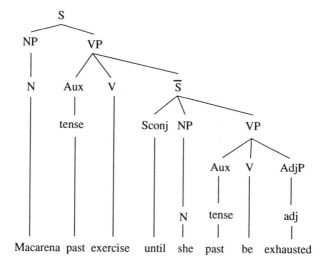

Sentence 2.51: Although he was uncultivated, Buggsy liked opera

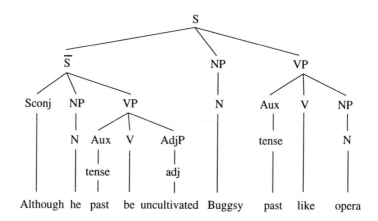

Sentence 2.52: Fritz wore a sweater, even though the evening was warm

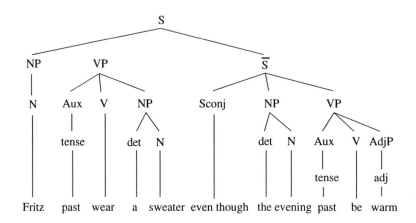

Sentence 2.53: Raul, because he was young, felt immortal

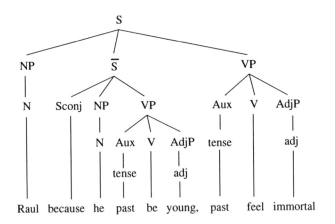

Sentence 2.54: We wondered whether the fish were fresh

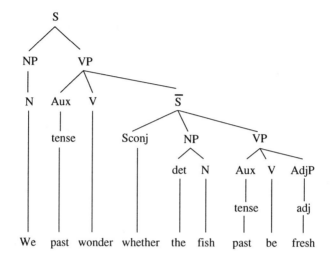

Sentence 2.55: They could not decide whether the trip was worth the cost

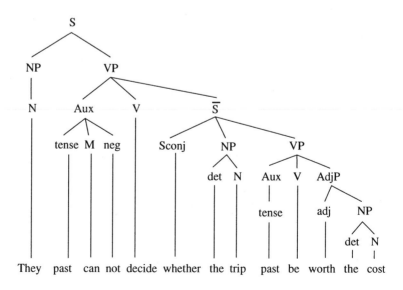

COMPLEMENT CLAUSES

Earlier we looked at a common problem in nonstandard usage that involves a subordinate clause and a linking verb:

*The reason is because it's important.

Subordinate clauses cannot follow linking verbs; only noun constructions, adjective constructions, and prepositional phrases can do so. With respect to this example sentence, formal standard usage therefore calls for:

The reason is *that it's important.*

The italicized portion of the sentence is a complex noun construction known as a complement clause.

These constructions are fairly versatile. They can function as subjects, objects, noun complements, verb complements (as shown earlier), and adjective complements. The following sentences illustrate these possibilities:

56. *That Macarena liked Buggsy* surprised everyone. (subject)
57. Raul knew *that he should get* a job. (object)
58. Mrs. DiMarco scoffed at the idea *that she should remarry.* (NP complement)
59. The problem was *that Buggsy's wife could be mean.* (VP complement)
60. Macarena was sad *that she had missed the concert.* (AdjP complement)
61. Raul knew nothing except *that he loved Maria.* (object of preposition)

A complement clause always has a subject and a predicate, and it begins with the complementizing conjunction (comp) *that.* In the case of complement clauses functioning as objects, however, we have the option of deleting the complementizer, which results in sentences like 57a:

57a. Raul knew *he should get a job.*

When such sentences are analyzed on a tree diagram, the null symbol (Ø) takes the place of the complementizer.

We can describe this construction by again adjusting the relevant phrase-structure rule. We simply need to add a complementizer to our S̄ rule.

$$\bar{S} \rightarrow \begin{Bmatrix} Sconj \\ comp \end{Bmatrix} NP\ VP$$

$$comp \rightarrow \begin{Bmatrix} that \\ \theta \end{Bmatrix}$$

The accompanying diagrams illustrate how to analyze these types of constructions:

Sentence 2.56: That Macarena liked Buggsy surprised everyone

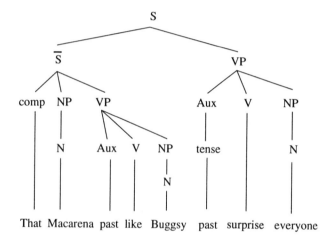

Sentence 2.57: Raul knew that he should get a job

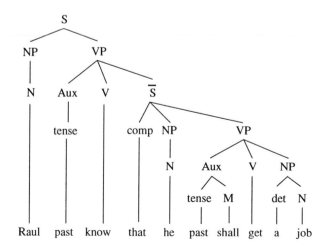

Sentence 2.58: Mrs. DiMarco scoffed at the idea that she should remarry

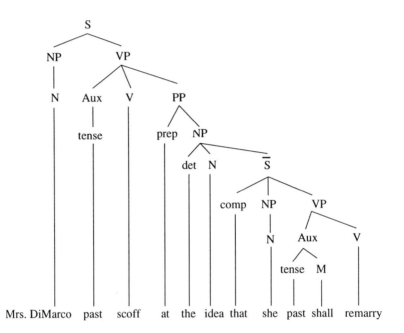

Sentence 2.59: The problem was that Buggsy's wife could be mean

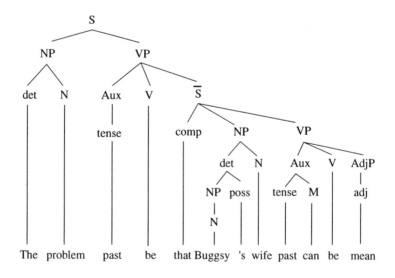

Sentence 2.60: Macarena was sad that she had missed the concert

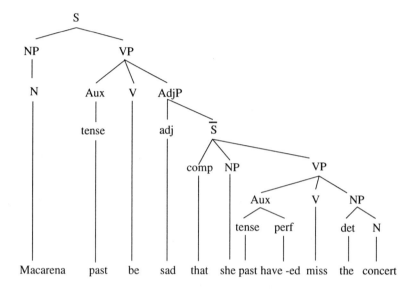

Sentence 2.61: Raul knew nothing except that he loved Maria

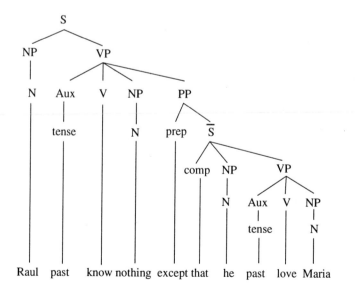

APPLYING KEY IDEAS

Directions: Draw tree diagrams for the following sentences.

1. Buggsy's goons had come from New Jersey.
2. Fritz realized that he could have forgotten the meeting.
3. Macarena did like Fritz, even though she hated his apartment.
4. That Buggsy flirted with Macarena and Rita de Luna shocked the host of the party.
5. Buggsy's goons got nice tans after they arrived in L.A. from the East Coast.
6. Macarena sometimes wondered whether she should settle down.
7. When she thought of her childhood in cold Chicago, Mrs. DiMarco was happy that she lived in L.A.
8. Mrs. DiMarco's nephew had lost his way after his parents died.
9. She knew that he ran with a dangerous crowd but was unsure that she could help him.
10. Although Fritz had had little success with women, he thought that he was a ladykiller.
11. The fact that he was obnoxious troubled everyone.
12. He did believe that he had bad luck.
13. Macarena's friends disliked Fritz immensely, and because they were her friends, they had suggested that she find a better beau.
14. Fred was more kind, but he brooded and often was downcast because he felt unappreciated.
15. Macarena felt bad when she thought about the men in her life.

RELATIVE CLAUSES

In many respects, relative clauses are among the more interesting structures in English. They are interesting, in part, because of how they work as modifiers. They supply information to noun phrases, but they also can function as sentence-level modifiers. When they do, they modify the *meaning* of the independent clause rather than a syntactic component—a curious arrangement. Another factor that makes relative clauses interesting is the relative pronoun. We have seen how other dependent clauses—subordinate clauses and complement clauses—are connected to an independent clause via a linking word (a subordinating conjunction and a complementizer, respectively). Relative clauses are linked to independent clauses via a relative pronoun, but relative pronouns are more than just linking words. They are like regular pronouns in that they replace a duplicate noun phrase in a sentence. In addition, they function as either the subject or the object of the relative clause. Thus, they perform three syntactic functions in a sentence, whereas subordinators and complementizers perform only one.

The more common relative pronouns are shown in the following table:

who	whom	that
which	whose	where
when	why	

A relative clause must always begin with a relative pronoun because it needs to be linked to the independent clause. We can see the linking function in the following sample sentences:

62. Buggsy bought the house *that had belonged to Liberace.*
63. The boy *who drove the van* played the blues.
64. The book *that Fritz borrowed* lacked an index.

It is always important to understand that any sentence with a dependent clause has undergone a process of combining that joins two (or more) clauses into a single sentence. In the case of relative clauses, the relative pronoun replaces a noun phrase duplicated in the two clauses. Sentences 62 through 64, for example, are made up of the following clauses.

62a. Buggsy bought *the house. The house* had belonged to Liberace.
63a. *The boy* played the blues. *The boy* drove the van.
64a. *The book* lacked an index. Fritz borrowed *the book.*

If we attempted to combine these clauses without using a relative pronoun, the results would be ungrammatical:

62b. *Buggsy bought the house the house had belonged to Liberace.
63b. *The boy played the blues the boy drove the van.
64b. *The book lacked an index Fritz borrowed the book.

The multiple functions that relative pronouns play in such sentences create a certain degree of confusion, at least with respect to sentences like 64, in which the relative pronoun replaces an object noun phrase. Sentence 64a clearly shows that *the book* functions as the object noun phrase in what becomes the relative clause. We know that objects follow nouns; that's a basic feature of English word order. In this case, however, the relative pronoun must link the relative clause to the independent clause, which means that the pronoun must shift from its position behind the verb to a new position in front of the subject, thereby violating the standard SVO word order. As a result, large numbers of native English speakers cannot recognize that the word *that* in Sentence 64 is functioning as an object.

Like other complex modifiers, relative clauses can function restrictively or nonrestrictively. Restrictive relative clauses supply defining or necessary information, so they are not set off with punctuation. Nonrestrictive relative clauses, on the other hand, supply additional or nonessential information; thus, they are set off with punctuation. The nonrestrictive constructions we have examined to this point have been adverbials, and they always have been sentence-level modifiers. Nonrestrictive relative clauses are different in this respect because sometimes they are sentence-level modifiers and sometimes they are not. Consider the following:

65. The book, *which was a first edition*, had a gold-inlaid cover.
66. Fred vacationed in Mexico, *which disturbed his parents*.

In Sentence 65, the relative clause, even though it is nonrestrictive, clearly modifies the noun phrase *The book*. In Sentence 66, however, there is no single head word; instead, the relative clause is modifying the meaning of the independent clause. That meaning might be described as the fact that Fred vacationed in Mexico. Because the entire clause is receiving the modification, we must consider the relative clause in Sentence 66 to be a sentence-level modifier. Relative clauses that function as sentence-level modifiers always begin with the relative pronoun *which* (*in which* is a common exception), but not all relative clauses that begin with the relative pronoun *which* are sentence-level modifiers.[7]

Following are some additional examples that show the difference between the two types of nonrestrictive modification:

---

[7]A curious exception seems to occur with sentences that begin with *there*. Consider the following:
There was a thunderous rip from Buggy's trousers that focused all eyes on him.
The relative clause, *that focused all eyes on him*, is similar to the one in Sentence 66 in that it lacks a head word. Clearly, *trousers* is not the head word. Equally unacceptable is a *thunderous rip*—for syntactic reasons. The relative clause would have to be attached to this NP if a *thunderous rip* were the head word, in which case the sentence would have to be:
*There was a thunderous rip that focused all eyes on him from Buggy's trousers.
Not only is this sentence ungrammatical, but it also is not the sentence we started with. On this account, we have to propose that the antecedent for the relative pronoun *that* is semantic rather than syntactic, such that the clause, before the relative pronoun replaces the NP subject, might be: *A thunderous rip from Buggy's trousers focused all eyes on him.*
In this case, however, the relative clause must function as a sentence-level modifier. Thus, we not only have a nonrestrictive sentence-level relative clause that begins with *that* rather than *which*, but we also have one that lacks the punctuation that normally distinguishes nonrestrictive relative clauses.

67. Fritz enjoyed walks in the park, *which drove Macarena crazy.* (sentence modifier)
68. The Malibu house, *which Buggsy used simply for relaxation,* was damaged in the mud slide. (NP modifier)
69. Buggsy took up golf, *which troubled his wife.* (sentence modifier)
70. Mrs. DiMarco's properties, *which were extensive,* provided her with a very comfortable living. (NP modifier)
71. China Club always had an attractive crowd, *which appealed to Fritz.* (sentence modifier)

We saw earlier that when complement clauses function as objects, English allows deletion of the complementizer, as in *She knew Fred was tired.* English also allows us to delete relative pronouns under the same conditions, as the following sentences illustrate:

72. The book *that Fritz borrowed* lacked an index.
72a. The book *Fritz borrowed* lacked an index.

To describe relative clauses, we must make a slight adjustment to our phrase-structure rules. Note that we must make NP optional to describe the fact that some relative clauses have a relative pronoun as the subject. Also note that the null marker is for deleted relative pronouns:

$$\bar{S} \rightarrow \begin{Bmatrix} \text{Sconj} \\ \text{comp} \\ \text{RP} \end{Bmatrix} \text{(NP) VP}$$

$$RP \rightarrow \begin{Bmatrix} \text{who} \\ \text{that} \\ \text{which} \\ \text{where} \\ \text{why} \\ \ldots \\ \theta \end{Bmatrix}$$

Now let's examine more carefully the structure of the previous sentences by seeing how they appear in tree diagrams. Of particular importance are the diagrams for sentences 65 and 66, which illustrate how the analysis of nonrestrictive relative clauses differs from that of restrictive.

Sentence 2.62: Buggsy bought the house that had belonged to Liberace

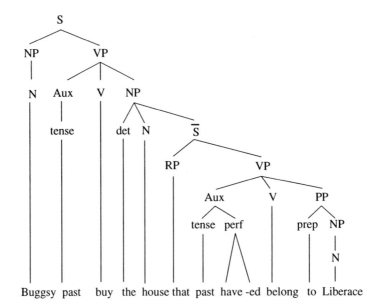

Sentence 2.63: The boy who drove the van played the blues

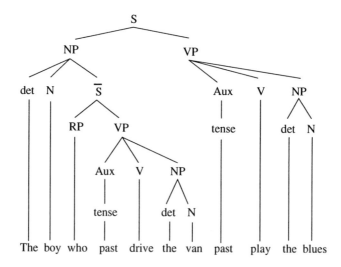

Sentence 2.64: The book that Fritz borrowed lacked an index

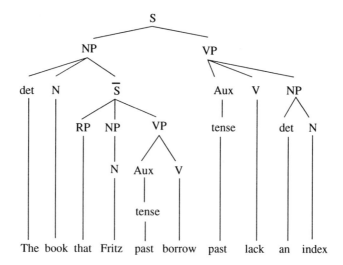

Sentence 2.65: The book, which was a first edition, had a gold-inlaid cover

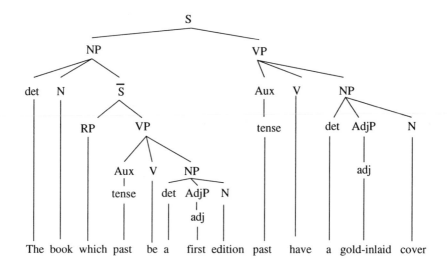

Sentence 2.66: Fred vacationed in Mexico, which disturbed his parents

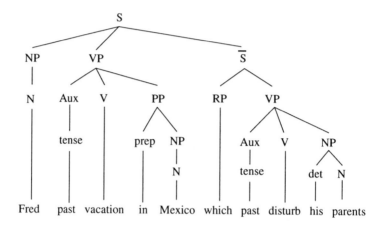

Sentence 2.67: Fritz enjoyed walks in the park, which drove Macarena crazy

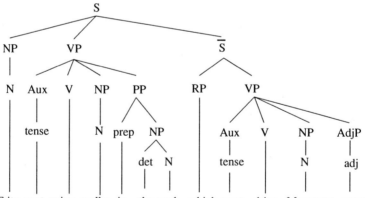

Sentence 2.68: The Malibu house, which Buggsy used simply for relaxation, was damaged in the mud slide

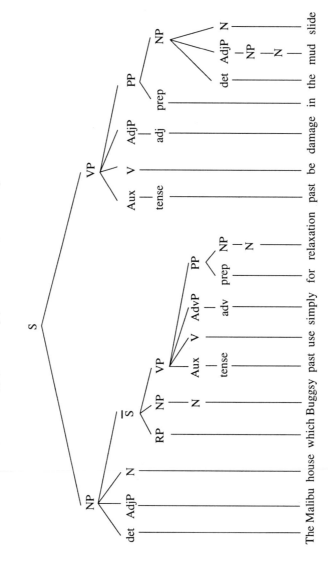

Sentence 2.69: Buggsy took up golf, which troubled his wife

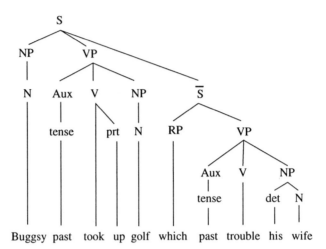

Sentence 2.70: Mrs. DiMarco's properties, which were extensive, provided her with a very comfortable living

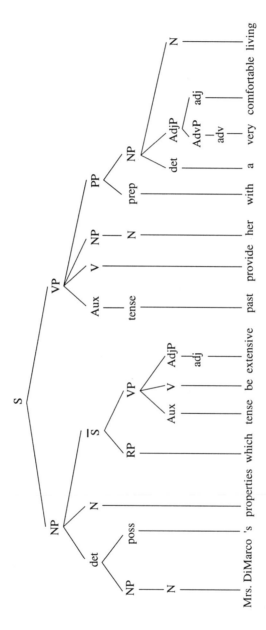

Sentence 2.71: China Club always had an attractive crowd, which appealed to Fritz

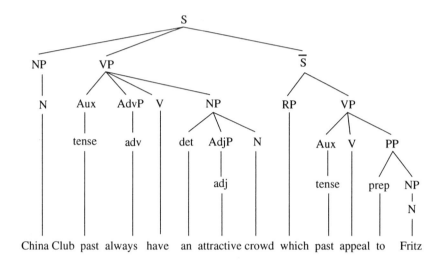

Usage Note

Most people treat the relative pronouns *that* and *which* as being identical. In fact, many teachers are known to tell students who ask about these words that they are interchangeable and that they should be used alternatively to add more variety to writing. Formal standard usage, however, differentiates them along a very clear line: *That* is used exclusively to introduce restrictive relative clauses, and *which* is used, generally, to introduce nonrestrictive relative clauses. The word "generally" is important because there are several types of relative clauses and some involve the relative pronoun *which* even though they are restrictive, as in: "The deposition *in which* the answer appeared had been sealed by the court."

We examine this construction in the next section but can say here that it does not really affect the convention.[8]

Earlier, the discussion noted that many people are not able to recognize when a relative pronoun is functioning as an object because relative clauses do not follow standard SVO word order. This difficulty appears to have affected usage significantly with respect to the pronouns *who* and *whom*. Even those who use Standard English fairly consistently have dropped *whom* from most of their speech, and increasingly it is being dropped from writing as well. In speech,

---

[8]The exception to this convention was discussed in note 7.

most people use *who* or *that*, and even in much journalistic writing we find *who* being used rather than *whom*. In English education, writers who still use *whom* frequently find that journal editors will change *whom* to *who* before publication. Clearly, usage is changing!

The difference between *who* and *whom* is related to case, which we examined on pages 16–18. *Who* always functions as the subject of a relative clause, so it is in the nominative case. *Whom*, on the other hand, always functions as an object, either of the verb of the relative clause or of a preposition, so it is in the objective case. And like other pronouns in English, the form of these relative pronouns is determined by their case—*whom* is the objective form of *who*. Consider the following sentences:

- The man *who owned the Porsche* worked at a bank.
- The man *whom I knew* worked at a bank.

The structure of these relative clauses is quite different. *Who* functions as the subject of *owned* in the first case, and *I* functions as the subject of *knew* in the second. *Whom* is the object of *knew*, even though it appears at the beginning of the clause. Most people do not pay much attention to this difference, especially when speaking: They have not had sufficient exposure to formal standard usage for it to have become internalized, so applying the *who/whom* distinction requires conscious application of grammatical knowledge that many do not possess. Even those with this knowledge commonly fail to apply it because the flow of the conversation interferes with application or because they fear that using *whom* will make them sound elitist.

As noted on page 113, when the relative pronoun is an object it is possible to drop it from the sentence (*The man I knew worked at a bank*), which helps a bit. People do this naturally, so they do not have to learn anything new.[9] More problematic, perhaps, are instances in which the relative pronoun functions as the object of a preposition: "Ask not for whom the bell tolls ... " Some speakers will use the nominative case in such constructions (*for who the bell tolls*), but many others simply avoid using these constructions entirely, thereby reducing their linguistic repertoire.

Another feature of formal standard usage involves differentiating between *that* and *who*. Again, as in the case of *that* and *which*, many people mistakenly believe that these words are interchangeable:

- ?The boy *that* found the wallet turned it in at the police station.

---

[9]An analysis of a sentence like *The man I knew worked at a bank* would show the null symbol (Ø) to mark the place of the dropped relative pronoun.

- The boy *who* found the wallet turned it in at the police station.

But they are not interchangeable in formal Standard English; they are quite different. Standard usage provides that *who* is used for people and *that* is used for everything else. This convention used to be followed with some consistency, as evidenced by the fact that not even nonstandard speakers use these pronouns interchangeably in sentences like the following:

- The lamp *that* is on the table cost $300.
- *The lamp *who* is on the table cost $300.

This interesting example raises the question of why English has two relative pronouns that are so similar. Both words have Old English roots, so the answer does not lie in English's famous ability to absorb words from other languages. Most likely, these pronouns reflect a time when English was more concerned about distinctions, much in the way that Spanish is concerned about identifying gender: *La muchacha es linda* (The girl is pretty) versus *El muchacho is lindo* (The boy is cute). In any event, we appear to be witnessing a shift in English to a single form—*that*—for use in all situations. If this shift continues, both *who* and *whom* eventually may disappear from contemporary English.

Relative Clauses and Prepositional Phrases

Another interesting feature of relative clauses is that they often involve a prepositional phrase. When they do, the noun phrase in the prepositional phrase is a relative pronoun. Consider the following sentences:

73. The triangle *in which they were embroiled* defied logic.
74. We knew several people *for whom banishment was too kind.*

It may be easier to understand these constructions if we look at the dependent clauses before they are relativized:

73a. The triangle defied logic. They were embroiled in the triangle.
74a. We knew several people. Banishment was too kind for several people.

In Sentences 73a and 74a, we can see the noun phrases that require shifting to relative pronouns in keeping with the general prohibition against duplicate noun phrases.

Earlier, we examined (and discarded) the common school injunction against ending sentences with prepositions. We are now in a better position to consider what is involved when at least one kind of sentence ends with a preposition. Consider Sentences 75 and 75a:

75. Macarena hated the clothes *which Fred arrived in.*
75a. Macarena hated the clothes. Fred arrived in the clothes.

Sentence 75 is very similar to Sentence 73 in that it involves a prepositional phrase with a relative pronoun in the NP. It differs, however, in that the prepositional phrase has been split; the relative pronoun is at the beginning of the relative clause, but the preposition still follows the verb. English allows this sort of construction. Examining 75a suggests an important pattern for relatives. When we take a clause like *Fred arrived in the clothes*, where the NP that gets relativized is an object—either of the verb or of the preposition—we move the resulting relative pronoun to the front of the clause. We do not have to do this when we relativize a subject NP because it is already at the beginning of the clause. When the relativized NP is the object of a preposition, as in Sentence 75, *we have the option of shifting the entire PP to the beginning of the clause or of shifting just the relative pronoun.* Exercising the second option results in sentences like 75, with a preposition at the end.

To describe these sentences, we need to make a couple of small adjustments to our phrase- structure rules:

$$\bar{S} \to \left\{ \begin{array}{c} \text{Sconj} \\ \text{comp} \\ \text{RP} \\ \text{PP} \end{array} \right\} \text{(NP) VP}$$

$$\text{PP} \to \text{prep} \left\{ \begin{array}{c} \text{NP} \\ \text{RP} \\ \theta \end{array} \right\}$$

These rules allow us to begin a relative clause with a PP as long as the object of the preposition is a relative pronoun. This restriction is important because it means that a prepositional phrase with a relative-pronoun object outside the domain of a relative clause will be ungrammatical.[10] The null marker fills the place of a shifted relative pronoun. As in some other cases, there is a feature here that we cannot write into the rule; we must consider it outside the expression. The

---

[10]This point is fairly simple if we look at an actual construction. Consider the following: **Raul parked the car in which.*

optional NP occurs only when the RP of a relative clause is functioning as the subject; otherwise the NP is obligatory.

The role of relative pronouns in prepositional phrases is much clearer if we use diagrams to analyze their structure. Consider the following examples:

Sentence 2.73: The triangle in which they were embroiled defied logic

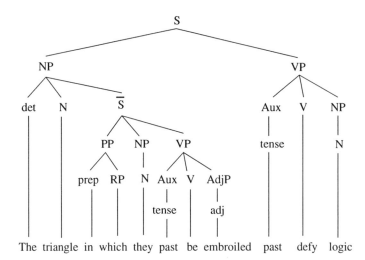

Sentence 2.74: We knew several people for whom banishment was too kind

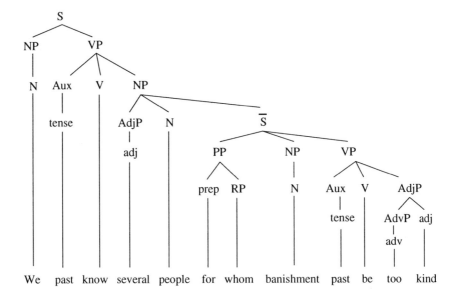

Sentence 2.75: Macarena hated the clothes which Fred arrived in

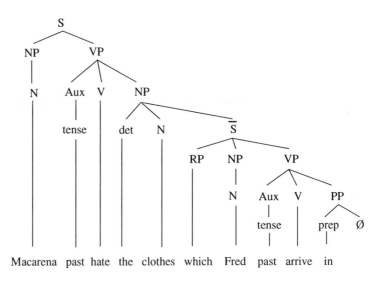

125

NEGATIVES

Although there are many ways to say *no* in English even when appearing to say *yes*, grammatically we form the negative using *no*, *not*, and *never*. Technically, these words are adverbials, but phrase-structure grammar analyzes them as negation markers in the Aux, as the following phrase-structure rule shows:

Aux → tense (neg) (do) (M) (prog) (perf)

$$\text{neg} \rightarrow \begin{Bmatrix} \text{no} \\ \text{not} \\ \text{never} \end{Bmatrix}$$

An interesting feature of the negative is that it triggers Do Support in the verb phrase of simple active sentences. Consider these examples:

76. Fred kissed Macarena.
76a. Fred *did not* kiss Macarena.

Strangely enough, negation does not have this effect on progressive or perfect verb forms, as the following sentences illustrate:

77. Buggsy is inviting Michael Star to his next party.
77a. Buggsy is not inviting Michael Star to his next party.
78. Buggsy had left the waiter a huge tip.
78a. Buggsy had not left the waiter a huge tip.

Again, diagraming can make the structure of the sentences clearer, as in the accompanying trees:

Sentence 2.76a: Fred did not kiss Macarena

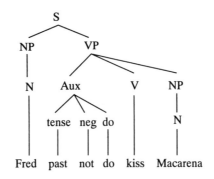

Sentence 2.77a: Buggsy is not inviting Michael Star to his next party

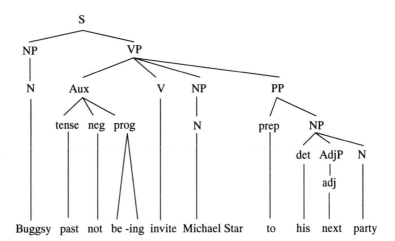

Sentence 2.78a: Buggsy had not left the waiter a huge tip

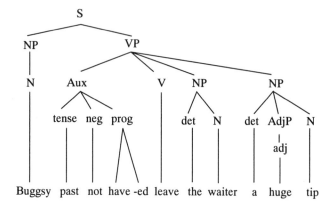

APPLYING KEY IDEAS

Directions: Draw tree diagrams for the following sentences.

1. The movie that Universal made on the USC campus disrupted classes.
2. Raul played the part of a man who won the lottery.
3. He liked the work, which thrilled his aunt.
4. Raul did not want the part.
5. Raul did not complain.
6. The actress who played his wife had amazing red hair.
7. The director whom Raul had met at a beach party gave him some acting lessons before filming.
8. Fritz, who knew Raul slightly, was jealous when he heard about the film.
9. Fritz was not happy with his career in banking because it lacked glamour.
10. He knew that Mrs. DiMarco had pawned the bracelet that he had given her for the rent.
11. The bracelet, which had been a gift for Macarena, looked like an heirloom.
12. Fritz thought that he could ask Buggsy for a loan that would buy back the bracelet, but he was afraid of the goons, who always looked mean.
13. Meanwhile, Fred had decided that Macarena, whom he loved, was the woman for him.

14. He did not have much money, but he went to Beverly Center for an engagement ring.
15. He knew a jeweler there who would give him a good price.
16. The ring that Fred wanted was very expensive, which did not surprise him.
17. Reluctantly, he turned his attention to a smaller ring that had been marked down.
18. The jeweler Fred knew was not working that day, which was a disappointment.
19. A young woman who had eyes as blue as the Pacific helped him at the counter.
20. She told him that some girl was really lucky, which made Fred blush.
21. Suddenly, he wondered whether he should ask Macarena about marriage before buying the ring.
22. The young woman, whose name was Maria, told him that most women do not like surprises of this kind.
23. At that moment, Raul, who had a date with Maria, walked into the store, which interrupted the moment.
24. Maria remembered the day when she met Raul.
25. Fred could not think of a reason why he had not talked to Macarena about his dream.

NONFINITE VERB FORMS

Up to this point, all the verb constructions we have worked with have included tensed, or what are called *finite*, verbs. Some of the more interesting constructions, however, involve untensed, or *nonfinite*, verbs. There are two major types of untensed verb forms: *infinitive* and *bare infinitive*. The infinitive involves *to* + *verb*, whereas the bare infinitive lacks the word *to*.[11] These constructions are significantly different from any we have looked at so far, and analyzing them requires a level of abstraction that is quite a bit higher than what we have needed in the other sections. For reasons that are beyond the scope of this book, nonfinite verb constructions are deemed to be clauses, even though they do not look much like any clauses we have considered.

Nonfinite verb forms function as subjects, noun phrase complements, predicate complements, and adverbial modifiers, as illustrated in these sentences:

79. *For him to invite Rod Harris* is crazy. (subject)

---

[11] It is easy to confuse the *to* that marks an infinitive verb form with the *to* that marks a prepositional phrase. A prepositional phrase always involves a noun and not a verb, whereas the infinitive verb form always involves a verb and not a noun.

Sentence 80 illustrates how this construction also can function as a noun phrase complement:

80. Mrs. DiMarco had a job *for him to do*. (NP complement)

The word *for*, which normally would be a preposition, is functioning as a complementizer in these sentences.

81. Macarena wanted *to hold the baby*. (predicate complement)
82. Fritz knew that he needed *to get a better job*. (predicate complement)

The bare infinitive verb form, illustrated in Sentence 83, also functions as a predicate complement:

83. Raul's mother made him *eat his vegetables*. (predicate complement)

As an adverbial modifier, infinitive verb forms are sentence-level modifiers, as in sentences 84 and 85:

84. *To appear calm*, Fred smiled. (adverbial)
85. Macarena, *to stay awake*, made a pot of coffee. (adverbial)

We also have instances in which nonfinite verb forms appear with negative markers, as in:

86. Macarena answered slowly, *not to be coy but to be clear.*

Our phrase-structure rules require a bit of adjusting to describe these structures. First, we have to modify the $\bar{S}$ rule, putting parentheses around the dependent clause markers; this indicates that the marker now is optional. We have to do the same thing for NP to describe the fact that our nonfinite verb clauses do not have a visible subject. Then we need to add a new constituent, $\overline{VP}$, which we call bar-VP. The $\overline{VP}$ will be the core of the new clause. Putting brackets around VP and $\overline{VP}$ indicates that we have to select one. The second line of the modified rules indicates that the new clause has a verb with an optional infinitive marker (inf) and optional NP, AdjP, AdvP, and PP. To describe negatives, we also must adjust the expression for Aux, transforming it so that all constituents are optional (we must include a null marker also). The last step is to allow comp to include *for* as well as *that*: As with some of our other rules, the grammar requires us to add restrictions that cannot be written into the expressions. For example, the NP in the $\bar{S}$ is optional only in the presence of $\overline{VP}$. Bare infinitives only appear with certain kinds of verbs, such as *make*, and tense is optional only in a VP.

The necessity of adding these extra-rule restrictions is clearly a problem for phrase-structure grammar. The grammar would be more elegant, perhaps, if we could write the rules in such a way as to include these restrictions, but no one has figured out how to do that. As we approach the end of this chapter, it may be tempting to anticipate the next by intuiting that transformational-generative grammar solves the problem of restrictions. In this case, however, intuition would be wrong. Transformational-generative grammar also has many extra-rule restrictions.

$$\bar{S} \rightarrow \left(\begin{Bmatrix} \begin{bmatrix} \text{Sconj} \end{bmatrix} \\ \text{comp} \\ \text{RP} \\ \theta \end{Bmatrix} \right) (\text{NP}) \begin{Bmatrix} \text{VP} \\ \overline{\text{VP}} \end{Bmatrix}$$

$$\overline{\text{VP}} \rightarrow \text{Aux (inf) V (NP) (AdjP) (AdvP) (PP)}$$

$$\text{Aux} \rightarrow \left(\begin{Bmatrix} \theta \\ (\text{tense})(\text{neg})(\text{do}) \\ (\text{m})(\text{prog})(\text{perf}) \end{Bmatrix} \right)$$

$$\text{comp} \rightarrow \begin{Bmatrix} \text{that} \\ \text{for} \\ \theta \end{Bmatrix}$$

With these rules, we can analyze sentences 79 through 86, as in the accompanying diagrams.

Sentence 2.79: For him to invite Rod Harris is crazy

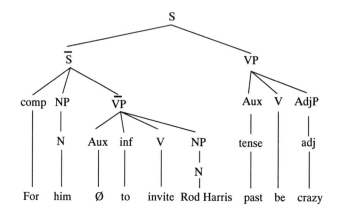

Sentence 2.80: Mrs. DiMarco had a job for him to do

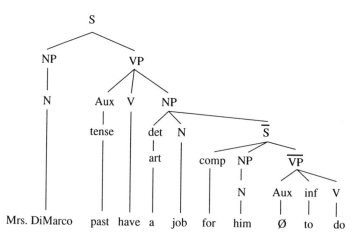

Sentence 2.81: Macarena wanted to hold the baby

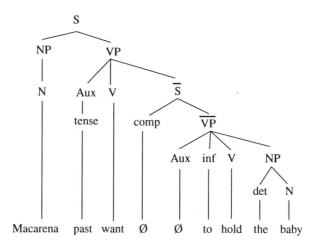

Sentence 2.82: Fred knew that he needed to get a better job

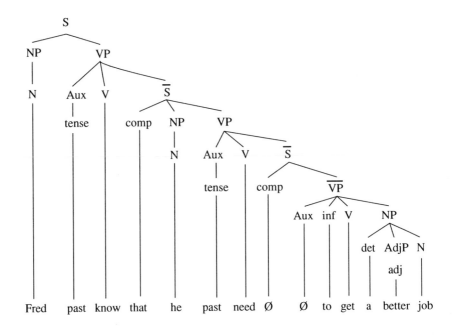

Sentence 2.83: Raul's mother made him eat his vegetables

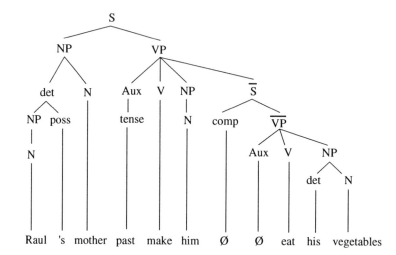

Sentence 2.84: To appear calm, Fred smiled

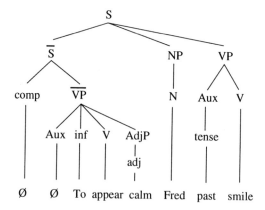

Sentence 2.85: Macarena, to stay awake, made a pot of coffee

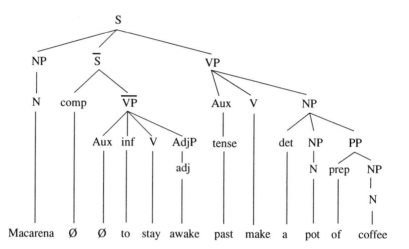

Sentence 2.86: Macarena answered slowly, not to be coy but to be clear

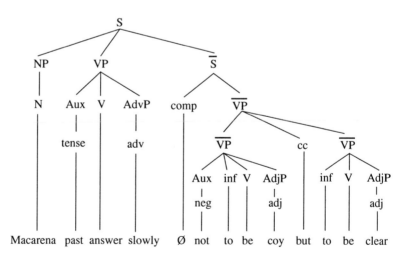

Directions: Draw tree diagrams for the following sentences.

1. Fred wanted to talk to Macarena about marriage.
2. For him to buy an engagement ring at this point would be foolish.
3. Fred decided to discuss the matter with his priest.
4. Her fondness for the two boys made Macarena tell them a lie.
5. Buggsy told his goons that he had a message for them to deliver.
6. Raul asked Maria to go with him to the dance.
7. Macarena was delighted to get the invitation to Buggsy's next party.
8. To tell the truth, she was impressed with Buggsy's money.
9. For her to turn down the invitation would have been unthinkable.
10. She decided to tell Fred and Fritz that she wanted to visit her sick aunt.

Usage Note

Infinitive verbs in Latin are one word; they have no separate infinitive marker. Consequently, it is impossible to split an infinitive form of a Latin verb. The fact that English does have a separate infinitive marker created a problem for traditional grammarians because it allows speakers to split the infinitive with an adverb, as in the following:

Their 5-year mission was to boldly go where no man had gone before.

The effort to get English to conform to Latin grammar probably is at the heart of the school injunction against splitting infinitives. Although English allows constructions like the one just shown, the prejudice against them is so strong that wise writers avoid them, if they can. There are situations in which shifting the adverb outside the infinitive makes for a less appealing statement. In the case of the example sentence just shown, some people might argue that it just does not have the same effect if we shift *boldly* to the rear of *go*.

SUMMARY OF PHRASE-STRUCTURE RULES

Before we go on to consider transformational-generative grammar in the next chapter, let's take a moment to review all the phrase-structure rules we've developed so far.

1. XP → XP CC XP

2. XP → XP S̄

3. S → NP VP

4. NP → (det) (AdjP) N (PP)

5. VP → Aux V (NP) (AdjP) (AdvP) (PP)

6. V → $\left\{ \begin{array}{l} V \\ V + prt \end{array} \right\}$

7. prt → particle

8. AdvP → $\left\{ \begin{array}{l} adv \\ NP \end{array} \right\}$

9. det → $\left\{ \begin{array}{l} pro \\ NP\ poss \\ art \end{array} \right\}$

10. pro → possessive pronoun

11. poss → 's

12. tense → $\left\{ \begin{array}{l} past \\ present \end{array} \right\}$

13. neg → $\left\{ \begin{array}{l} no \\ not \\ never \end{array} \right\}$

14. $\text{AdjP} \rightarrow \begin{Bmatrix} \text{adj} \\ \text{NP} \end{Bmatrix} \text{(AdvP) (PP)}$

15. $\text{M} \rightarrow \begin{Bmatrix} \text{will} \\ \text{shall} \\ \text{must} \\ \text{may} \\ \text{can} \end{Bmatrix}$

16. prog $\rightarrow$ be -ing

17. perf $\rightarrow$ have -ed/-en

18. $\text{PP} \rightarrow \text{prep} \begin{Bmatrix} \text{NP} \\ \text{RP} \\ \theta \end{Bmatrix}$

19. $\bar{\text{S}} \rightarrow \left(\begin{Bmatrix} \text{Sconj} \\ \text{comp} \\ \text{RP} \\ \theta \end{Bmatrix} \right) \text{(NP)} \begin{Bmatrix} \text{VP} \\ \overline{\text{VP}} \end{Bmatrix}$

20. $\overline{\text{VP}} \rightarrow \text{Aux (inf) V (NP (AdjP) (AdvP) (PP)}$

21. $\text{comp} \rightarrow \begin{Bmatrix} \text{that} \\ \text{for} \\ \theta \end{Bmatrix}$

22. $\text{Aux} \rightarrow \begin{Bmatrix} \theta \\ \text{(tense)(neg)(do)(M)(prog)(perf)} \end{Bmatrix}$

APPLYING KEY IDEAS

Directions: Draw tree diagrams for the following sentences.

1. Mrs. DiMarco's nephew was Raul, who had a crush on Maria.
2. Maria worked in a jewelry store, but she did volunteer work at a hospital.
3. Raul dreamed of being a movie star.
4. When Macarena accepted Buggsy's invitation to the party, she did not know that Fred and Fritz would be there.
5. The party was at Buggsy's house in Beverly Hills, which Liberace had owned.
6. Macarena was impressed when she saw the stars at the party, and she was thrilled when Michael Star shook her hand.
7. Buggsy, who was drinking too much champagne, pulled Macarena into a dark corner and whispered sweet nothings in her ear.
8. He promised to take her to Mexico if he could get his wife to go to Paris for a holiday.
9. Macarena knew that she really wanted to take the trip.
10. Later, Macarena was stunned as Fred and Fritz walked into the party.
11. She set her drink down and walked over to her guys with an angry expression on her face.
12. Fred looked guilty because he remembered the party in Malibu when the paramedics had taken Buggsy away.
13. They gave Macarena a kiss, and she decided to mingle.
14. By accident, she stumbled upon Buggsy and Rita de Luna, who was wearing a white spandex jumpsuit that barely covered her anywhere.
15. Macarena could not believe her eyes, because Buggsy was trying to whisper sweet nothings into Rita's ear.
16. Rita, although aware of Buggsy's status, seemed uninterested.
17. Macarena slipped away, but Michael Star grabbed her and pulled her to the dance floor, where he started to boogie.
18. Suddenly, three goons lifted Michael up and carried him outside.
19. Macarena began to think that Buggsy might be rather selfish and possessive.
20. In that moment, she worried about Fred and Fritz because Buggsy would send the goons after them.
21. She also felt flattered that Buggsy wanted her, but the matter of Rita de Luna presented a big problem.
22. Macarena picked up another drink and thought about solutions as the music played.
23. She saw Fred and Fritz across the room, where they were talking intensely with Senator River Run and four young women.

24. Because she watched the news, Macarena knew that the women were Brazilian quadruplets who had discovered a cure for baldness in the Amazon jungle.

25. These Hollywood parties were just wonderful, and she really wanted nothing except to attend more of them.

APPLYING KEY IDEAS

Applying grammatical analysis to one's own writing can be an interesting experience for a couple of reasons. Choose a paper you wrote for one of your classes, select 10 consecutive sentences at random, and try to analyze them using phrase-structure trees. Then write a paragraph or two discussing what you learned from this activity.

3

Transformational-Generative Grammar

THE CHOMSKY REVOLUTION

It is often said that academics hate theoretical vacuums. Clearly, one existed with respect to phrase-structure grammar, which, although effective at describing languages, was not very theoretical. Structuralists were interested primarily in application, not in theory. In the mid-1950s, a young linguist named Noam Chomsky set out to fill the theoretical vacuum by challenging most of the dominant assumptions underlying phrase-structure grammar. Although trained as a structuralist, Chomsky was intrigued by the idea that grammar could reflect a theory of language and, in turn, a theory of mind. He explored this idea around 1955 in a mimeographed paper titled "The Logical Structure of Linguistic Theory," which formed the foundation for his first book, *Syntactic Structures* (1957). In this book, Chomsky argued that phrase-structure grammar was inadequate, and he proposed an alternative that proved to be so powerful that it revolutionized linguistics.

Many books have been devoted to exploring the significance of *Syntactic Structures* and related works, so these few pages provide just a short summary. *Syntactic Structures* dismantled phrase-structure grammar as a viable intellectual enterprise, offered a new grammar to replace it, reasserted rationalism as the *sine qua non* of linguistics, and established language study firmly as a branch of psychology. It vitalized the emerging field of cognitive psychology, gave birth to a new area of language study called psycholinguistics, influenced philosophers working in the philosophy of language, and gave English teachers a new tool for helping students become better writers. It also laid the groundwork for a redefinition of the nature of language study. Given such intellectual influence, Chomsky has been, with good reason, widely characterized as one of the more important thinkers of the 20th century. Among modern intellectuals cited by other writers, Chomsky ranks fourth, following Marx, Lenin, and Freud (Harris, 1993, p. 79).

What was it that Chomsky found lacking in phrase-structure grammar? He had several criticisms, but perhaps the two most important involved describing and explaining language. Phrase-structure grammar focused on languages rather than language. Structuralists studied a given language in order to record as many features of it as possible, building a corpus, or body, of utterances that formed the foundation of the grammar for that language. These utterances were sentences and expressions that native speakers actually used, what are called *attested* utterances. The corpus was made up only of attested utterances, and the grammar was constructed so that it described them.

Chomsky argued that this approach cannot lead to an adequate description of language for the simple reason that it is based on a finite set of utterances/sentences whereas language itself is infinite. Consequently, no matter how large the corpus, it never can constitute a significant portion of the language.

A related problem is that the resulting grammar may describe the corpus, but it does not describe all the grammatical sentences of the language. It fails to account for the fact that language is inherently creative, with few sentences ever being repeated from one situation to the next. That is, phrase-structure grammar can describe just attested utterances; it cannot describe the infinite number of grammatical sentences that may have been uttered before the corpus was compiled, that have yet to be uttered, or that never will be uttered but are potential utterances. Even though phrase-structure rules such as those we developed in the previous chapter are sufficiently general to describe a vast array of sentences, this array is insignificant in the context of an infinite number of possible sentences.

Sentence 1 below, which is quite a common sentence, illustrates this point:

1. The day was hot.

This sentence reasonably would appear in the corpus of English, as would Sentence 1a:

1a. The day was very hot.

We might even imagine Sentence 1b in the corpus, because it, too, is fairly common:

1b. The day was very, very hot.

At some point, however, we find that we reach the limit of the number of *verys* we can put in front of the adjective and still be congruent with attested utterances. It is unlikely that anyone has ever uttered this sentence with, say, 53 *verys*. Nevertheless, such a sentence would be grammatical. In fact, we can imagine Sentence 1c quite easily (where *n* equals an infinite number of iterations of the word *very*), and we also understand that it is grammatical:

1c. The day was very ... *n* hot.

Chomsky correctly observed that phrase-structure grammar did not have the means to account for our ability to insert an infinite number of adverbial intensifiers (*very*) in front of the adjective and still have a grammatical sentence. He concluded (1957) that "it is obvious that the set of grammatical sentences cannot be identified with any particular corpus of utterances obtained by the linguist in his field work" (p. 15). In other words, a given body of sentences cannot identify a grammar of the language.

Chomsky's second major criticism focused on our intuitive understanding that certain types of sentences have some underlying relation, even though they look quite different from each other. Active and passive sentences are the most significant example. The most common type of sentence in English follows SVO word order, has an agent as the subject, and an object, as in Sentence 2:

2. Macarena kissed Fritz.

The passive form of this sentence reverses the order of subject and object, modifies the verb phrase, and adds the preposition *by*, converting the subject to an object of the preposition, as in Sentence 3:

3. Fritz was kissed by Macarena.

Although these sentences do not look the same, Chomsky argued that they express the same meaning and that the passive form is based on the active form. Phrase-structure grammar does not address the connection between such sentences; in fact, it would assign different sentence grammars to them:

Sentence 3: S → NP VP

VP → V NP

Sentence 4: S → NP be -en V PP

PP → prep NP

prep → by

In Chomsky's view, this approach fails to explain what our intuition tells us is obvious: These sentences are closely related. Sentence 2 somehow has been transformed into Sentence 3. However, the only way to get at that relation was with a grammar that examined the *history of sentences*, one that looked beneath the surface and into what we may think of as *mentalese*, language as it exists in the mind before it reaches its final form, before it is transformed. In other words, Chomsky was keenly interested in exploring how people produce language. He proposed that the ability to look into the history of a sentence gives a grammar a *generative component* that reveals something about language production—about how people connect strings of words into sentences. On these grounds, Chomsky developed a grammar that focused on the transformation of mentalese into actual language—and he called it *transformational-generative* (T-G) grammar.

Deep Structure and Surface Structure

In *Syntactic Structures*, Chomsky hinted that transformations work in the background. We do not really see them at work; we only see the consequences of their application on an underlying structure. In *Aspects of the Theory of Syntax* (1965), Chomsky developed this idea by resuscitating the prestructuralism idea that there is something underneath language, some universal feature of the human mind, such as logic, that determines the substance of utterances. In the case of a sentence like *Fritz was kissed by Macarena*, what lies underneath the passive construction is its corresponding active.

Chomsky had identified a basic grammatical structure in *Syntactic Structures* that he referred to as *kernel sentences*. Reflecting mentalese, kernel sentences were where words and meaning first appeared in the complex cognitive process that resulted in an utterance. In *Aspects*, Chomsky abandoned the notion of kernel sentences and identified the underlying constituents of sentences as *deep structure*. The deep structure was versatile insofar as it accounted for meaning and provided the basis for transformations that turned deep structure into *surface structure*, which represented what we actually hear or read. Transformation rules, therefore, connected deep structure and surface structure, meaning and syntax.[1]

Central to the idea that transformation rules serve as a bridge between deep structure and surface structure was the notion that transformations do not alter meaning. If they did, it would be difficult to justify the rules. Not only would they interfere with understanding, but they also would fail to realize Chomsky's goal of developing a grammar that looks into the history of a sentence. Deep structure was a convenient means of countering an alternative and nagging argument: that meaning is in the surface structure, that the words we hear and read mean pretty much what the person who created them intended. Understanding the consequences of this argument is important. If meaning is in the surface structure, there is no need for a mediating structure between mind and utterances, which makes transformation rules irrelevant.[2]

Unfortunately, it was clear that some transformations did change meaning. In the early version of the grammar, negatives are generated from an underlying affirmative through a transformation rule. That is, the negative transformation turns a positive statement into a negative one, as in these sentences:

4. Maria wanted to dance with Raul.
4a. Maria did not want to dance with Raul.

The deep structure of 4a is 4, and the meanings are different. The question transformation results in a similar change, turning an assertion into a question. Just prior to the publication of *Aspects*, however, Lees (1962) and Klima (1964) proposed that such difficulties could be eliminated by specifying certain phrase-structure markers in the deep structure of sentences, like 4a, that triggered transformation. These markers, governing, for example, negatives and questions, reside in the deep structure of all utterances and are activated by contextual cues. Once activated, they trigger the transformation. The result is that Sentence 4a would not have Sentence 4 as its deep structure but instead would have Sentence 4b:

4b. neg Maria wanted to dance with Raul.

---

[1]It is important to note, however, that Chomsky usually denied any connection between meaning and syntax. He proposed, for example, that the sentence, *Colorless green ideas sleep furiously*, doesn't mean anything, but it nevertheless is grammatical. But if meaning lies in the deep structure, as Chomsky suggested, the application of transformation rules would be the only way it could be realized in the surface structure. Hence, the connection between semantics and meaning is inescapable.

[2]This issue is discussed in more detail on pages 232–233.

This approach solved the problem in a clever way, and Chomsky adopted it. Unfortunately, the solution was highly artificial and not very satisfactory. In fact, the solution fairly quickly created many more problems than it solved. For example, there is no evidence to suggest that markers of any type exist in the deep structure. Psychological research on language processing has shown that meaning seems to reside solely in the surface structure. This finding has created even more problems. A rationalistic response is that evidence counts for very little, but there also is no intuitive basis for specifying such markers in the deep structure. We explore these problems later, but we can note now that they have their roots here, in the effort to adjust the grammar so that it would preserve Chomsky's claim that transformations do not affect meaning.

Language Acquisition: The Standard Account

One of the more visible characteristics of T-G grammar is that it reflects an interest in linguistic universals that we do not find in phrase-structure grammar. As Comsky conceptualized transformations, they were indeed universal—a part of every language because they reflected certain psychological principles of language and language processing.

These principles were evident, for example, in how children acquire language. One of Chomsky's assumptions was that transformation rules have a psychological reality. Humans are genetically programmed to use language, so they consequently are genetically programmed to develop grammar. How children acquire grammar and language is therefore an interesting question, particularly in light of the fact that acquisition takes place on the basis of limited and highly distorted input. Adults do not have long or complex conversations with infants; speech focuses on a narrow range of actions, such as going "bye-bye," and it uses a narrow range of words. In addition, adults do not always use standard syntax when speaking to infants. Their language lapses into "baby talk," which has a different syntax and even a different pitch from adult conversations. Nevertheless, infants in all societies somehow manage to sort through this language, develop the grammar, and begin speaking at about age one.

To account for this process, Chomsky proposed the *language acquisition device* (LAD). The LAD is a metaphor or psychological construct for the genetic programming that makes language and grammar possible; it does not really exist. The LAD is capable of processing all possible human languages, and as adults use language to interact with children, the LAD begins examining the strings of words to identify underlying patterns. In the case of English, it determines that the dominant word order is SVO, that adverbs can move to specific spots in a sentence vis-à-vis the verb, that sentences cannot have duplicate noun phrases but must replace one noun phrase with a pronoun, that particles may appear next to a verb or after a noun phrase, and so forth. In other words, the LAD induces the grammar rules that govern the language.[3]

The LAD is considered to be a subsystem of the language mechanism, with the sole role of inducing the grammar rules of the child's home language.[4] The LAD hypothesizes the rules on the basis of input, and the hypotheses are accepted or rejected on the basis of their ability to enable processing of the sentences children hear. Hudson (1980) and Slobin and Welsh (1973) argued that inducing accurate rules on the basis of inaccurate and distorted data presented a major problem for children, and they proposed that the LAD has an innate knowledge of the possible range of human languages and therefore considers only those hypotheses within the constraints imposed on grammar by a set of linguistic universals.

Transformational-generative linguists focus on an overgeneralization phenomenon involving regular and irregular verbs to support this standard account of acquisition. For example, when children start developing language, they use a small number of past-tense verbs, but more often they use present-tense verbs to indicate a past action. In addition, they tend to use irregular, high-frequency forms, such as *go* and *eat*. Because the lexicon includes regular as well as irregular verbs, there is no evidence that the child is using a past-tense rule. The regular and irregular verbs simply appear to be separate items in the lexicon (Pinker, 1994).

Around 2.5 years of age, a change occurs. Children start using more past-tense verbs, but the number of irregular verbs does not increase significantly. In the standard account, two new linguistic behaviors emerge at about this time: Children develop the ability to generate a past tense for an invented word, and they incorrectly attach regular past-tense endings to irregular verbs that they used correctly earlier. That is, they seem to overgeneralize these past-tense endings to irregular verbs. As a result, irregular verbs such as *go* and *eat* are expressed as *go-ed* and *eat-ed*. These two events suggest that children have developed a rule for marking the past tense, a rule that applies to regular

---

[3]Induction involves forming a generalization on the basis of a small amount of data, of reasoning from the specific to the general; deduction, on the other hand, involves forming a specific conclusion on the basis of a generalization, of reasoning from the general to the specific. For example, a person who observes an apple fall from a tree to the ground would use induction to conclude that there is some force that attracts the apple to the earth. A person who understands the law of gravity would be able to predict that if an astronaut dropped an apple on the surface of the moon, the apple would fall to the ground. That's deduction. The most well-known form of deduction is the logical syllogism: All men are mortal; Socrates is a man; therefore, Socrates is mortal.

[4]Fodor (1983), Johnson-Laird (1983), and others have argued that these rules are explicit but inaccessible; they can be described but not consciously altered.

verbs but, of course, not to irregular ones. Because they have not figured out the rule, children apply it to both types of verbs.

After about 8 months, the regular and irregular forms begin to coexist. Children start to use the correct irregular forms of the past tense and to apply the regular form correctly to new words they learn. It is widely believed in linguistics that these developments indicate that children have successfully induced the grammar rules and that after this developmental shift they are able to use the rules to compute the appropriate output for both regular and irregular verb forms. The rules operate automatically from that point on, in what Fodor (1983) characterized as a reflex. The grammar rules that the LAD induces, of course, are transformational-generative rules.

Errors in Language: Competence and Performance

The standard account of language acquisition raised a problem. If the LAD induces correct grammar rules, why is human speech full of errors? People make frequent mistakes with language, slips of the tongue that jumble up their utterances, slips of the pen that cause visible errors. We use prepositions incorrectly, saying that someone "got *in* the plane" rather than "*on* the plane," and we produce other ungrammatical utterances, as when we fail to shift a particle behind a pronoun:

*Macarena called up him.

Sometimes we recognize the flaw and repair the problem, but commonly we are not even aware that we have made a mistake, and so the ungrammatical construction slips by undetected.

As Chomsky formulated the grammar, however, it will not produce ungrammatical sentences under any circumstances. He defined T-G grammar as a system that produces all the grammatical sentences of the language but no ungrammatical ones, so the generative component of transformational-generative grammar was not congruent with actual language use. Chomsky was aware of the difficulty, of course, so he accounted for the inconsistency by distinguishing between the sentences that the grammar generates and the sentences that people actually produce. This approach put the burden for error on people rather than on the grammar.

The distinction was based on what Chomsky referred to as *competence* and *performance*. Linguistic competence may be understood as the inherent ability of a native speaker to make correct grammaticality judgments. This ability is what the LAD gives us after it figures out the grammar rules; thus all native speakers have linguistic competence. Performance, on the other hand, is what we actually do with the language given the fact that a range of environmental factors can upset our fairly delicate competence. Fatigue, distraction, hunger, and numerous psychosocial factors can interfere with our linguistic competence to such a degree that we generate ungrammatical utterances. Even though all native speakers possess linguistic competence, only an ideal speaker, a mental construct, is able to translate competence into error-free performance.

The competence-performance distinction is very clever, much in the way that negative markers in the deep structure are clever. It solves a problem that greatly undermines the validity of T-G grammar: It accounts for the occurrence of ungrammatical sentences and also for the occasional inability of listeners to analyze grammatical sentences.[5] Such difficulties are due to errors of performance, errors made somehow between the application of the rules and the articulation of an utterance. They are not due to errors in the grammar.

Grammar and Writing

During the 1960s, many people reasoned that the competence-performance distinction could be turned into an instructional agenda. The goal was to shift tacit knowledge on the level of competence into explicit knowledge on the level of performance. Numerous efforts were made at teaching transformational-generative grammar to raise performance to the level of competence (see Gale, 1968; Mellon, 1969; O'Hare, 1973; White, 1965). Chapter 1 summarized some of the more important studies investigating grammar instruction and writing; these studies showed that the efforts were not successful. Grammar instruction, regardless of the type of grammar taught, has no measurable effect on writing performance. The question is, why?

The central problem appears to lie in the area of language acquisition. Normally, children are immersed in language at the moment of birth, and they

---

[5]This inability can be significant in some situations, even though the errors that make a given sentence ungrammatical are small—such as errors with prepositions—or when the ungrammatical sentence is widely accepted—such as *The reason is because*. For example, many standardized tests of writing, such as the Test of Standard Written English (TSWE), are based in large part on small errors in grammar or usage that make test sentences ungrammatical or unacceptable. Students read a sentence and have to determine whether it displays an error and, if it does, how to fix it. Although such tests are able to predict fairly accurately how well students can write, they have been criticized as being invalid because they are not tests of writing per se—instead, they are tests of reading. In most instances, the issue of validity is not relevant in measuring writing skill because the goal is to *predict success at writing*, which these tests and others, such as the SAT verbal, do very well. Good readers are frequent readers, and for reasons that are beyond the scope of this book, they do something that, in the context of language in general, is unnatural—they attend to both the meaning and the form of language. When people listen to language in normal situations, such as conversations, they do not attend to form and, indeed, generally cannot repeat verbatim a sentence that they just heard. Good, frequent readers therefore possess a skill that poor, infrequent readers lack—the ability to deal with language consciously on the levels of form and meaning. This ability is central to writing skill.

begin acquisition immediately. Moreover, the human brain is designed to develop and use language, so acquisition occurs easily and unconsciously. The language that children acquire is the language of the home and their immediate community of family and friends. In fact, we usually refer to acquired language as *home language*.

Few children are reared in families where the home language is close to formal Standard English, which characterizes most writing. As a result, the language they bring to school and to classroom writing assignments is measurably different from the language they use for oral communication. Some of the differences are related to grammar. For example, Black English and Chicano English have grammars that vary significantly from Standard English. Most of the differences, however, are related to usage, as we have seen in the Usage Notes throughout this text. Nevertheless, our schools operate under the mistaken belief that nearly all of the differences between home language and Standard English are based on grammar, with the result being that children begin studying grammar in the third grade and usually continue through junior high school. There are important reasons for studying grammar, but these reasons rarely find their way into curriculum guides. No school district has a guide that addresses the idea that grammar can be interesting or that it helps students develop analytical skills that are central to an effective education. Instead, the goal is to give students a tool (grammar) that will allow them to move their home language closer to Standard English, especially with respect to writing. In other words, the study of grammar is viewed as the bridge between home language and Standard English. The assumption is that once this bridge is in place (once students learn the grammar), they will speak and write Standard English.

The lack of any evidence to support this approach has not motivated school districts or teachers to abandon it. On the contrary, declines in verbal test scores have lead to greater emphasis on "basics" such as grammar (Healy, 1990). Even if such a cause-effect relationship existed, the expected outcome would be hard to achieve. The reason is that the mind processes *acquired* knowledge of language in a way that is significantly different from *learned* knowledge of language. For the most part, acquired knowledge operates unconsciously, whereas learned knowledge operates consciously. (The Key Ideas activity on page 48 reflects this principle.) Whenever most people try to apply such learned knowledge, their language processing ability is seriously impaired. Part of the problem is related to differences in form and meaning. In nearly all situations, people focus on the meaning of an utterance or a piece of writing (text). They find that when they try to focus also on form, it is harder to attend to meaning. We see extreme examples of this phenomenon among people with writer's block. Rose (1984) reported that students in his study of writer's block were so concerned with getting the form correct that they could not focus on meaning; moreover, they never felt that the form they used was correct, so they became caught in a cycle of writing a sentence or two, crossing them out, rewriting them, crossing them out, rewriting them, and so on. Completing even one paragraph was difficult. On a less serious level, we see students who study and understand the difference between *who* and *whom*, for example, who nevertheless either fail to make the distinction when speaking or writing or who must think for several moments about which form is appropriate.

Some people recognize the cognitive difficulty of applying learned knowledge and argue that the issue is *time*. Students need to study grammar for many years, and given sufficient time the learned knowledge will become so ingrained that application becomes automated. That is, they will be able to use a feature such as *whom* correctly without having to think about it. In theory, this is a sound argument, and there is no doubt that some students are able to automate learned linguistic behavior. It appears, however, that for the majority this is quite difficult. Furthermore, all available evidence indicates that years of grammar study result essentially in producing students who know a great deal about grammar. Many foreign students, for example, especially those from Asia, commonly know more about English grammar than their teachers do, but these students nevertheless speak and write English quite poorly, on the whole, because they have not been immersed in contexts that require speaking and writing in English. In addition, the automation argument usually ignores motivation. The question of why students might be motivated to use formal Standard English rather than their home language is very important, for without such motivation no change is possible.

As we see later in this text, there are compelling reasons for students to resist change. Also, many people now question whether schools should be trying to move students to use Standard English. Even so, there are perhaps more reasons than ever before for our schools to help students master Standard English. Since 1967, standardized test scores have declined in all areas—math, science, history, analytical reasoning—but the most precipitous decline has been in verbal scores (Chall, 1996; Coulson, 1996). This fact is particularly disturbing because verbal ability is closely linked to performance in all other academic endeavors. The decline has been so great that American students now rank last in international comparisons of academic performance among the world's 25 most developed countries (Healy, 1990; Herrnstein & Murray, 1994). Herrnstein and Murray (1994) correctly pointed out that in an agricultural or even an industrial economy, high levels of academic achievement are not, strictly speaking, a necessity for the society as a whole. In the technological economy that has developed with the growth of the computer industry, however, high levels of academic achievement among a large percentage of the population is a fundamental requirement for growth and stability. Such an economy simply cannot survive in a society with large numbers of poorly educated people who cannot read and write well.

Yet the performance levels of our students at all age groups have become so low as to be shocking. For many years, the average reading level of high school graduates was Grade 9; the National Assessment of Educational Progress report of 1994 indicated that the level now is Grade 8. In an unpublished study that this author conducted in 1996, only 15% of ninth-grade student participants could look at a map of the United States and locate the state they lived in, only 5% of college freshmen could correctly recount how God created woman in the Book of Genesis, and only 22% could correctly name the current President.

Critics argue that such studies are meaningless because they assess elitist cultural literacy rather than pop cultural literacy. One claim is that students may not know the name of the current President, but they know the names of all the characters in TV programs such as *The Simpsons* and *The X-files*. The issue, therefore, is the value assigned to the different types of knowledge. By the same token, today's students may not be able to read or write very well, but they are adept at watching TV and surfing the Internet. *They are video literate.* From this perspective, what our schools try to teach our children is, at best, out of date; at worst, it is a form of social engineering designed to perpetuate a cultural hegemony. Admittedly, a value judgment is involved whenever we make choices, but the issue of real literacy—not the make-believe kind that informs too much social policy and influences too many curricula—goes beyond cultural preferences linked to SES and level of education. There appears to be inherent value to a society when its citizens have the intellectual tools necessary to move it forward materially. As yet, not one critic has been able to explain how a storehouse of trivia about *The X-files* or any other pop culture icon can help anybody build a better computer or a more durable road.

Grammar instruction, as currently conceived, will do nothing to resolve these problems. In addition, it probably is naive to hope that anything we do in our schools will have more than a modest effect on the dominant social forces that celebrate ignorance and deride intelligence, that glamorize mediocrity and mock excellence. Having recognized this reality, it is important to understand that linguistics has taught us two uncontrovertible facts over the last 30 years. First, language change occurs when someone is highly motivated to modify his or her language. Second, change must occur in an environment that immerses a person in the target language. Teachers may not be able to do much to address the issue of motivation, but they can do a great deal with respect to environment. From this perspective, teachers must serve as models of spoken Standard English—a difficult challenge. In addition, they must do everything possible to get students to become readers and writers. Reading is the key to better writing—grammar study is not. What we know about language acquisition suggests that reading immerses students in written language in the way that a child's family immerses him or her in spoken language. Reading leads to acquisition of the features of language that characterize the formal standard of texts, which in turn facilitates composing.

It is important to recognize that knowledge of grammar does play a role in writing, but that role is not what many people believe it is. Knowledge of grammar gives teachers and students a common vocabulary for talking about language and makes discussions of writing tasks more efficient and clear. This role is too passive for many educators, and in the 1960s and early 1970s there was widespread hope that T-G grammar offered an aggressive tool for curing the numerous ills associated with teaching writing in a formulaic way. It would allow teachers to tap into students' innate competence. Consequently, T-G grammar replaced traditional grammar in numerous schools across the country during this period.

Unfortunately, many people were confused by the notions of competence and performance, and in some quarters that confusion still exists. The problem is that *competence* is a slippery term. It has two meanings in everyday usage, referring both to skill level and to potential ability. With respect to skill level, a person may be a competent pianist if he or she can play a tune on a piano. With respect to potential ability, a person may be competent *to play the piano* if he or she has functional arms, hands, fingers, legs, and feet. Consequently, the typical person may not be able to play at all but certainly is competent to do so. On this account, this level of competence has no real connection to actual performance. Even with training there is no assurance that a person ever will be competent in the first sense of the word.

When composition studies adopted the competence-performance distinction, the tendency was to ignore the technical definition of competence in favor of the popular one related to *potential ability*. Many teachers contributed to the confusion by bringing in folk notions of innateness, until "writing competence" came to mean something along the lines of "the innate ability to write." They equated linguistic competence with composing. Competence therefore suggested a classroom environment where students have ample opportunities to write, where they have the chance to practice *what they already know how to do* (Berthoff, 1981, 1983; Elbow, 1973; Graves, 1981; Murray, 1982; Parker, 1979).

Ironically, this view is antithetical to grammar study. As it spread, many schools, especially colleges and universities, jettisoned grammar instruction. The response in public schools was influenced by the general difficulty of T-G grammar. Numerous teachers just couldn't get it, no matter how they tried. Moreover, there was no evidence that T-G grammar worked any better than traditional grammar when it came to students' language skills. Politics and the long history of grammar instruction militated against dropping grammar in public schools, so they reverted to traditional grammar. The problem, of course, never was the type of grammar students learned but instead the fact that teachers tried (and continue to try) to use grammar instruction to improve students' speaking and writing skills.

Grammar and Psychology

Chomsky's ideas about grammar and language stimulated intellectuals in many fields, but perhaps no group was more intrigued than psychologists. The proposal that transformation rules had psychological reality offered a ready means for researchers to study cognitive processing, using language as the principal tool. Psychologists therefore were among the most ardent early supporters of Chomsky's new grammar.

However, conflict was inevitable. Chomsky was (and is) a rationalist, whereas psychology is predicated on empiricism, Freudian psychoanalysis notwithstanding.[6] Chomsky could argue that the empiricism of the structuralists was inadequate with respect to developing a viable grammar, and he could base his theories of language and grammar on the power of his intellect to see into the nature of things, but psychologists are compelled to find hard data to substantiate theories. With respect to transformational-generative grammar, the research question was simple: If language users actually apply transformation rules to underlying structures, they should take longer to process transformed sentences—but do they?

George Miller (1962) attempted to answer that question. He compiled a list of sentences and then directed subjects to signal as soon as they understood each one. Passives and actives were of particular interest because the passive transformation has such a significant effect on the structure of the active form. Miller's data indicated convincingly that transformed sentences like passives took subjects longer to process (also see Miller & McKean, 1964), and for some time the question of the psychological reality of transformation rules seemed answered. Only much later did it become clear that other factors may have caused the longer processing times. Passives, for example, generally are longer

---

[6]Although psychoanalysis played a vital role in the development of psychology, today it is little more than a curiosity. The biomedical model so thoroughly dominates modern psychology that references to psychoanalytical theories and principles are totally absent from the diagnostic manual (DSM IV) that therapists use to describe disorders. Freudian analysis was fundamentally rationalistic, whereas the biomedical model is fundamentally empirical.

than their corresponding actives, which influences processing time. In addition, the proposal that transformations do not affect meaning became harder to support. Tinkering with the deep structure did not affect sentences like 6 and 6a:

6. Everyone at the party spoke a foreign language.
6a. A foreign language was spoken by everyone at the party.

These sentences do not mean the same thing, which suggests that transformations do alter meaning. If they alter meaning, any measure of processing time necessarily involves more than the application of a rule affecting structure. The problem suddenly is complex; one is not just measuring the application of a rule or rules to a deep structure string of words but is measuring the time it takes subjects to adjust to the subtle differences in meaning that exist between deep structure and surface structure. Any results are hopelessly confounded, so what they mean is uncertain.

In addition, it turned out that some transformations that do not affect meaning also do not involve longer processing time. Particles, for example, are attached to the verb in the deep structure, but the particle-movement transformation shifts the particle behind the object NP, as in sentences 7 and 7a:

7. Buggsy looked up the number.
7a. Buggsy looked the number up.

The fact that 7a does not require a longer processing time than 7 is extremely problematic for the claim that transformation rules have psychological reality.

After several years of attempting unsuccessfully to find empirical verification for T-G grammar, most psychologists gave up. They came to view it as an interesting theory that lacked empirical validity. Expressing the view of many, Wanner (1988) noted that for most psychologists, "The adventure into transformational grammar reached a dead end" (p. 150).

APPLYING KEY IDEAS

1. Explain two differences between phrase-structure grammar and transformational grammar.
2. The idea that there are internalized rules for generating sentences might lead to an assumption regarding composition. What might this assumption be?
3. The question of whether the theoretical features of transformational grammar are important for teachers has been debated for many years. What do you think might be the central issues in the debate, and what is your position?

TRANSFORMATION RULES

One of the criticisms of T-G grammar is that over the years it moved away from the elegance and simplicity of *Syntactic Structures*. In doing so, the transformation rules have become more abstract and more difficult to understand for those who are not specially trained in linguistics. For this reason, the transformations that we examine here are based primarily on Chomsky's early work. The goal is to provide some understanding of the general principles of T-G grammar rather than an in-depth analysis. The current version of T-G grammar, known as Extended Standard Theory, is different in many respects from what we examine in this section, but numerous similarities still exist. Thus, we can explore the substance of T-G grammar even though we pass over many of the details that characterize the current version. In addition, it is important to recognize that grammar is an everchanging field. Linguists always are making adjustments to existing theories and rules in an effort to improve what we currently know. As a result, grammar is dynamic rather than static. Any attempt to provide a definitive set of rules therefore would be futile. By understanding the underlying principles, however, we can be participants, making our own adjustments to the grammar as necessary. It also allows us to understand better the proposals made by others. Understanding principles is the objective here.

Chomsky proposed a variety of transformation rules, some obligatory and others optional. The rules themselves specify their status. Rather than examining all possible transformation rules, only a few are presented, those that govern several common constructions in English. Before turning to these rules, however, it is important to note that transformations are governed by certain conventions. The two that we consider here are the *ordering convention* and the *cycle convention*. When a sentence has several transformations, they must be applied in keeping with the *order* of the rules. The rules that appear in this chapter are ordered appropriately, with the exception of the morphophonemic rule that follows. In addition, when a sentence has embedded clauses, we must begin applying the transformations in the clause at the lowest level and work our way up. This is the cycle convention. Failure to abide by these conventions may result in ungrammatical sentences.[7]

The Morphophonemic Transformation

Consider for a moment the phrase structure rules governing the auxiliary that we examined in the last chapter:

---

[7]The question of how children induce the grammar rules may be straightforward, but how they induce the order and the cycle of the rules is not.

$$VP \rightarrow Aux\ V\ (AdvP)\ (NP)\ (AdjP)\ (PP)$$

$$Aux \rightarrow \begin{Bmatrix} \theta \\ (tense)(neg)(do) \\ (M)(prog)(perf) \end{Bmatrix}$$

$$tense \rightarrow \begin{Bmatrix} past \\ present \end{Bmatrix}$$

$$neg \rightarrow \begin{Bmatrix} no \\ not \\ never \end{Bmatrix}$$

$$M \rightarrow \begin{Bmatrix} will \\ shall \\ must \\ may \\ can \end{Bmatrix}$$

prog → be -ing

perf → have -ed/-en

In a sentence such as *Fred was eating macaroni*, our analysis is quite different from the actual sentence; tense and the progressive participle are under the auxiliary, to the left of the words that eventually are marked with tense and the progressive. The accompanying diagram (see following page) illustrates this analysis.

How these elements, these morphemes, end up where they belong is not much of an issue in phrase-structure grammar, but T-G grammar proposes a rule that shifts the morphemes and attaches them to the appropriate words. This rule is the *morphophonemic transformation*. In most accounts, it is the only transformation that applies to all sentences as well as the last transformation in any sentences affected by other transformation rules.

Why discuss this rule first? From most perspectives, the rule is not very interesting, and it does not reveal much about grammar in particular or language in general. Consequently, we do not apply it. Our analyses therefore end one step short of the surface structure of each sentence. Having this information in advance prevents any later confusion on this issue.

Example Sentence: Fred was eating macaroni

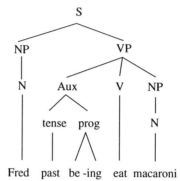

Passive

The passive transformation is an optional rule, which means that we may or may not apply it to certain types of sentences. Essentially, the rule states that some active sentences can be changed into a passive form. Consider Sentence 8:

8. Fred bought a ring.

Applying the passive transformation results in 8a:

8a. A ring was bought by Fred.

Sentence 8 represents the deep structure of 8a. If we analyze the two sentences, we can see what the transformation did to the deep structure. First, the object NP *(a ring)* shifted into the subject position. Second, the preposition *by* appeared, and the deep-structure subject *(Fred)* became the object of the preposition. Third, *be* and the past participle suffix appeared in the auxiliary, turning the deep structure verb *buy* into a passive verb form.

We can represent these changes symbolically through a rule that specifies the structure of 8 (and similar sentences) and the corresponding structural change. In this rule, the symbol ⇒ means "is transformed into":

Passive Transformation Rule

NP_1 Aux V NP_2

$\Rightarrow$

NP_2 Aux + be -ed/ en V by + NP_1

With respect to Sentence 8:

NP_1 = Fred

NP_2 = a ring

V = bought

It is important to note that only sentences with a transitive verb can undergo the passive transformation, which means that if we were to express the rule more formally we would have to include this condition as a constraint.

The following sentences further illustrate how this rule applies:

  9. The bank repossessed Fritz's car.
  9a. Fritz's car was repossessed by the bank.
 10. Buggsy owned the casino.
 10a. The casino was owned by Buggsy.
 11. Prada made Macarena's new bag.
 11a. Macarena's new bag was made by Prada.

Because T-G grammar is predicated on examining the history of a given sentence, our analysis is different from the analysis under phrase-structure grammar. T-G grammar requires a minimum of two trees, one for the deep structure and one for the surface structure. For more complicated sentences, there are more trees, each one reflecting a different transformation and a different stage in the history of the sentence. A convenient guideline is that the number of trees in a T-G analysis will consist of the number of transformations plus one. The accompanying diagrams illustrate the analyses of our sample sentences.

Sentence 3.8a: A ring was bought by Fred
Deep Structure:

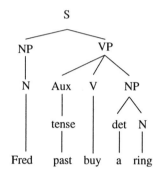

T-Passive:
Surface Structure:

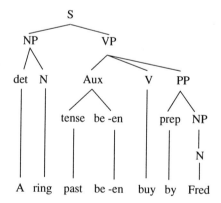

Sentence 3.9a: Fritz's car was repossessed by the bank
Deep Structure:

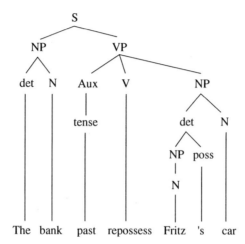

T-Passive:
Surface Structure:

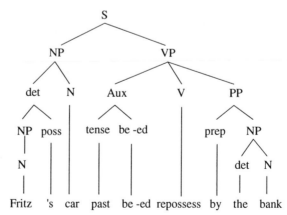

Deep Structure:

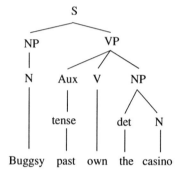

T-Passive:
Surface Structure:

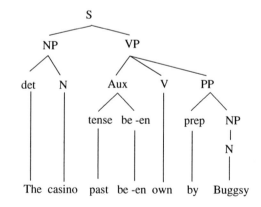

Sentence 3.11a: Macarena's new bag was made by Prada
Deep Structure:

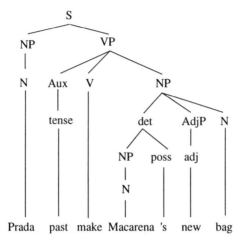

T-Passive:
Surface Structure:

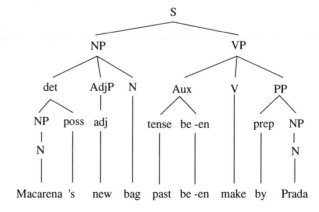

Passive Agent Deletion.   The subject agent in Sentences 9a through 11a
is stated in each case, but sometimes a sentence does not specify the subject, as in
Sentence 12:

12. The cake was eaten.

Because the subject agent is not identified, we have to use an indefinite pronoun to fill the slot where it would appear in the deep structure, as in 12a:

12a. [Someone] ate the cake.

This deep structure, however, would result in the surface structure of Sentence 12b:

12b. The cake was eaten by [someone].

To account for Sentence 12, T-G grammar proposes a deletion rule that elim-
inates the prepositional phrase containing the subject agent. We can say, therefore, that Sentence 12 has undergone two transformations, passive and passive
agent deletion.

Agent Deletion Rule

NP_2 Aux + be -ed/ en V by + NP_1

$\Rightarrow$

NP_2 Aux + be -ed/ en V

Sentences 13 through 16 are other examples of sentences that have undergone
this transformation, and the accompanying diagrams illustrate their analysis:

13. The plot was developed slowly.
14. The accident occurred when the driver's forward vision was impaired.
15. Their family was driven into bankruptcy.
16. Buggsy's favorite goon was attacked.

Sentence 3.12: The cake was eaten

Deep Structure:

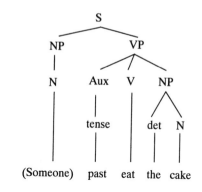

T-Passive:

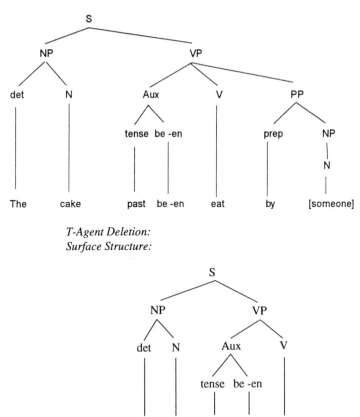

T-Agent Deletion:
Surface Structure:

165

Sentence 3.13a: The plot was developed slowly

Deep Structure:

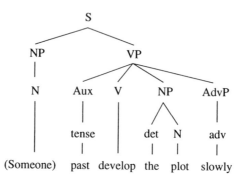

T-Passive:

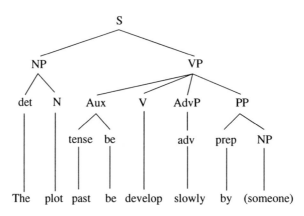

T-Agent Deletion:
Surface Structure:

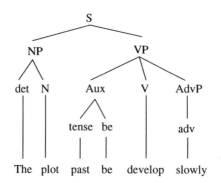

Sentence 3.14: The accident occurred when the driver's forward vision was impaired

Deep Structure:

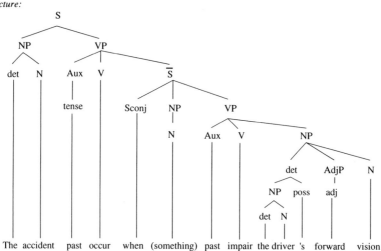

T-Passive:

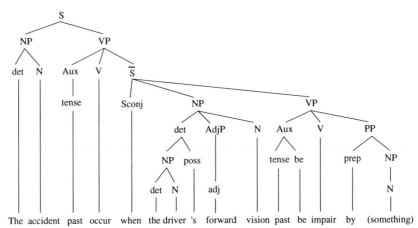

T-Agent Deletion:
Surface Structure:

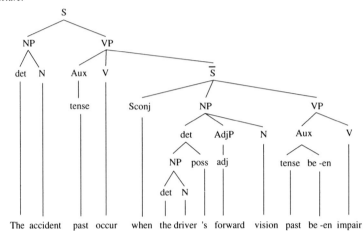

Sentence 3.15: Their family was driven into bankruptcy
Deep Structure:

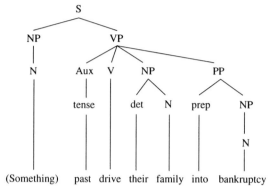

```
                          S
              ┌───────────┴───────────┐
             NP                       VP
              │              ┌────┬────┴──────────────┐
              N            Aux    V     NP            PP
              │             │           ╱╲           ╱╲
              │           tense       det  N      prep  NP
              │             │          │   │       │    │
              │             │          │   │       │    N
              │             │          │   │       │    │
       (Something)        past drive their family into bankruptcy
```

T-Passive:

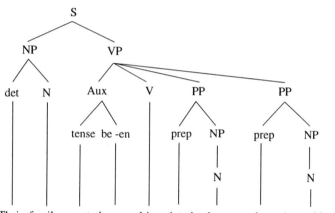

```
                    S
          ┌─────────┴─────────┐
         NP                   VP
         ╱╲          ┌────┬────┴────────┬──────────┐
       det  N      Aux    V            PP          PP
        │    │     ╱│╲     │           ╱╲          ╱╲
        │    │ tense be -en │        prep NP     prep NP
        │    │    │  │   │   │         │   │       │   │
        │    │    │  │   │   │         │   N       │   N
        │    │    │  │   │   │         │   │       │   │
      Their family past be -en drive into bankruptcy by (something)
```

T-Agent Deletion:
Surface Structure:

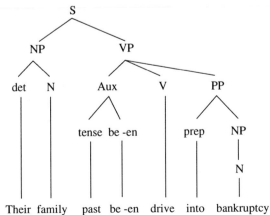

```
                    S
          ┌─────────┴─────────┐
         NP                   VP
         ╱╲          ┌────┬────┴────────┐
       det  N      Aux    V            PP
        │    │     ╱│╲     │           ╱╲
        │    │ tense be -en │        prep NP
        │    │    │  │   │   │         │   │
        │    │    │  │   │   │         │   N
        │    │    │  │   │   │         │   │
      Their family past be -en drive into bankruptcy
```

169

Sentence 3.16: Buggsy's favorite goon was attacked

Deep Structure:

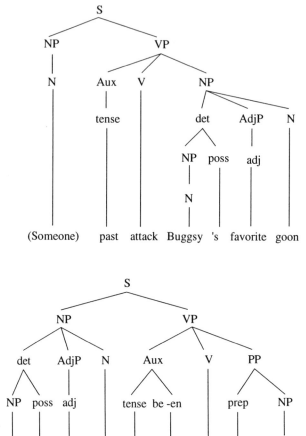

```
                         S
          ┌──────────────┴──────────────┐
         NP                             VP
          │                ┌────────────┼────────────┐
          N               Aux           V            NP
          │                │            │      ┌──────┼──────┐
          │              tense          │     det    AdjP    N
          │                │            │    ┌─┴─┐    │      │
          │                │            │   NP poss  adj     │
          │                │            │    │       │       │
          │                │            │    N       │       │
          │                │            │    │       │       │
      (Someone)          past        attack Buggsy  's  favorite goon
```

T-Passive:

```
                              S
               ┌──────────────┴──────────────┐
              NP                             VP
       ┌───────┼───────┐             ┌────────┼────────┐
      det     AdjP      N           Aux        V        PP
    ┌──┴──┐    │        │         ┌──┴──┐      │      ┌──┴──┐
   NP poss    adj       │       tense be -en   │     prep   NP
    │          │        │         │    │       │      │      │
    N          │        │         │    │       │      │      N
    │          │        │         │    │       │      │      │
  Buggy  's favorite  goon      past be -en  attack   by  (someone)
```

T-Agent Deletion:
Surface Structure:

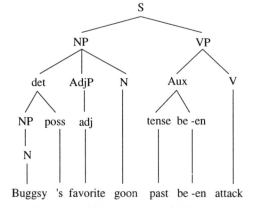

```
                            S
             ┌──────────────┴──────────────┐
            NP                             VP
      ┌──────┼──────┐                  ┌────┴────┐
     det    AdjP     N                Aux        V
   ┌──┴──┐   │       │              ┌──┴──┐      │
  NP poss   adj      │            tense be -en   │
   │         │       │              │    │       │
   N         │       │              │    │       │
   │         │       │              │    │       │
 Buggsy  's favorite goon         past be -en  attack
```

APPLYING KEY IDEAS

Directions: Draw tree diagrams for the following sentences. Remember: T-G grammar requires two trees for any sentence that has undergone transformation.

1. Maria was thrilled by the music in the park.
2. Mrs. DiMarco was stunned by the news.
3. The door was opened slowly.
4. Fred was stung by a swarm of bees.
5. The nest had been stirred up deliberately.

Usage Note

Many writing teachers tell students not to use the passive in their work, and they urge students to focus on "active" rather than "passive" verbs. However, teachers usually do not link passive verbs to passive constructions but instead identify them as forms of *be*, which creates quite a bit of confusion. For example, students who write something like "The day was hot" might find their teacher identifying *was* as a passive verb—even though it is not—and recommending a revision into something like "The sun broiled the earth." Of course, this revision changes entirely the meaning of the original, and in some contexts it will be inappropriate. This injunction against passives is meaningful in the *belles-lettres* tradition that has shaped the critical essay in literature, but it is misplaced in the broader context of writing outside that tradition.

In science and social science, the passive is a well-established and quite reasonable convention. It normally appears in the methods section of scientific papers, where researchers describe the procedures they used in their study and how they collected data. The convention is based on the worthwhile goal of providing an objective account of procedures, one that other researchers can use, if they like, to set up their own, similar study. Of course, this objectivity is largely a fiction because anyone reading a scientific paper knows that the authors were the ones who set up the study and collected the data. Nevertheless, the passive creates an air of objectivity by shifting any focus away from the researchers as agents and toward the actions: "The data were collected via electrodes leading to three electromyograms." Moreover, contrary to what some teachers claim, there is nothing insidious about the fiction of objectivity.

The widespread use of passive constructions outside the humanities indicates that blanket injunctions against them are misguided. It is the case, however, that the passive is inappropriate in many situations. Even in a scientific paper, the passive usually appears only in two sections—methods and results. In the introduction and conclusion sections, writers tend to use active constructions. In addition, most school-sponsored writing is journalistic in that it does not address a specific audience of insiders, as a scientific paper or even a lab report does. Journalistic writing by its very nature is written by outsiders for outsiders, and it follows conventions associated with the goals of clarity, conciseness, and generating audience interest. Any writing with these goals will not use passives with much frequency. Quite simply, it is easier for people to process sentences in the active voice with a readily identifiable subject. This fact appears to have nothing to do with transformations but very much to do with the way people tend to classify the world into agents and actions.

Because the passive allows us to delete subject agents, many people use it to avoid assigning responsibility or blame. Sentence 14 on page 164, for example, came from an automaker's report on faulty hood latches in a certain line of cars. The driver's forward vision was impaired *by the hood* (subject agent undeleted) of his car, which unlatched at 60 miles an hour and wrapped itself around the windshield. The report writers could not include the subject agent without assigning responsibility and potential liability to the company, which they avoided for obvious reasons. Using the passive, with agent deleted, allowed them to describe the circumstances of the accident without attaching blame, which was left to a court to determine.

Industry and government are the primary but not the sole sources of such evasiveness. Passives appear spontaneously in the speech and writing of people who strive, for one reason or another, to be circumspect. The usage question regarding passive constructions, consequently, revolves around situation.

APPLYING KEY IDEAS

Directions: Examine a paper you've written for another class and see whether you can find any passive constructions. If you find some, determine whether they are appropriate to that context, given the previous discussion. If they are not appropriate, rewrite them to active form.

Relative Clause Formation

Relative clauses are immensely interesting structures. They generally function as modifiers that supply information about nouns. In addition, they generally allow us to avoid repeating a noun. Consider the following sentences:

17. The message, *which Macarena had left near the flowers*, baffled Fred.
18. The wallet *that held Macarena's money* was in the trunk.
19. The woman *whom I love* has red hair.

Each of these sentences contains an independent clause and a relative clause. Each relative clause is introduced by a relative pronoun. The respective clauses are as follows:

17a. the message baffled Fred/*which* Macarena had left near the flowers
18a. the wallet was in the trunk/*that* held Macarena's money
19a. the woman has red hair/*whom* I love

T-G grammar examines the history of sentences; thus, being able to identify the underlying clauses in a sentence that has a relative clause is important. The clauses listed previously, however, are one step short of the deep structure necessary for an appropriate analysis. We must identify the noun or noun phrase that serves as the antecedent for the relative pronoun. Doing so results in the clause pairs that follow:

17b. the message baffled Fred/Macarena had left *the message* near the flowers
18b. the wallet was in the trunk/*the wallet* held Macarena's money
19b. the woman has red hair/I love *the woman*

It is easy to see in Sentences 17b through 19b that each relative clause has a duplicate NP in the underlying structure. The relative clause transformation turns the duplicate NP into a relative pronoun. In the event that the relativized NP is an object in the dependent clause, the transformation also shifts the relative pronoun to the front of the clause. This second step is necessary because the relative pronoun links the relative clause to the independent clause.

Chapter 2 dealt with this topic without the benefit of a formal rule. The mechanism, however, is the same: Relativization shifts the object NP to the front of the relative clause, where it functions both as object and as a connector joining the independent clause and the dependent clause.

Relative Clause Rule

$NP_{1\,s}\ [Y\ NP_2\ Z]_s$

$\Rightarrow$

$NP_{1\,s}\ [\text{wh-pro}\ Y\ Z]_s$

$$\text{wh-pro} \rightarrow \left\{ \begin{array}{c} \text{RP} \\ \text{prep} + \text{RP} \end{array} \right\}$$

This rule looks more complicated than it is. Y and Z are variables that T-G grammar uses to account for constituents that do not affect the transformation. The important factors are that NP_1 must equal NP_2 and that there is a clause, represented by the S and brackets, that branches off NP_1. The transformation takes NP_2 and turns it into a relative pronoun, which is designated as *wh-pro* because so many relative pronouns begin with the letters *wh*. In the event that NP_2 is the subject of the clause, the variable Y will be empty. In the event that NP_2 is the object, Y will be everything in front of the object. Note that this transformation rule cannot account for relativization of noun phrases that are objects of prepositions. Consequently, we must add a phrase-structure rule that allows us to include prepositional phrases as part of the overall transformation. In the context of a relativized object of a preposition, *wh-pro* may include the preposition as well as the relative pronoun.

Now let's examine how to diagram the relative clauses in Sentences 17 through 19:

Sentence 3.17: The message, which Macarena had left near the flowers, baffled Fred

Deep Structure:

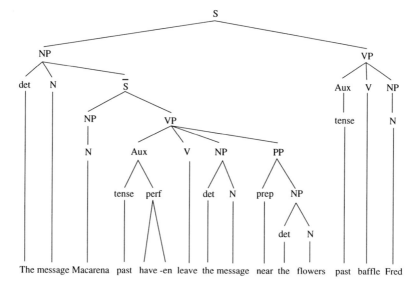

T-Relative
Surface Structure:

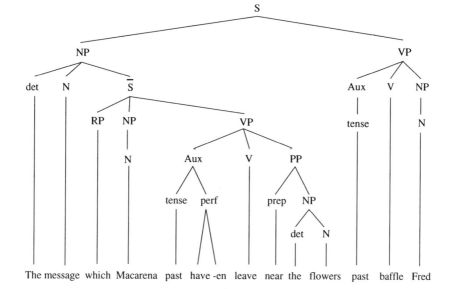

Sentence 3.18: The wallet that had Macarena's money was in the trunk

Deep Structure:

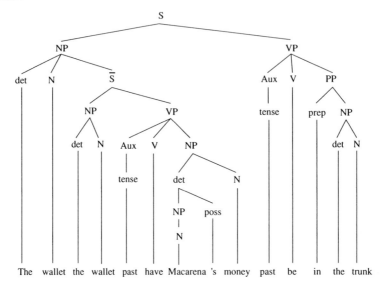

T-Relative:
Surface Structure:

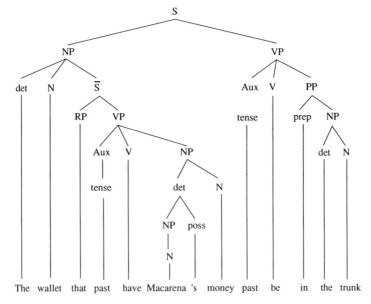

Sentence 3.19: The woman whom I love has red hair
Deep Structure:

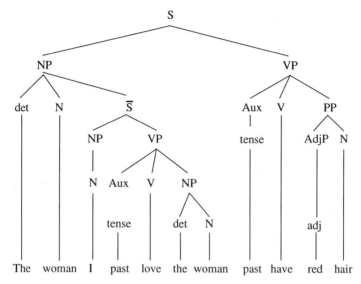

T-Relative
Surface Structure:

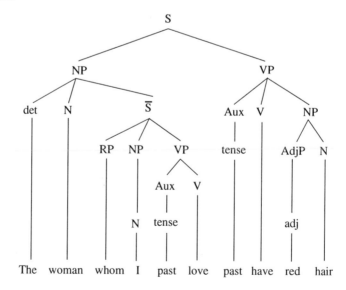

Directions: Use the relative clause transformation to analyze the following sentences using tree diagrams.

1. Macarena was the woman who danced on the bar at China Club.
2. The high heels that she was wearing almost slipped on the slick surface.
3. A bartender who knew her grabbed Macarena's arm.
4. The patrons who were seated at the bar laughed at her in good fun.
5. The drink that Macarena had in her hand went flying.

Relativizing Noun Phrases in Prepositional Phrases

Sometimes a duplicate NP appears as the object of a preposition, and we have to relativize it, as in Sentence 20. This procedure raises some interesting grammatical questions:

20. Fred loved the house *in which the couple lived.*

This sentence is made up of the following clauses:

20a. Fred loved the house/the couple lived in the house.

Relativization affects the noun phrase, but the grammar allows us to shift either the NP or the entire prepositional phrase to the beginning of the relative clause. In Sentence 20, we see that the entire PP was shifted. Sentence 20b shows the effect of shifting just the NP:

20b. Fred loved the house *which the couple lived in.*

On pages 40–41, we examined traditional injunctions against ending a sentence with a preposition, but here we see that the grammar provides for this option; the injunction is not supported by the grammar.

Usage Note

The usage note on page 120 mentioned that most people use the relative pronouns *which* and *that* interchangeably. Although these words are very similar, they are not exactly the same; *which* generally is used in nonrestrictive relative clauses, whereas *that* is used in restrictive ones. There is another difference, however, as Sentence 20b illustrates—*which* can function as the object of a preposition, but *that* cannot. T-G grammar suggests that there is an intermediary step that lies between sentences 20a and 20b, in which the underlying form is:

*Fred loved the house/the couple lived in which.

Nevertheless, common usage treats *which* and *that* as being the same, with one result being that Sentence 20b more often than not is uttered as 20c:

20c. ?Fred loved the house *that the couple lived in.*

Even though this sentence is common, it appears to violate the rules of the grammar. Sentence 20c would have the following as an intermediary underlying form:

Fred loved the house/the couple lived in that

The problem becomes even more evident if we perform the option of shifting the entire prepositional phrase to the front of the relative clause. In fact, doing so creates an ungrammatical sentence:

*Fred loved the house *in that the couple lived.*

This breach of the underlying grammar suggests that Sentence 20c may not be acceptable in formal standard usage; it certainly is not allowed by the version of T-G grammar presented here.

Other Relative Pronouns

Perhaps even more interesting than sentences with relativization in a prepositional phrase are sentences like 21:

21. They drove to Big Sur, *where the sea otters play.*

The deep structure of this sentence would have to be something along the lines of 21a:

21a. They drove to Big Sur/the sea otters play *at Big Sur.*

We can duplicate *Big Sur* in both clauses, but we cannot readily duplicate the prepositional phrase that governs this NP. It is possible to suggest that the preposition *at* is not necessary in the deep structure, that we can substitute a marker for the prepositional phrase, (e.g., Z). The transformation then would delete this marker as it relativizes the NP. This approach seems ad hoc and counterintuitive, however. It is also incongruent with analysis of sentences like 20 (Fred loved the house in which the couple lived), where the preposition *in* is a real preposition in the deep structure as well as the surface structure. In Sentence 20, the preposition cannot be deleted because doing so produces an ungrammatical construction:

*Fred loved the house *which the couple lived.*

We therefore are forced to propose that the prepositional phrases in the deep structure for sentences of this type simply do not match. To make this proposal more reasonable, we also would have to propose that relative clauses involving the relative pronoun *where* are different from those involving relative pronouns such as *which, who,* and *whom*. Once we accept these proposals, accounting for

Sentence 3.20: Fred loved the house in which the couple lived
Deep Structure:

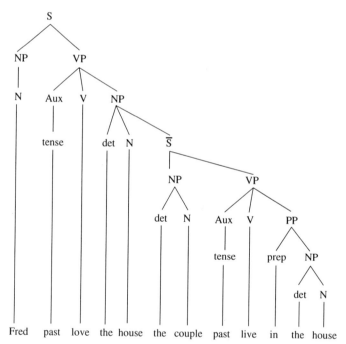

T-Relative
Surface Structure:

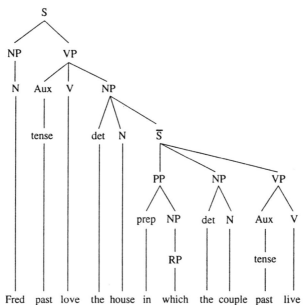

Sentence 3.21: They drove to Big Sur, where the sea otters play

Deep Structure:

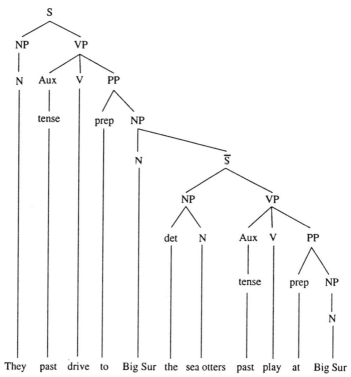

T-Relative
Surface Structure:

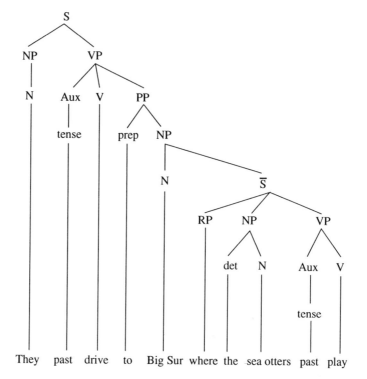

what happens to the preposition *at* is fairly straightforward: It is absorbed into the relative pronoun.

This analysis presages what lies ahead. From the beginning, T-G grammar proposed that its focus on the history of sentences was a significant strength. However, as the previous analysis suggests, reconciling deep structure with surface structure presents problems. As we move further into the grammar, we see that these problems become more severe, forcing increasingly ad hoc—or even far-fetched—explanations of deep structure.

Consider the nonstandard question:

*Where is he at?

In this common sentence, *at* is redundant because it is implicit in the word *where*. The same principle applies in relative clauses of the type illustrated in Sentence 21. The relative pronoun must include both the noun phrase and the preposition.

Equally troubling are sentences such as 22 and 23:

22. The reason *why Fred was late* was unknown.
23. Fred bought a thong swimsuit, *which horrified his mother.*

We must analyze Sentence 22 as consisting of the following clauses:

22a. The reason was unknown/Fred was late *for the reason.*

As in Sentence 21, we must assume that relativization alters the entire prepositional phrase, not just the NP.

Sentence 23 perhaps is even more problematic because there is no antecedent for the relative pronoun. The relative pronoun does not duplicate a noun phrase in the independent clause; instead, it seems to replace the semantic content of the independent clause. We might analyze Sentence 23 as consisting of the following clauses:

23a. Fred bought a thong swimsuit/*the fact that Fred bought a thong swimsuit* horrified his mother.

As Chomsky initially formulated the grammar, there was a clear separation between syntax and semantics, yet sentences of this type indicate that this separation is artificial. The relative pronoun's chief syntactic function in sentences like those just given is to link the dependent and independent clauses. However, it also has a clear semantic component that cannot be described in the grammar. One result is that the transformation rule presented on page 173 for relative clauses does not work for Sentences 21 through 23. It is possible to formulate additional rules to account for Sentences 21 and 22, but such rules would be contrary to the goal of T-G grammar to provide general rather than specific rules. It is not possible to formulate an additional rule for Sentence 23 because transformation rules do not, and cannot, address issues of semantic content. Consequently, we have to rely on intuition and guesswork to analyze the deep structure of such sentences. Such a reliance is not desirable in T-G grammar, which from the beginning strove to eliminate guesswork through rigorous formulation of rules. It is one of several problems with T-G grammar that has not been satisfactorily solved.

Sentence 3.22: The reason why Fred was late was unknown

Surface Structure:

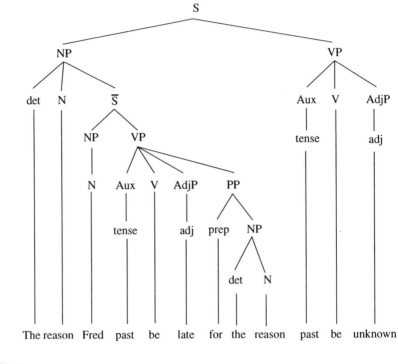

T-Relative:
Deep Structure:

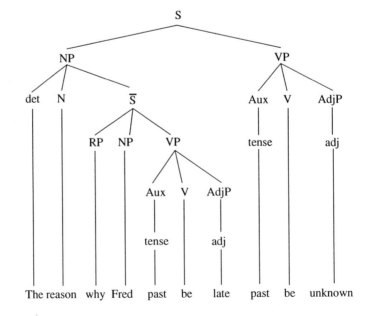

Sentence 3.23: Fred bought a thong swimsuit, which horrified his mother

Note: When diagramming sentences like this one, linguists use a convention to make the analysis easier. Rather than diagram the construction *The fact that Fred bought a thong swimsuit*, we can put the entire string of words under a *triangle* governed by an NP. We know that the construction is an NP, even though we may not know exactly what it is composed of; thus this convention facilitates the analysis while recognizing the uncertain nature of the NP that is being replaced in the transformation. Also note that the relative clause branches off the main S because it is a sentence-level modifier.

Deep Structure:

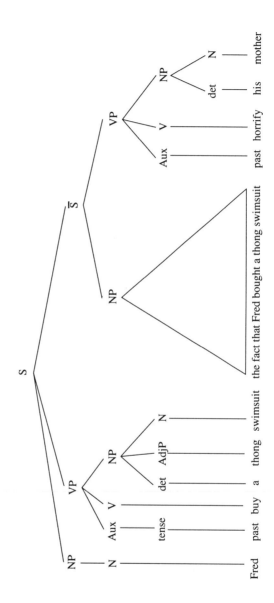

T-Relative
Surface Structure:

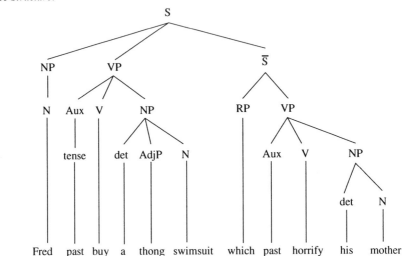

Relative Pronoun Deletion

English allows us to delete relative pronouns in sentences when the pronoun is functioning as an object in a restrictive relative clause. Consider the following sentences:

24. The book *Maria bought* was a first edition.
25. All of the people *we know* will be dead in 50 years.

The relative clauses, set in italics, have had their relative pronouns deleted. Before this operation, the sentences would exist as:

24a. The book *that Maria bought* was a first edition.
25a. All of the people *whom we know* will be dead in 50 years.

Sentence 3.24: The book Maria bought was a first edition

Deep Structure:

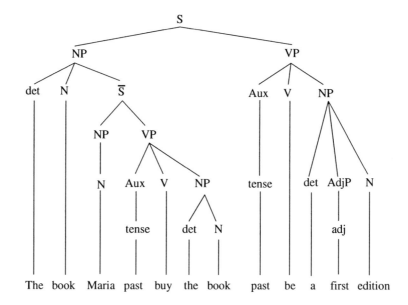

T-Relative:

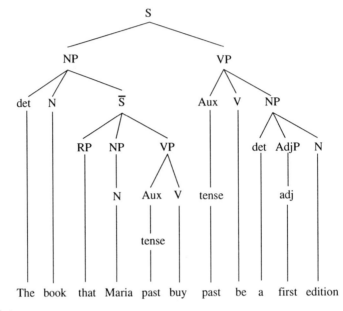

T-RP Deletion:
Surface Structure:

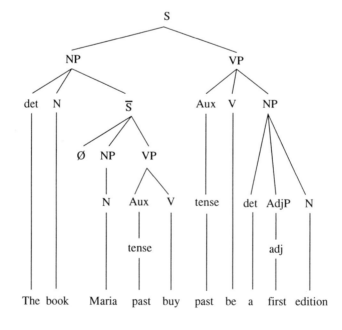

188

Sentence 3.25: All of the people we know will be dead in 50 years
Deep Structure:

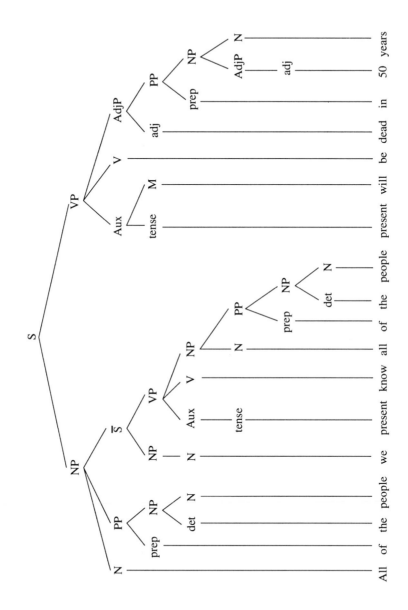

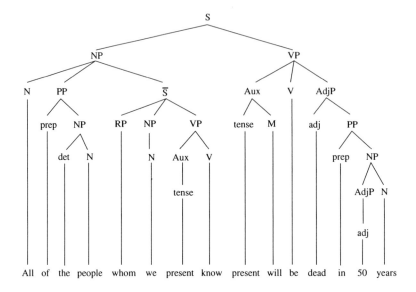

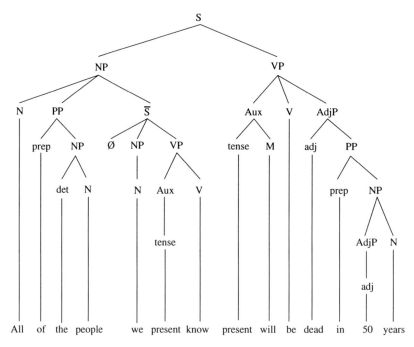

190

Relative Pronoun Deletion Rule

NP$_{1 \, s}$ [wh-pro Y Z]$_s$

$\Rightarrow$

NP$_{1 \, s}$ [Ø Y Z]$_s$

The null symbol, Ø, signifies that the place of the relative pronoun is empty.

APPLYING KEY IDEAS

Directions: Show derivations for the following sentences.

1. Fritz pocketed the money that was on the counter.
2. Fred, who loved the beach, lived in the Valley.
3. Fred reached a decision which Macarena agreed with.
4. Fritz remembered the day when Macarena gave him that first kiss.
5. The new house that Fritz wanted cost about $500,000, which was too expensive.
6. They drove to Big Sur, where the sea otters play, and stopped at the house that Buggsy had built.
7. She was astounded that someone who was so unpleasant could have millions.
8. The keys Raul lost opened a safety deposit box.
9. Rita de Luna, who always enjoyed Las Vegas, was intrigued by Buggsy and wanted to know more about him.
10. They made an incongruous couple because Rita was short, which made Buggsy look very tall.
11. Buggsy's face had the appeal of month-old cottage cheese, and she was certain that he had learned his manners at the zoo, yet his mansion displayed impeccable taste and was furnished in the ultramodern style that she loved.
12. The junior found the book that the senior who lives in the dorm with the leaky roof lost.
13. Fritz scolded the boy whose harsh language hurt the feelings of the girl who earned an *A*.
14. Meanwhile, Fritz had picked up a vase that was made by someone with the improbable name of Ming, but his habitually sweaty palms could not hold it, and it slipped to the marble floor in an instant.
15. The three-carat diamond ring that Fritz had given her for Christmas became a cheap bauble in her eyes, and in her fantasy Macarena envisioned a gem that was the size of a museum piece on her finger, which seemed wonderfully enhanced in the light from its many facets.

Particle Movement

On page 42 we noted that particles can appear in two positions: They can come immediately after the verb, or they can come after the noun phrase object. Sentences 26 and 26a illustrate these possibilities:

  26. Maria took off her apron.
26a. Maria took her apron off.

    Transformational grammar accounts for these sentences through the *particle movement* rule.

Particle Movement Rule

    X V → prt NP

    ⇒

    X V NP prt

Here *X* is a variable that includes the NP subject, and prt is the particle. This rule shows that in the deep structure the particle is attached to the verb, whereas in the surface structure it follows the object NP and, as a verbal constituent, would be attached to the VP. Thus, Sentence 26 is the underlying form of 26a, as illustrated in the following tree diagram:

Sentence 3.26a: Maria took her apron off
Deep Structure:

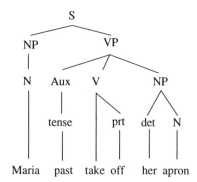

Surface Structure:

```
                      S
             _____/_____
            NP                 VP
            |           _____/\_____
            N    Aux   V    NP       prt
            |     |    |   /\         |
            |   tense  | det  N       |
            |     |    |  |   |       |
          Maria  past take her apron off
```

The particle-movement transformation works well for simple sentences like 26, but it does not seem to work very well with sentences that include an additional location indicator, as in Sentence 27 below:

27. Buggsy took the books *back up*.

Our rule indicates that the underlying structure is 27a:

27a. *Buggsy took *back up* the books.

Although with many sentences we do not expect the deep structure to be grammatical, we do with sentences involving a particle because particle movement is an optional transformation. With any optional transformation, the underlying form must be able to serve as the surface structure.

Some linguists have proposed switching the underlying structure with the surface structure as a way of solving the problem presented by sentences like 27. In this approach, particles would be attached to the VP and would follow the NP object in the underlying structure; the transformation would shift the particle to the verb. Fig. 3.1 illustrates the two possibilities. With more complex sentences, neither approach seems acceptable. In Chapter 1, we examined the following sentence:

　　　Fritz picked up the book that Macarena had dropped.

If we move the particle behind the NP object, we have:

　　　Fritz picked the book up that Macarena had dropped.

Sentence 3.1: Shifting the Position of the Particle. The two proposals for the underlying structure of sentences with particles result in different movement.

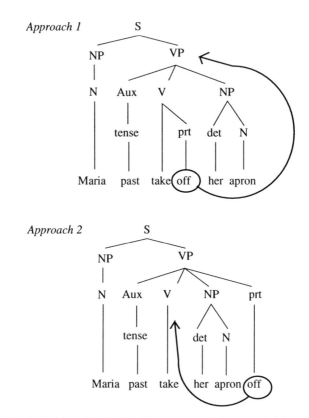

FIG. 3.1. Shifting the Position of the Particle. The two proposals for the underlying structure of sentences with particles results in different movement.

    No matter which underlying structure we choose, there is no way to account for the relative clause unless we specify that the particle attaches to the NP rather than to the VP, as in the accompanying diagram. If we propose that the particle exists behind the NP object in the underlying structure, the transformation would shift *up* so that it attaches to the verb; if, however, we propose that the particle is attached to the verb in the underlying structure, the transformation would shift the particle and attach it to the NP object. In this latter case, it is impossible to shift the particle to the VP because movement is blocked by the relative clause. This analysis, unfortunately, is not very satisfying because particles are related to verbs, not noun phrases. Moreover, we are faced with the

Example Sentence: Fritz picked the book up that Macarena had dropped

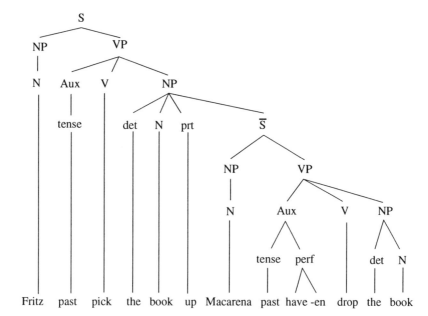

difficult task of explaining how the transformation allows a constituent to be verbal in one condition and nominal in another.

Although this problem is quite troubling for T-G grammar, we must note that phrase-structure grammar does not offer a better solution. True, with phrase-structure grammar we do not have to concern ourselves with the question of underlying structure, but we do have to wonder about the dual functions that the particle has in such sentences.

Dative, or Indirect Objects

The term *dative* refers to indirect objects. It is the Latin translation of the Greek word *dotike*, which roughly means "giving." Linguists commonly use the term dative instead of indirect object when discussing grammar. As we saw on pages 26–27, the indirect object receives the action of ditransitive verbs, as in the following sentences:

28. Buggsy gave *Rita de Luna* free tickets to the show.
29. Mrs. DiMarco sent the flowers *to Raul*.
30. The night in jail taught *Buggsy's goons* an important lesson.
31. Buggsy asked a great deal *of his friends*.

These sentences show that the indirect object can have two forms. It can be a noun phrase that immediately follows the verb and that precedes the direct object, as in sentences 28 and 30, or it can be the object of a preposition, as in sentences 29 and 31. In the second case, the entire prepositional phrase is considered to be the indirect object. These two forms raise the question of which one represents the deep structure. Some linguists have proposed that the deep structure is the prepositional form, whereas others have proposed that it is the noun-phrase form. In *Syntactic Structures*, Chomsky identified the noun-phrase form as the deep structure, and here we follow his example.

Dative Transformation Rule

$X \ V \ NP_1 \ NP_2$

$\Rightarrow$

$X \ V \ NP_2 \ prep + NP_1$

As in other instances, X is a variable, V is a ditransitive verb, NP_1 is the indirect object, NP_2 the direct object, and prep is the prepositions *to*, *of*, and *for.*

Sentence 3.28: Buggsy gave Rita de Luna free tickets to the show
Deep Structure

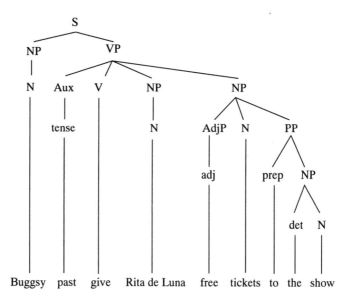

No transformation

Sentence 3.29: Mrs. DiMarco sent the flowers to Raul
Deep Structure

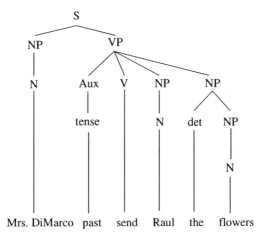

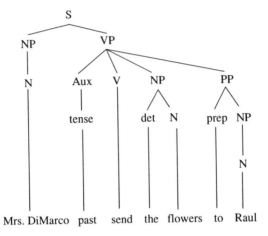

Sentence 3.30: The night in jail taught Buggsy's goons an important lesson
Deep Structure

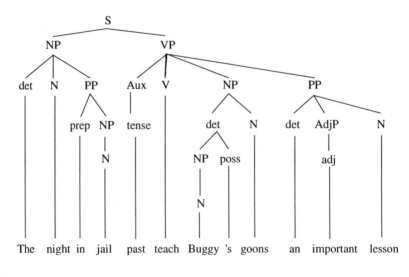

No transformation

Sentence 3.31: Buggsy asked a great deal of his friends
Deep Structure

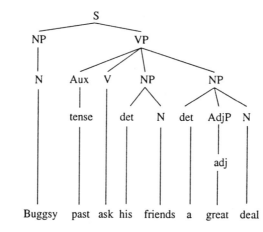

T-Dative:
Surface Structure

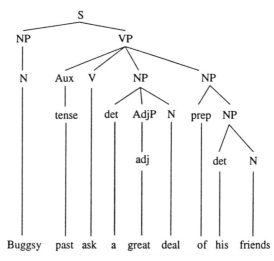

Sometimes a sentence may appear to have an indirect object when it does not, as in the following:

Raul bought a cake for the birthday party.

In many respects, this sentence resembles Sentence 31. Notice, however, that if we try to put this sentence in its alternative form it does not sound right:

*Raul bought the birthday party a cake.

We cannot always use the way a sentence sounds in the deep structure to determine its grammaticality, but in this case we can because the deep structure also can exist as the surface structure.

199

When indirect objects are part of other transformations, such as relative clause formation, the result can be syntactically interesting sentences. For example:

32.   Fred was the man whom Macarena gave the kiss to.

Whom is the indirect object, but through relative pronoun deletion we can produce:

32a. Fred was the man Macarena gave the kiss to.

In this surface structure, we really don't have an indirect object in the dependent clause, even though the ditransitive verb *gave* requires it. One option is to consider *the man* as being both the NP complement of the first clause and the indirect object of the second.

Sometimes, an indirect object functions with a complement clause that is functioning as a direct object, as in Sentence 33:

33.   Maria showed Raul that she could dance the pachanga.

Raul is the indirect object, and *that she could dance the pachanga* is the direct object. What's interesting about this construction is that the prepositional form does not seem to be accepted in all dialects:

33a. ?Maria showed that she could dance the pachanga to Raul.

Usage Note

Indirect objects raise some fascinating questions when we consider their structure in passive sentences. In those cases in which the indirect object is part of a prepositional phrase, applying the passive transformation to a ditransitive verb is straightforward, as in Sentence 34:

34. Mrs. DiMarco sent the money to Raul.
34a. The money was sent to Raul by Mrs. DiMarco.

However, in those instances in which the indirect object is not part of a prepositional phrase, there appears to be variation with regard to the acceptability of the passivized form. Consider these examples:

35.   Fritz gave Macarena a kiss.
35a. ?A kiss was given Macarena by Fritz.

Sentence 35a is not acceptable in some American dialects, although it seems to be acceptable, but not preferred, in British English dialects.

When the indirect object is a pronoun, the resulting passive seems not only unacceptable but ungrammatical:

36. Macarena fixed me a drink.
36a. *A drink was fixed me by Macarena.

The acceptable form is shown in Sentence 36b:

36b. A drink was fixed for me by Macarena.

Yet we should be able to passivize Sentence 36 without this problem, given the formulation of the transformation rule. This problem suggests that the rule requires that we restrict its operation in the context of ditransitive verbs and pronoun indirect objects.

Although we can add this restriction fairly easily, it is not satisfactory because it cannot account for certain ditransitive verbs, (e.g., *made*), that do not lend themselves to passivization at all when the indirect object is not part of a prepositional phrase:

37. Someone made a motion to the court.
37a. ?Someone made the court a motion.
37b. A motion was made to the court by someone.
37c. *A motion was made the court by someone.

Given such sentences, it appears as though the simplest grammatical approach is to bar passivization of NP indirect objects. This approach would eliminate ungrammatical and even questionable sentences by requiring that the passive apply only to indirect objects in a prepositional phrase. A consequence would be that the order of the rules, as shown on pages 221–223, would change: The dative transformation necessarily would have to come before the passive so as to ensure that the indirect object always appeared in the PP prior to passivization.

APPLYING KEY IDEAS

Directions: Show derivations for the following sentences.
1. Macarena picked the books up and ran to her car.
2. Raul bought a huge cake for his friends.
3. Michael Star put on a wig to hid his bald spot.

4. Maria sent her mother a fruit basket for Mother's Day, but it got lost in the mail.
5. Fritz went to a dance club to mingle, but he struck out with the women.
6. Buggsy's wife put the cat out before she went to bed.
7. Raul did a huge favor for his aunt when he stopped at the market for cat food.
8. A night out with Buggsy taught a valuable lesson to Rita de Luna.
9. Macarena became so angry that she stuck her tongue out at Fred.
10. Buggsy asked a question of the station attendant, who could not understand him.
11. Rita sent a farewell card to Buggsy before she left for London.
12. Buggsy had two goons at Heathrow Airport who picked Rita up after she landed.
13. Rita put her sunglasses on and said nothing.
14. Macarena saw the new car she wanted when she drove into Beverly Hills.
15. She thought about the mock rabbit fur coat that Fritz had given to her.

Reflexive Pronouns

We saw on page 21 that English uses a reflexive pronoun whenever a subject performs an action on itself, as in the following sentences:

38. Fred shaved himself.
39. The dog scratched itself.

In transformational grammar, the reflexive pronoun appears in the deep structure as a duplication of the subject noun phrase. The deep structures of Sentences 38 and 39, for example, would have the form of 38a and 39a:

38a. Fred shaved Fred.
39a. The dog scratched the dog.

The reflexive transformation therefore changes the duplicate noun phrase into a reflexive pronoun.

Reflexive Rule

NP_1 V NP_2

$\Rightarrow$

NP_1 V ref-pro

In this statement, *ref-pro* is a reflexive pronoun. This transformation is obligatory when NP_1 equals NP_2.

Sentence 3.38: Fred shaved himself
Deep Structure

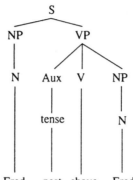

T-Reflexive:
Surface Structure

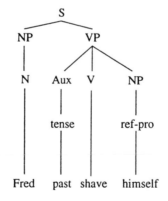

Sentence 3.39: The dog scratched itself
Deep Structure

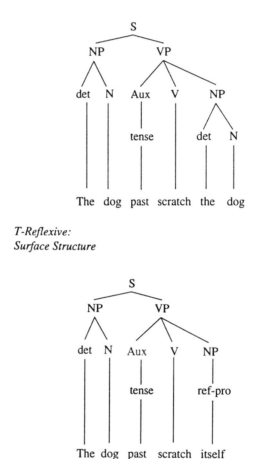

T-Reflexive:
Surface Structure

Imperatives

Imperative is the term we use to signify commands, as in Sentence 40:

40. Stop the car.

Most imperatives in English lack a subject; normally, we include the subject only when we want to make the command stronger, as in *You stop the car.* The deep structure of imperatives always includes the subject, so the transformation itself consists of deleting the subject *you.*

Imperative Rule

NP V X

⇒

Ø V X

In this rule, NP is the subject, and X is a variable. The rule simply deletes the subject. The accompanying diagram illustrates this analysis.

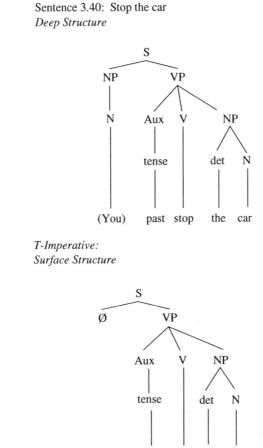

Sentence 3.40: Stop the car
Deep Structure

T-Imperative:
Surface Structure

There Insertion

A certain type of sentence in English begins with the word *there*, which is followed by a form of *be*, a *noun phrase*, and a *prepositional phrase*, as in:

41. There was a bug in my salad.
42. There is an ugly spot on my tie.

These are existential sentences, and *there* has many of the characteristics of a noun (or pronoun), but it is not the subject. Because it also has many non-noun characteristics, we might think of *there* as a pseudo-noun. Notice also that *there* is not functioning as an adverbial. The adverbial use is easily seen in sentences like 43:

43. There are my keys.

The difference becomes clearer if we examine the deep structure of these sentences:

41a. A bug was in my salad.
42a. An ugly spot was on my tie.
43a. My keys are there.

These sentences illustrate that, in 41 and 42, *there* is inserted by the transformation, whereas in 43a *there* is not because it exists in the deep structure. It is worth mentioning, however, that even in 43 *there* is not functioning as a regular adverbial, as we see if we replace it with the adverb *somewhere*:

My keys are somewhere.

*Somewhere are my keys.

There Insertion Rule

NP be PP

⇒

There be NP PP

The accompanying diagrams show the application of this rule.

Sentence 3.41: There was a bug in my salad
Deep Structure

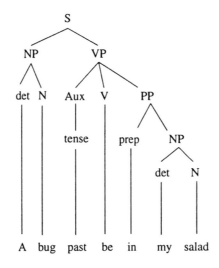

T-There Insertion
Surface Structure

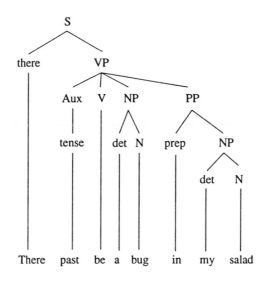

Sentence 3.42: There is an ugly spot on my tie
Deep Structure

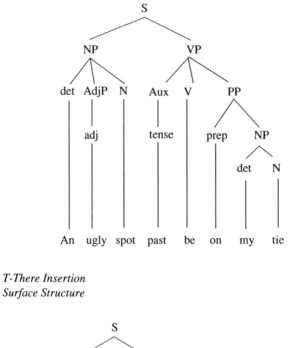

T-There Insertion
Surface Structure

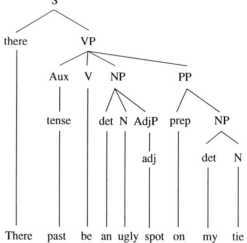

Directions: Show derivations for the following sentences.

1. Macarena saw herself in the mirror after her haircut and screamed.
2. Find a towel!
3. There were several of Buggsy's goons at the party in Hollywood.
4. Buggsy's last girlfriend hurt herself when she tried skiing.
5. Stop at the market and buy a box of doughnuts.
6. There was a strange glow on her face, and it frightened the guests.
7. Raul told himself that he could make it in Hollywood in spite of the odds.
8. Rita de Luna sang for herself that night, but she told Buggsy that she sang for him.
9. There were high rollers everywhere in Buggsy's casino.
10. Put the flowers on the table.

Adverbial Movement

We have already seen in the previous chapters that different types of constructions can function as adverbials. The most common are adverbs, subordinate clauses, and prepositional phrases. These discussions indicated that adverbials can appear in different parts of a sentence, but they did not propose any type of rule for governing movement. Again, because phrase-structure grammar is descriptive rather than generative, there is no need for such a rule. Transformational grammar, of course, does provide a movement rule. For example, consider Sentences 44 through 44b:

44. Fred loaded the Mack 10 slowly.
44a. Fred slowly loaded the Mack 10.
44b. Slowly, Fred loaded the Mack 10.

Sentence 44 is deemed to be the deep structure of both 44a and 44b, which means that in the deep structure adverbials appear at the end of the VP. The transformation rule takes two forms, one for sentences of the type illustrated in 44a and one for sentences of the type for 44b. The first form moves the adverbial from the end of the verb phrase to before the verb, a movement that is called *preposing*. The second form moves the adverbial from the end of the verb phrase to the beginning of the clause, a movement that is called *fronting*.

Adverbial Movement Rule

Form 1: Preposing

X V NP AdvP Y

⇒

X AdvP V NP Y

Form 2: Fronting

X V NP AdvP Y

⇒

AdvP X V NP Y

Preposing. The T-G analysis of preposed adverbials is straightforward, as long as we are dealing with simple adverbs:

45. Macarena *carefully* placed her napkin on the table and stood up.
46. She *quickly* walked to the window of the restaurant.

However, prepositional phrases and subordinate clauses also function adverbially. When we prepose these constructions—unlike their simple adverb counterparts—they change from restrictive to nonrestrictive modifiers and thus become sentence-level modifiers, as shown in the following sentences:

47. Macarena kissed Buggsy *with fire in her heart.*
47a. Macarena, *with fire in her heart*, kissed Buggsy.
48. Fritz forgave Macarena's indiscretion *because he loved her.*
48a. Fritz, *because he loved her*, forgave Macarena's indiscretion.

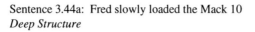

Sentence 3.44a: Fred slowly loaded the Mack 10
Deep Structure

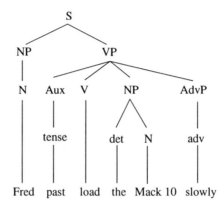

T-Adverb Movement (preposing):
Surface Structure:

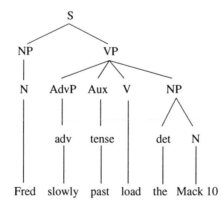

Sentence 3.44b: Slowly, Fred loaded the Mack 10
Deep Structure

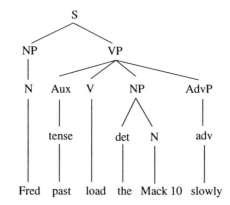

T-Adverb Movement (fronting):
Surface Structure:

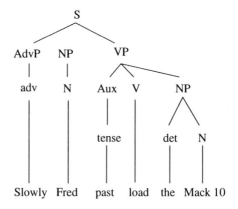

Sentence 3.47a: Macarena, with fire in her heart, kissed Buggsy
Deep Structure

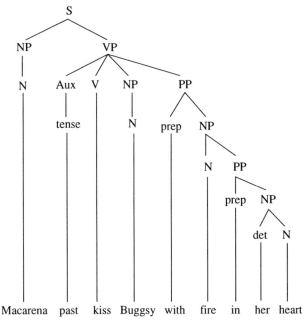

T-Adverb Movement (preposing):
Surface Structure

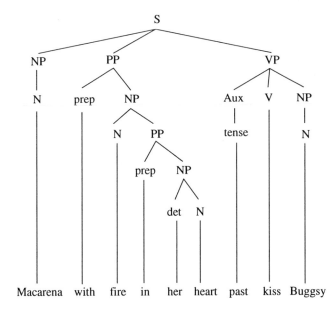

Sentence 3.48a: Fritz, because he loved her, forgave Macarena's indiscretion
Deep Structure

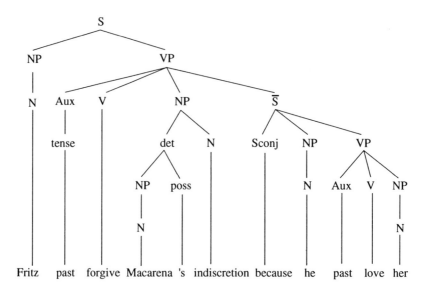

T-Adverb Movement (preposing):
Surface Structure:

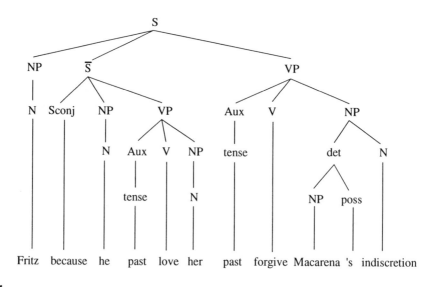

Fronting. Fronting an adverbial of any kind also makes it a nonrestrictive, or sentence-level, modifier. The nonrestrictive nature of the fronted adverbial is captured in the writing convention that requires setting off such constructions with punctuation. Other conventions, such as the one used by most journalists, do not provide for punctuation of fronted prepositional phrases. From a grammatical perspective, however, even when a fronted adverbial is not set off with punctuation, our analysis must treat it as a sentence-level modifier, as in the following examples:

49. *After the dinner at Spago's* Macarena saw Buggsy and Rita de Luna in a limo.
50. *With his usual aplomb* Fritz undertipped the waiter.
51. *In a smooth gesture* the waiter returned the tip.

Sentence 3.49: After the dinner at Spago's Macarena saw Buggsy and Rita de Luna in a limo*
Deep Structure

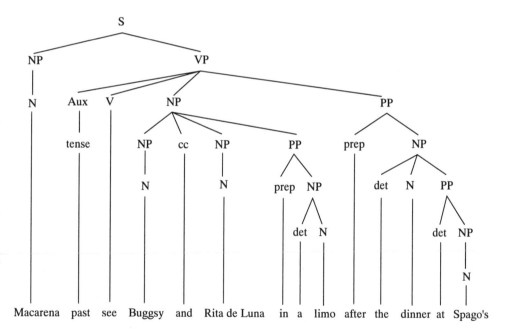

*Although we might be tempted to analyze *Spago's* as a *det* that is rewritten as NP poss, such analysis is contrary to how we use such terms. It would be based on the idea that *Spago's* is part of *Spago's restaurant*. However, Spago's was opened by an entrepreneur named Wolfgang Puck; there is no person named Spago. In such instances, the possessive must be considered as a proper noun, as indicated in the tree above.

T-Adverb Movement (fronting)
Surface Structure

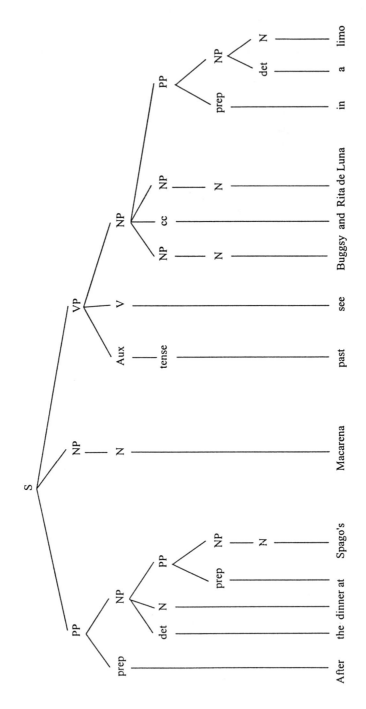

Deep Structure

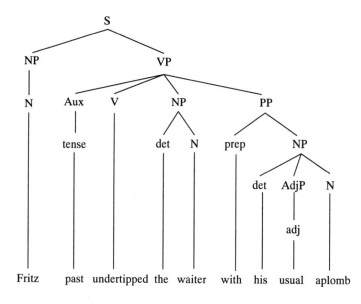

Fritz past undertipped the waiter with his usual aplomb

T-Adverb Movement (fronting)
Surface Structure

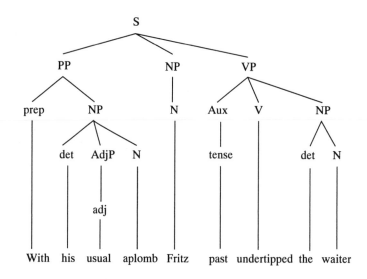

With his usual aplomb Fritz past undertipped the waiter

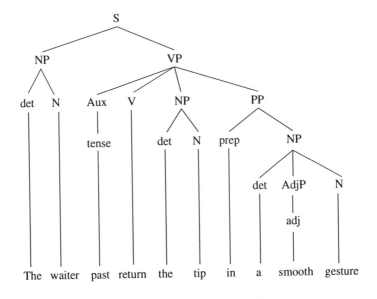

T-Adverb Movement (fronting)
Surface Structure

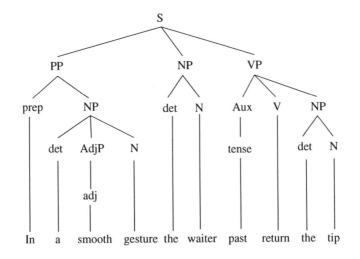

Applying Key Ideas

1. Slowly, Buggsy and Rita de Luna got into the limo.
2. Michael Star, because he needed a ride, ran after them, but he was too late.
3. With genuine concern, Fritz held Macarena's trembling hand.
4. Macarena clearly had seen Buggsy with Rita de Luna, and she was greatly upset with him.
5. Although she wanted the planned trip to Mexico, Macarena knew that it was hopeless.
6. Fred did not buy the engagement ring because his friend could not give him a discount.
7. He carefully counted his money and thought about a simple wedding.
8. Suddenly, he heard a loud crash from outside, and he ran to the front door.
9. He saw an armored truck that had turned over at the corner, and bags of money, as though the hand of Providence had scattered them like rice, were lying in his front yard.
10. He quickly ran outside and grabbed three of the biggest bags in each hand, as sirens sounded in the distance.
11. After he was safely in his house, he opened the bags, and hundreds of neatly wrapped stacks of $100 bills fell out.
12. Fred was stunned, because he now had $1.2 million on his kitchen table.
13. Before he went on a buying spree, he considered carefully his current situation.
14. His conscience bothered him badly, and although he knew it was wrong, he really wanted the money.
15. He wondered whether Macarena would love him more if he was rich and decided that she would, unless he landed in jail for taking those bags.

Usage Note

The adverbial movement rule allows adverbials to occupy only three positions in a sentence. They can come at the end of the verb phrase, before the verb, or in the front of a clause. Nevertheless, it is very common to find adverbs in a fourth position, as illustrated in these sentences:

*   ?Fritz could *still* win Macarena's heart if he applies himself.
*   ?Fred had *almost* given up hope of getting Macarena to settle down.

In these sentences, the adverbs—*still* and *almost*—literally are inside the verb phrase, separating the auxiliary from the main verb.

Some writing conventions do not allow this particular construction. Instead, they require the adverbial to be either at the end of the VP or preposed, as in:

Example Sentence: Fred had almost given up hope of getting Macarena to settle down

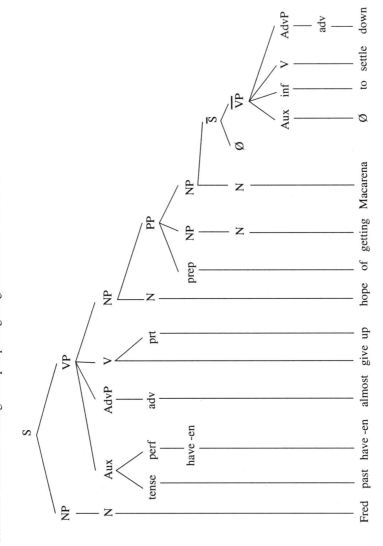

- Fritz could win Macarena's heart *still* if he applies himself.
- Fred had given up hope *almost* of getting Macarena to settle down.
- Fritz *still* could win Macarena's heart if he applies himself.
- Fred *almost* had given up hope of getting Macarena to settle down.

In some dialects, however, the first two instances are not entirely acceptable, and the last two are preferred.

Although no such rule exists, we could develop a transformation rule that would allow us to split the auxiliary and the verb with an adverbial, but it would create a difficulty that the grammar cannot readily overcome. For example, in the case of *Fred had almost given up hope of getting Macarena to settle down*, the adverbial phrase governing *almost* blocks the morphophonemic transformation that attaches the past-participle marker to the verb. This problem leads to the interesting conclusion that, in T-G grammar, sentences with an adverbial separating the auxiliary and the verb are ungrammatical. This conclusion supports the formal standard convention that deems such constructions inappropriate. We should note, however, that phrase-structure grammar does not have the same difficulty because of the descriptive nature of the rules.

APPLYING KEY IDEAS

Using your own writing, as well as one or two of your textbooks, select samples of 20 consecutive sentences. Determine whether any sentences have an auxiliary split from the verb with an adverbial. What conclusion can you draw from your results?

SUMMARY OF TRANSFORMATION RULES

Passive Transformation Rule

NP$_1$ Aux V NP$_2$

$\Rightarrow$

NP$_2$ Aux + be -ed/en V by + NP$_1$

Agent Deletion Rule

NP_2 Aux + be -ed/en V by + NP_1

$\Rightarrow$

NP_2 Aux + be -ed/en V

Relative Clause Rule

NP_1 $_S$ [Y NP_2 Z] $_S$

$\Rightarrow$

NP_1 $_S$ [wh-pro Y Z] $_S$

Relative Pronoun Deletion Rule

NP_1 $_S$ [wh-pro Y Z] $_S$

$\Rightarrow$

NP_1 $_S$ [Ø Y Z] $_S$

Particle Movement Rule

X V - prt NP

$\Rightarrow$

X V NP - prt

Dative Transformation Rule

X V NP_1 NP_2

$\Rightarrow$

X V NP_2 prep + NP_1

Reflexive Rule

NP_1 V NP_2

$\Rightarrow$

NP_1 V ref-pro

Imperative Rule

NP V X

⇒

Ø V X

There Insertion Rule

NP be PP

⇒

There be NP PP

Adverb Movement Rule

Form 1: Preposing

X V NP AdvPY

⇒

X AdvP V NP Y

Form 2: Fronting

X V NP AdvP Y

⇒

AdvP X V NP Y

APPLYING KEY IDEAS

Directions: Show derivations for the following sentences.

1. After Macarena spurned his proposal, Fred was devastated.
2. He looked at the loaded Mack 10 that he had borrowed from Raul's cousin.
3. He picked the weapon up and pressed it against his cheek.
4. Meanwhile, Macarena and Fritz were having an intimate party.
5. The rain was pouring down, but Fred did not mind because he knew that soon he would be dry.
6. Macarena looked at herself in the mirror as she poured more champagne, and she adjusted a strap on the evening gown Buggsy had given to her.
7. The gown had been made in Paris, which thrilled her a great deal.

8. Suddenly, there was a knock on the door, even though she was not expecting more company.
9. Macarena gave a strained look to Fritz, who was ready to open the door.
10. Fred, with the Mack 10 in one hand, lunged inside, where he sized the situation up.
11. The Mack 10 quickly sputtered, and Fritz went down with more holes than a round of Swiss cheese.
12. Macarena saw that Fritz had been shot, and because she could not think of anything else to do, she screamed.
13. She reached for the small Barretta she kept in her purse.
14. A passing policeman heard the scream and quickly turned to the apartment building.
15. He started running up the steps but cursed himself and the jelly-filled doughnuts he had been eating for 20 years.
16. After two flights, he had to walk, but finally he reached the crime scene, where another Hollywood triangle lay in ruins.
17. Buggsy heard the news as he was admiring himself and the new Rolls that was given to him by a producer in Bel Air.
18. There was a dead bug on the grill, and he flicked it off with one finger.
19. After a moment of silence, he told a goon to pick up some flowers.
20. He then called Rita and invited her to dinner at Le Dome, where he had reserved a special table for the evening.

4

Cognitive Grammar

OVERVIEW

- **Psychology and Grammar**
- **Connectionism: Changing the Model of Cognition**
- **The Implications for Grammatical Analysis**

Professional fields rely on models to explain how they understand and describe reality. Often, these models are referred to as *paradigms*. Periodically, a field will abandon the dominant model and adopt a new one. For example, in physics the Newtonian model was largely replaced by the quantum model, and in psychology the psychoanalytic model was replaced by the biomedical model. When the dominant model is replaced by another one, we call the process a *paradigm shift*. We can see that the earlier chapters described two paradigm shifts in grammar: The first was the move from traditional to phrase-structure grammar, and the second was the move from phrase-structure to transformational grammar.

We appear to be witnessing yet another paradigm shift. Since the mid-1980s, the transformational model has been challenged by a very powerful alternative—*cognitive grammar* (Langacker, 1987, 1990). It is important to note immediately, however, that cognitive grammar does not consist of a new set of rules. There are no diagrams, no new classifications, no new analyses. Instead, cognitive grammar involves a new way of looking at language and its relation to mind.

The first step in understanding cognitive grammar lies in reexamining transformational-generative grammar and its aims. Chomsky initially justified replacing phrase-structure grammar by arguing that it was awkward, complex,

225

and incapable of providing adequate accounts of language. Transformational grammar offered a simple and elegant way to understand language, and it promised new insights into the underlying psychological mechanisms.

As the grammar matured, however, it lost its simplicity and much of its elegance. In addition, transformational grammar always has been plagued by Chomsky's ambivalence and ambiguity regarding meaning. In *Syntactic Structures*, he noted that transformational grammar "was completely formal and non-semantic" (1957, p. 93). Nevertheless, as we saw in the last chapter, there are strong indications that meaning in transformational-generative grammar is represented in the deep structure of sentences, and as a result many people suspected that Chomsky was interested in meaning but could not decide exactly how to integrate semantics into the grammar. Numerous linguists were ready to step forward and attempt what Chomsky did not, and throughout the 1970s there was a concerted effort to bring syntax and semantics together through what is called *generative semantics*. Chomsky alternately supported and opposed this effort for many years, and it was hard to determine his position at any given time (Harris, 1993). Meanwhile, Chomsky continued to tinker with transformational grammar, changing the theories and making it more abstract and in many respects more complex, until all but those with specialized training in linguistics were befuddled.

Change per se is not problematic. From one perspective theories are models that try to describe the way the world operates, and as new information becomes available, we alter theories to make them more effective. The increasing complexity of the transformational model, however, was a problem for two reasons. First, the goal in science is to reduce theoretical complexity, not increase it. Second, a growing number of people began challenging the descriptive adequacy of the model, arguing that the changes were ad hoc and failed to address basic principles of language. That is, the tinkering failed to solve most of the problems because Chomsky refused to abandon the idea of deep structure, which is at the heart of T-G grammar but which also underlies nearly all of its problems.[1] Such complaints have fueled the paradigm shift to cognitive grammar.

PSYCHOLOGY AND GRAMMAR

The criticisms of transformational-generative grammar become clearer when we consider that, from the beginning, one of the more exciting features of transformational grammar was how it linked grammar and language to psy-

---

[1] In the most current version of T-G grammar, Chomsky refers to deep structure as *d structure*, but the essence is unchanged.

chology. Cognitive psychologists, as a result, were among the earliest supporters of transformational-generative grammar, because they saw it as offering
interesting ways to examine how the mind operates. It is far harder to understand how Chomsky came to advocate the connection. Chomsky's
anti-empirical sentiments are notorious; yet cognitive psychology is grounded
in empiricism and experimental method. Thus, the two fields have incompati-
ble approaches. Cognitive psychologists ignored the incompatibility for years,
not only because they were seduced by T-G grammar's superficial elegance but
also because the grammar is congruent with the computational, rule-governed
model of mind that had dominated psychology for decades. In this model, explicit, inaccessible rules compute input and output of all types: logic, decision
making, reading, and so forth. With respect to language, computation involves
combining small units to create larger ones. We can say, then, that the underlying mechanisms for transformational-generative grammar and cognition were
deemed to be identical but that the approaches for understanding those mechanisms were different. Chomsky relied on intuition, whereas psychologists relied on empirical observation.

At work were two different ways of knowing, two different standards of
proof. From a psychological perspective, transformational grammar was not a
theory of mind, as Chomsky had proposed, but instead was merely a reflection
of the underlying computational model. Thus, the grammar could be tested to
determine whether it truly was congruent with the model. The ultimate goal of
such testing, however, would not be to substantiate the model of grammar but
rather the model of mind.

As noted in the previous chapter, one of the first attempts to apply experimental methods to Chomsky's theory occurred in 1962, when George Miller set
out to evaluate the psychological reality of transformation rules. He hypothe-
sized that transformed sentences would require longer processing times than
would nontransformed sentences, and he developed a study to measure the differences in processing rates. If the rules were "psychologically real"—if they
truly existed in the brain as Chomsky proposed—then transformed sentences
indeed would take longer to process. Negatives would take longer than
positives and passives longer than actives. Sentences with multiple transformations would take even longer.

Miller's results confirmed his hypothesis; he found that subjects indeed took
more time to process the transformed sentences in the study than they did the
nontransformed sentences. Initially, these results were accepted as empirical
validation of Chomsky's intuition, and for several years the psychological reality of transformation rules was deemed a given. Problems began to emerge
when some researchers noted that passive sentences generally are longer than

their corresponding active form and that sentence length could have accounted for Miller's results. A variety of studies soon followed that took into account such factors as sentence length and subtle changes in meaning. The results showed that transformations had no effect on processing time (Baker, Prideaux, & Derwing, 1973; Bever, 1970; Fodor, Bever, & Garrett, 1974; Fodor & Garrett, 1966; Glucksberg & Danks, 1969). Neither transformations nor deep structure seemed to have any psychological reality. Transformational-generative grammar had failed to lend itself to empirical validation.

Chomsky was unaffected by such findings, but psychologists took them seriously. Without empirical validations, Chomsky's claims had no merit, and it appeared that the grammar did not really reflect the underlying computational model in any meaningful way. Transformational-generative grammar became widely viewed as an interesting theory that had no measurable support, and by the late 1970s most cognitive psychologists had abandoned it.

CONNECTIONISM: CHANGING THE MODEL OF COGNITION

A characteristic of rule-driven systems is that they consistently produce correct output. They are deterministic, so after a rule is in place there is no reason to expect an error. Transformational-generative grammar is deterministic with a vengeance. It proposes that after a person has induced grammar rules, they are invoked unconsciously whenever he or she intends to produce a sentence. The rule necessarily must produce the same result each time. The process is similar to a game like basketball: There is a rule that stipulates that when a player makes a basket outside the three-point line his or her team gets three points. As long as a player makes a basket outside this line, he or she always gets three points; the result is the same each time.

The situation is quite different with respect to language. People produce frequent errors in speech, which suggests that whatever mechanisms are responsible for generating sentences, *they in fact do not produce correct output consistently.* As Chomsky recognized, this is a huge problem for a generative grammar.[2] The competence/performance distinction was his way of solving it. Without this distinction, the grammar fails either to describe or explain language in any principled way because it purports to describe how people generate language, but the rules for this generation commonly produce error-free sentences.

---

[2]Phrase-structure grammar does not face this problem because it does not purport to be generative.

Cognitive grammar simplifies matters immensely by rejecting the rule-governed model of mind and language, replacing it with an association model based on the work in cognitive science by Rumelhart and McClelland (1986) and others working in an area known as *connectionism* (also see Searle, 1992). Rejecting the rule-governed model of mind offers significant insight into how we process language, but it presents insurmountable problems for T-G grammar as a theory of language.

Connectionism describes learning in terms of *neural networks*. These networks are physiological structures in the brain that are composed of cells called *neurons* and pathways—*dendrites* and *axons*—that allow neurons to communicate with one another. This basic structure is illustrated in Fig. 4.1. Learning involves changes in the brain's cell structure, changes that literally grow the network to accommodate the new knowledge.[3] The more a person learns, the more extensive the neural network becomes.

Neuron A   Neuron B

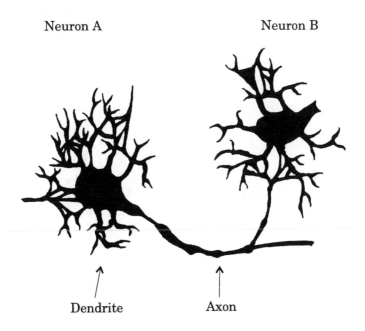

Dendrite   Axon

FIG. 4.1.   Neurons, dendrites, and axons. Each neuron has numerous dendrites that connect it to other neurons via connecting pathways called axons. From Carlson (1994). Copyright © 1994 by Allyn & Bacon. Adapted with permission.

---

[3]Sometimes the network contracts.

Contrasting Views of Language Acquisition

Language acquisition provides insight into the different principles that inform the rule-governed model of language and cognition and the connectionist view. Transformational-generative grammar proposes that language acquisition proceeds on a computational basis. In this account, the language acquisition device (LAD) has an inherent, gene-based knowledge of grammar that is stimulated by parental input. The argument for this process depends on two related observations: Input is severely distorted and limited, and the complexity of grammar and language are such that only some higher-order induction/computation mechanism can adequately explain the richness of language. In other words, given what they have to work with, children should not be able to develop language so easily, but they do. The only way to explain the outcome is to propose that language is genetic and emerges even under adverse conditions.

Cognitive grammar discounts these ideas as being both simplistic and unverifiable. It is grounded on research in connectionism that has shown that the parental input is neither as distorted nor as sparse as transformational linguists have proposed. Elman et al. (1996), for example, noted that "considerably more information may be latent in the environment—and extractable, using simple learning algorithms—than was previously thought" (p. 16). Furthermore, various strands of research have shown that organic systems are efficiently self-organized and do not rely on extensive or explicit guidance from the environment (Elman, et al., 1996; Kelso, 1995). Self-organized systems usually are in a state of delicate equilibrium determined in large part by preexisting conditions and to a lesser extent by the dynamics of their environment, which provide data through a feedback mechanism (Smolin, 1997). One result for cognition is that even meager input can have a significant influence (Elman et al., 1996). Perhaps more important is that, although to adult observers the linguistic input children receive may appear to be limited and distorted, to a child's developing brain this input is both rich and meaningful. Adult language is absolutely necessary if children are to develop language, but infants bring resources to the endeavor that we are only now beginning to understand. Under such circumstances, there is no need to postulate the existence of an autonomous subsystem to explain the ease and regularity with which children acquire language.

Pattern Recognition. An advantage of cognitive grammar is that it explains language acquisition on the basis of pattern recognition without recourse to a black-box metaphor or induction. Rule-governed models like Chomsky's assume that mental activity or thought is verbal—any given sentence begins as mentalese.

Some of the early versions of transformational-generative grammar attempted to capture the nature of mentalese in the deep structure. Sentence 1 illustrates a simple example:

1. Macarena bought the refrigerator that had the automatic ice maker.

This sentence, according to transformational grammar, has the following deep structure:

1a. Macarena bought the refrigerator/the refrigerator had the automatic ice maker

According to T-G grammar, the underlying form exists verbally in the mind, having been compiled using the grammar and the lexicon. In response to the obvious question—*How do we know that sentences exist in mentalese before they are translated into surface structures*—the typical answer is that everyone reports hearing a mental voice when thinking (Pinker, 1994).

This response is not satisfactory. Cognitive grammar proposes that it is a mistake to assume that cognitive activities are verbal just because we recognize a voice in our heads when we think. It is quite reasonable to propose, for example, that the voice is the end product of some other, nonverbal process. Researchers have known for many years, for example, that language comprehension proceeds on the basis of *analysis by synthesis*, a psychophysiological process in which what we hear and read is filtered through the articulatory mechanisms before reaching working memory. Quite literally, we reproduce the language we hear, read, and write through micromovements of the articulatory musculature (Williams, 1985, 1987). Cognitive grammar and connectionism discount the idea that mental activities are verbal and instead propose that they are primarily, although not exclusively, based on images rather than words. At best, the language of the mind—linked to micromovements of the articulatory musculature—is a mediating mechanism between images and the words we speak and write. But even this limited proposition may be too strong. The significance of this position is that it allows language processing to be understood as a matter of matching words with mental representations and internalized models of reality. No rules are involved. Instead, language is governed by patterns of regularity (Rumelhart & McClelland, 1986).[4]

---

[4]Some educators have proposed that, if mentation is largely imagistic, then immersing children in highly visual activities will enhance learning. As Katz (1989) noted, however, such activities usually do not include a verbal component. Images appear to be native to mental operations, whereas language is not. Thus, language must arise out of social interactions.

The idea that language does not involve grammar rules strikes some people as nonsensical because in so many respects language gives the appearance of operating on the basis of rules. Addressing this issue, Rumelhart and McClelland (1986) noted that a bouncing ball may give the appearance of adhering to certain rules, even though there are no rules governing its behavior.[5] From their perspective, language also gives the appearance of operating on the basis of rules.

Adopting this position, cognitive grammar proposes that grammar is nothing more than a system for describing the patterns of regularity that are inherent in language. It follows that grammar is not specifically a theory of language or of mind, although the study of grammar may shed light on both. Because mental activities are deemed to be imagistic rather than verbal, cognitive grammar has no need to postulate an underlying grammatical form for sentences—there is no deep structure. The free association of images makes the question of underlying structure irrelevant. Consequently, the surface structure of sentences is linked directly to the mental proposition and corresponding phonemic and lexical representations. A formal grammatical apparatus to explain the relatedness of actives and passives, for example, and other types of related sentences is not necessary because these patterns coexist in the neural network. The role of the grammar is merely to describe surface structures.

Cognitive grammar proposes that the patterns of regularity that typify language begin establishing themselves at birth (see Kelso, 1995). As Williams (1993) noted, when children encounter the world, their parents and other adults provide them with the names of things. The children see dogs, and they immediately are provided the word *dog*, with the result that they develop a mental model related to "dog-ness." On a neurophysiological level, this mental model consists of modifications to the cerebral structure: Cells change; the network grows.

It seems reasonable to propose that in an infant the mental model for "dog-ness" includes the sound of the word *dog* and a range of physical features that typify dogs. These features are connected to the mental representation as well as to the string of phonemes that make up the word *dog*, and it is fairly cer-

---

[5]It is important to differentiate rules of behavior in this case from a range of factors that, without question, influence the bouncing of the ball. Gravity, temperature, air pressure, and so forth influence the bouncing, but we do not speak in terms of rules of air pressure, rules of temperature, or rules of gravitation. We may, however, speak of the law of gravitation or the law of thermodynamics, but we cannot say that these laws influence the bouncing of the ball beyond the most general comments. The law of gravitation, for example, specifies an attraction between two bodies on the basis of their mass and distance, and it accounts for the acceleration of the ball to the ground, but it does not specify the bouncing of the ball.

tain that the connection is via neural pathways (Rumelhart & McClelland, 1986). Over time, or owing to some other factors, such as interest, the connection becomes stronger, like a well-worn path, until the image of a dog is firmly linked to the word *dog*. From that point on, the child is able to process the image of "dog-ness" and the phonemic representation of the word *dog* simultaneously, but there is no reason to assume that the processing is verbal. There is simply a sound to symbol correspondence that, as far as we can determine, is imagistic.[6] Stated another way, "Hearing the word [*dog*] or deciding to utter it triggers an association between one set of patterns of regularity, the string of phonemes, and another set that contains subsets of the various features related to 'dog-ness'" (Williams, 1993, p. 558).[7] This account does not mean that cognitive operations lack a verbal component or that certain linguistic expressions cannot begin and end as words. It does suggest, however, that the verbal component is subordinate to the imagistic.

Language acquisition in this account has nothing to do with inducing the rules of the grammar, but it has very much to do with recognizing and practicing the patterns of regularity that typify language. At this point, it is reasonable to ask whether there is any evidence to suggest that this cognitive account is accurate. Anyone who has raised children or spent a great deal of time with children knows that acquisition depends significantly on a matching procedure. Beyond the cooing and baby talk that is part of the bonding that parents and children experience, there is a fairly consistent instructional agenda that involves introducing children to objects in their world and providing them with the names for those objects. In the case of a ball, for example, a parent will hold up a ball and utter the word "ball." Eventually, the day will come when the child makes his or her first attempt at producing the word, and in most instances it comes out as something other than "ball." "Ba" is a very common first effort. Normally, the parent will correct the child's utterance, stretching out the word and emphasizing the /l/ sound, and the child will respond by trying his or her best to mimic the parent. This procedure ultimately results in a close match between the two utterances.[8] In rejecting the rule-governed model of mind, cognitive grammar

---

[6]Focusing on the imagistic properties of language can mask the fact that there also is a range of affective factors associated with words. The strength of these factors is apparent when we consider the ways pets respond to language. There is no question that the cognitive abilities of animals are extremely limited, but they nevertheless have a wide range of emotions. They cannot think, but they can feel, and they respond to the language of their owners. Given the limited cognitive abilities of infants and their obvious emotional responses to language, it may be that the first neural pathways for language establish emotional rather than imagistic connections. Images would come later.

[7]Although the emphasis here is on intentional activities, clearly other factors can have a similar effect. Most people have the experience of encountering a certain fragrance or hearing a certain song that evokes detailed images from the past. The process of association is similar, if not identical, to the account here.

[8]The inability to achieve an exact match results in language change over generations.

also rejects the idea that language is computational and rule governed. Sociolinguistic conventions still play a significant role in our understanding of language, but rules do not, because syntax is determined by the patterns of regularity that develop in childhood.

Cognitive grammar proposes that language acquisition is intimately allied with experiences and internal representations of reality rather than with some metaphorical cognitive subsystem responsible for inducing the grammar. As Williams (1993) noted, sentence production and grammaticality, indeed language as a whole, are "tied to associations between various patterns of regularity generalized through interaction with the environment" (p. 561). From this perspective, the act of producing an utterance involves matching a mental model of the intended representation of reality against the range of linguistic patterns available from experience.

A reasonable objection to this model is based on the observation that language is infinite and that the cognitive grammar model fails to account for our inability to store an infinite number of patterns in our brains. Only a system composed of a small set of rules that rearrange sentences can be stored and still account for the infinite number of sentences that can exist. This objection ignores, however, the fact that the number of sentences people actually use is not infinite, just as the range of numbers they use is not infinite. We do not have to deal with infinity to balance a check book. The acceptable patterns in English, for example, tend to be variations of the two dominant patterns for sentences—SVO and SVC. Other patterns exist, of course. Although the number of variations within these patterns is large, it does not approach infinity, and the basic patterns remain unchanged.

This objection also does not take into account the fact that the brain contains approximately 100 billion neurons (Kalat, 1995; Williams & Herrup, 1988). Each neuron branches into many dendrites, and each dendrite contains many synapses, at which the dendrites receive and transmit information from other neurons. Some dendrites branch further into dendritic spines that have specialized synapses that play an important role in memory and learning. Finally, neurons tend to be linked to another neuron via an axon (not all neurons are so linked). The goal here is not to provide a summary of neurophysiology. It is to suggest that the brain has the potential of performing trillions of operations (100 billion neurons interacting through perhaps a trillion connections). If we consider that the average speaking vocabulary contains about 2,500 words, and if we generously propose that English allows 10 million variations of basic sentence patterns (which is probably too large by a factor of 20), we still would not come close to taxing the resources of the brain. The brain has a processing capacity that far exceeds the demands language places on it. The issue of storage is moot.

From the cognitive-grammar perspective, language production involves selecting a given pattern and then filling it with words that match the mental model of the proposition that the speaker wants to convey. The grammar itself has no generative component—it is purely descriptive. The high degree of creativity observed in language is the result of an essentially limitless supply of mental propositions and the flexibility inherent in English word order. Moreover, cognitive grammar involves no special rules to explain the relation between, say, actives and passives, because it simply notes that these two sentence patterns are alternative forms available for certain propositions. The forms themselves are described as being linked psychophysiologically in the neural network, coexisting simultaneously.

Explaining Errors in Language

Critics of transformational-generative grammar have noted that Chomsky's explanation of error does little to explain the nature of error. The suggestion that errors are the result of environmental factors does not provide any insight into the mechanism of error, nor does it explain why errors are congruent with standard syntax. That is, someone who intends to utter "My cat eats too much" might actually utter "My dog eats too much," particularly if he or she has both a cat and a dog. But we never observe anyone who intends the cat utterance but who actually says "Too eats my much cat."

Cognitive grammar explains errors in language on the basis of the connecting pathways that link the various components of language. In the case of cats and dogs, for example, the neural network will contain similar patterns of regularity with many overlapping features: Cats and dogs have four legs, tails, and fur; they are pets, they require a great deal of care, they shed, and so forth. When an association is triggered, the connecting pathways become excited. Thus, whenever a person's intention causes a phoneme or phoneme sequence to become active in a particular utterance, all the words in the lexicon that are similar to the target word become active as well. These words compete with one another on the basis of their connecting strengths to their corresponding mental representations. Normally, the target word has the greatest connecting strength. There is a match, and the person's intention is realized. On a probabilistic basis, however, an incorrect match, or error, will occur owing to the competition among the connecting pathways. When it does, a speaker may replace the word *dog* with the word *cat* because the associations between the words are close. We see this sort of competition most frequently among children, who commonly call their mothers "Daddy," and vice versa. Fig. 4.2 shows a schematic rendering of a developed neural network.

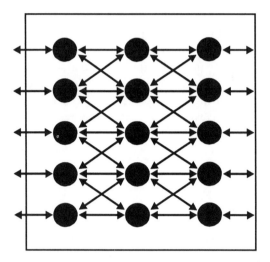

FIG. 4.2.   Schematic of neural network. This schematic representationally show neurons
and their corresponding pathways. Note how the neurons are interconnected.

There is no question that age increases the connecting strengths within the
network, so as people grow older they produce fewer language errors. Nevertheless, the model predicts that, statistically, errors always will occur on a random basis, regardless of age. This prediction is borne out by the fact that
everyone produces errors of one type or another while speaking.

Earlier, we examined the phenomenon of tense overgeneralization and saw
how it is used to support the standard account of language acquisition. In this account, children apply the past-participle affix to irregular verbs consistently after
they supposedly formulate the rules associated with verb forms. However, this
account is incongruent with reality. Sometimes children use the regular and irregular forms correctly, sometimes incorrectly; moreover, adults make the same errors, indicating that, contrary to the standard account, consistency does not come
with age. As Williams (1993) noted, this "inconsistent behavior is almost impossible to explain adequately with a rule-governed model" (p. 560). However, it is
easily understood in terms of competing forms: The connecting associations related to past-tense forms are insufficiently developed in children to allow one
form to dominate. In adults the connecting associations are fully developed, but
the competition among the pathways results in probabilistic error.

THE IMPLICATIONS FOR GRAMMATICAL ANALYSIS

Cognitive grammar is not a grammar at all in the sense that we have used the term in the earlier chapters. Instead, it is a way of understanding the relation between mind and language. The more important features of this relation have been examined in the earlier sections, such as the fact that cognitive grammar proposes that grammar is a descriptive system rather than a theoretical one. Cognitive grammar operates from the position that grammar cannot claim to provide either a theory of mind or a theory of language. It does not propose a new system for examining the relations among words that make up sentences, nor does it propose a new set of descriptive tools for grammatical analyses. As Langacker (1987) noted, cognitive grammar "is defined as those aspects of cognitive organization in which resides a speaker's grasp of established linguistic conventions. It can be characterized as a structured inventory of conventional linguistic units" (p. 57). If cognitive grammar is concerned with the structured inventory of conventional linguistic units, it follows that grammatical analyses will focus on conventional linguistic knowledge, that is, the knowledge gained from experience with real language rather than language manufactured to meet the needs of some syntactic analysis. *Consequently, cognitive grammar relies on phrase-structure grammar for the symbolic representation of syntax.*

Using phrase-structure grammar for syntactic analysis raises the question of phrase-structure rules, but those working in cognitive grammar do not recognize the formulaic descriptions familiar from Chapter 2 as being rules in any meaningful sense. Langacker (1990), for example, referred to phrase-structure rules as "general statements" (p. 102). Thus, there is no reason to assume that the NP VP notation specifies a rule, but there is every reason to recognize that it describes a grammatical relation. In fact, we may think of phrase-structure analysis as consisting, in part, of a set of synthetic symbols that allow us to talk about language more easily.

As in phrase-structure grammar, issues of meaning become fairly self-evident because there is no effort to develop an intervening stage between cognition and utterance—there is no deep structure. This position has the immediate benefit of linking syntax and semantics, which Langacker (1987, 1990) supported when he cautioned against efforts to separate syntax and semantics, arguing that in cognitive grammar "symbolic structure is not distinct from semantic or phonological structure" (p. 105).

Other criticisms of phrase-structure analysis are equally irrelevant. For example, Chomsky's charge that it fails to provide a theory of language is viable only if one assumes that grammar should be theoretical. There is no compelling reason to make this assumption. Far more reasonable is to take Chomsky's own proposal a step farther and assign responsibility for theories of language to psychology, genetics, and biology. Cognitive grammar takes this step and therefore proceeds from a different assumption—that the first goal is to develop a viable theory of cognition that will include language and grammar. From this perspective, Chomsky got things backward.

By the same token, the criticism that phrase-structure analysis is not descriptively adequate because it is based on a finite corpus is based on the dubious premise that a grammar should be able to account for all the possible sentences in a language. Yet no grammar can analyze a sentence until it has been uttered or written, in which case it no longer is a possible sentence but instead is an actual sentence. Speculating on the realm of possible sentences is not particularly productive because these sentences do not exist. Phrase-structure analysis is sufficiently powerful to describe any actual sentence. Moreover, the syntactic patterns in any language are sufficiently regular to allow us to predict, with great accuracy, what form possible (as opposed to actual) sentences may take. We do not need a rule to tell us that grammatical sentences in English generally will follow the SVO pattern and that ungrammatical ones will not.

Cognitive Grammar and Writing

The value of cognitive grammar with respect to writing is that it offers insight into the act of composing. Writing is difficult for many reasons, but one of the more visible is the need to coordinate local concerns (e.g., word choice, paragraph development, sentence structure, and spelling), with global concerns (e.g., aim, rhetorical stance, audience, and purpose). For many people, the task proves too difficult. Cognitive grammar suggests that both local and global features of discourse exist as mental models and that many of these features will be in competition with one another as a person composes. It also suggests that significant experience with a wide range of texts is necessary to establish and elaborate the mental models. People who lack the experience will not be successful writers, which explains the often perceived relation between reading and writing. From this perspective, poor writers have not read enough to develop the mental models required to produce written language beyond the most rudimentary.

Even vast experience, however, will not automate the process of writing. Writers must match their mental models of audience, for example, with language—perhaps initially in the form of mentalese but certainly at some point with language in the form of the actual words on the page or computer screen. This matching process has been identified as an important factor in writing success: Good writers read what they compose as they develop a text (Williams,

1998). Examining this process, Williams (1993) noted that "there is a sense in which writers, even experienced ones, must approach every writing task as though it were their first. They are faced with individual acts of creation each time they attempt to match a mental model of the discourse with the premises, paragraphs, examples, proofs, sentences, and words that comprise it" (p. 564).

From this analysis, cognitive grammar provides a deeper understanding of what many teachers already know—the key to helping students become better writers lies in getting them to become effective, self-motivated readers and in giving them frequent opportunities to write. The feedback from peers and teachers that are part of theory-based composition classes strengthens the connecting pathways that build the neural network. Cognitive grammar also helps us better understand why grammar instruction does not lead to improved writing. The ability to identify a noun or a verb is linked to a specific set of mental models that have, at best, only a tenuous association through the neural network with those models for local and global features of written discourse. Stated another way, there are indications that knowledge of grammar may be stored in an area quite far removed from knowledge of writing, stored in different parts of the network in such a way that association is difficult. Grammar instruction is likely to strengthen connecting associations in that part of the network responsible for grammar, but there is no evidence that it strengthens connections between the two parts of the network.

APPLYING KEY IDEAS

1. In what ways does the rejection of grammar "rules" affect notions of correctness in language?
2. Parents and people who work with children know that the very young never seem to tire of repetitive interactions. How might this observation be linked to cognitive grammar?
3. Some people see important connections between critical thinking skills and the idea that thought is largely imagistic rather than verbal. Reflect on this notion, and then list some of the connections you see.
4. What are some of the pedagogical implications of cognitive grammar with respect to teaching grammar to students?
5. Although linguists focus almost exclusively on spoken language, teachers generally focus on writing, and historically grammar has been seen, incorrectly, as a means of improving writing skill. Does cognitive grammar have any implications for teaching reading and writing?

5

Dialects

WHAT IS A DIALECT?

Language varies over time, across national and geographical boundaries, by gender, across age groups, and by socioeconomic status. When the variation occurs within a given language, we call the different versions of the same language *dialects*. Thus, we describe English, for example, in terms of British English, Canadian English, American English, Australian English, Caribbean English, and Indian English. Within the United States, we speak of Southern English, Boston English, New York English, West Coast English, and so on. Dialects are the result of geographical and socioeconomic factors, although many people mistakenly associate dialects with ethnicity (Haugen, 1966; Hudson, 1980; Trudgill, 1974; Wolfram, Christian, & Adger, 1998).

Language always is undergoing subtle changes, largely as a result of children's efforts to match the adult speech they hear around them. The match never is exact, and over time the minute variations between the language of children and the language of adults produces changes in lexicon, accent, and even grammar. Within a given group, the changes are fairly uniform; thus everyone in that group is essentially using the same language at any point in time. Geographical barriers inhibit uniform change whenever they prevent easy and frequent travel between any two groups. In cases where travel is infrequent, the language of any two groups always is moving in different directions at any given time. As a result, significant dialectical differences might appear within two generations.

Socioeconomic factors play a more complex role. Every language has a *prestige dialect* associated with education and financial success. The prestige dialect in the United States is known as Standard English, and it is spoken by a large number of people, in part because those who do not grow up speaking Standard English are motivated to learn it because it is the language of school and business. In this text, we have referred to *formal* Standard English, which is a level above Standard English and is most often associated with writing and conventions of spoken language that commonly are linked to members of the educated elite. The number of people who use formal Standard English is relatively small, but it nevertheless is the most widely *accepted* dialect. Students who want to succeed academically have good reasons to shift from their home dialect to formal Standard English, and many do so. This motivation continues in the workplace, where employers deem home dialects unacceptable for many positions. Language is perhaps the most important factor in defining who we are, and we judge and are judged continually on the basis of the language we use. Consequently, the desire to be identified with an elite group leads many people to drop their home dialect for Standard English, if not the formal standard.

Abandoning one's home dialect is not easy. There is the linguistic challenge, of course, but highly motivated people are able to meet this challenge without great difficulty. The number of professional actors and actresses who have replaced their New York or Southern or even Australian dialects is testimony to our adaptability. More problematic is the fact that much of our definition of self is linked to identification with those closest to us, so there is a sense in which adopting the prestige dialect involves a loss of identity and connection. Some students coming home for a college break often experience this loss when they find that the language they now use is different from what their parents and friends speak. They may feel that they are outsiders in their own homes. First-generation college students—those who are the first in their families to attend university—are especially prone to this experience. Although nearly all parents want their children to get a college education, ours is a very class-conscious society, and education that threatens to move children too far outside the boundaries of their communities often is seen as a threat by friends and family, in spite of their good intentions and best wishes.

The question of what makes people insiders and outsiders with respect to given groups is important in any discussion of dialect. Those who do not master the prestige dialect are likely to remain insiders in their communities but outsiders with respect to the workplace and the broader society. Most people try to solve this problem by becoming *bidialectical,* over time learning how to use both dialects with varying degrees of success. Others may find jobs that do not require much proficiency in the prestige dialect. This issue is particularly important with respect to those who speak Black English Vernacular and Chicano English, the two most pervasive "nonprestige," or *nonstandard*, dialects in the country. Many students whose home dialect is Chicano English or Black English resist using Standard English in school because they do not want to be identified with the white mainstream. Many students who do use Standard English find that they are ostracized by their nonwhite peers.

Standard English may be thought of as consisting of a continuum ranging from informal to formal, with conversations being representative of informal and writing of formal usage. Few people actually use *formal* Standard English all the time, although some do. Even the most conscientious speakers may periodically use informal features, as when one says "It's me" rather than "It's I." The difficulty associated with using formal Standard English consistently in speech suggests that prescriptive notions of language are hard to defend.

Dialects differ with respect to accent, grammar, and lexicons. A person in California, for example, is highly unlikely to utter "I have plenty enough," whereas this utterance is common in parts of North Carolina. By the same token, someone from the upper third of the socioeconomic scale would be likely to utter "I'm not going to the party," whereas someone from the lower third would be more likely to utter "I ain't goin' to no party." Other features differ both by region and socioeconomic status, as in the case of:

- Fred jumped *off* the table.
- Fred jumped *off of* the table.

Slang

Although slang is a variation of a language, it is not the same as a dialect. Slang differs from a dialect in several ways. For example, it is a limited to a relatively small group of people, whereas a dialect is used by vast numbers. Slang typically is associated with young people between the ages of 12 and 25, who use it as a means of group bonding that distinguishes insiders from outsiders, especially with respect to age and gender—boys tend to use more slang than girls. The lexicons of dialects remain fairly stable over time, as we see in the case of the word *elevator* in American English and *lift* in British English. Slang, on the other hand, is in perpetual motion even within a given group, which results in the rapid emergence and disappearance of terms.

An important factor in the dynamic character of slang is that the sociological factors that stimulate it—the changes that are part of adolescence—become less important as people mature into adulthood. Teenagers feel that they are different from other people, so they use slang as a way of validating their perception, attempting to solidify their group identity by erecting linguistic barriers to all who are different, particularly adults. As they themselves become adults, the imperative disappears for most, which is why we encounter few adults who use slang. When we do, the effect usually is discomfort; it just doesn't seem appropriate.

Some people argue that adults have their own version of slang, called *jargon*. Jargon signifies technical terms used in trades and professional work. It performs nearly all of the same functions as slang, for it also separates insiders from outsiders. Some professions, such as law, make their domain even more opaque to outsiders by seasoning jargon with Latin. Likewise, physicians write prescriptions in Latin, which has the effect of preventing most people from knowing what they are purchasing at the pharmacy. Like slang, jargon commonly serves as a kind of insider code that allows people to reduce into a single term complex ideas that may require dozens of words to explain. Teachers, for example, often use the expression *zone of proximal development*, coined by Vygotsky (1978), to describe a sophisticated concept in education. A significant difference between slang and jargon, however, is that jargon does not disappear over time; indeed, in many instances it becomes more dense.

HOW DOES A PRESTIGE DIALECT DEVELOP?

All countries have prestige dialects, and, in most cases, sheer historical accident led to the dominance of one variety of a language rather than another. Haugen (1966) suggested that all standard dialects undergo similar processes that solidify their position in a society. First, a society will select, usually on the basis of users' socioeconomic success, a particular variety of the language to be the standard. At some point, the chosen variety will be codified by teachers and scholars who write grammar books and dictionaries for it. The effect is to stabilize the dialect by reaching some sort of agreement regarding what is correct and what is not. The dialect then must be functionally elaborated so that it can be used in government, law, education, technology, and in all forms of writing. Finally, the dialect has to be accepted by all segments of the society as the standard, particularly by those who speak some other variety (Hall, 1972; Macaulay, 1973; Trudgill, 1974).

Nonstandard Dialects

Although many people think of nonstandard dialects exclusively in terms of Black English and Chicano English, dialects cannot and should not be viewed in terms of ethnicity. They cross this line. In fact, some of the more troubling aspects of dialects today are found among white middle-class youngsters.

For most of America's history, the difficulties of travel in such a large country made geography the most important factor in language variation. Regional dialects still abound, but Wolfram et al. (1998) reported a leveling of regional differences. The reasons for this leveling are not very clear, but many people point to television as the dominant cause, noting that TV has spread Standard English to regions where it was not heard frequently in the past. The problem with this proposal is that it assumes that people respond to the presence of language that is not interactive. Yet we know that an infant placed in front of a TV and lacking normal contact with people using language interactively will not acquire language. To an infant, the voices from the TV are noise, not meaningful sounds. Likewise, older children and adults will not be influenced in any direct way by the presence of standard speakers on the airwaves. At best, they might be motivated to adopt Standard English as a result of some desire to identify with broadcasters and TV stars, but without any concrete possibility of entering those groups, of becoming entertainment insiders, the motivation would be fairly weak.

The leveling of dialects therefore is probably the result of some other factor, and the increased mobility of Americans appears to be the most likely. People relocate more frequently today than ever before, and the result is an unprecedented blending of various dialects, especially in the South, which has seen tremendous population growth owing to an influx of Northerners looking for jobs, lower taxes, and warm weather.

Another, related factor in the issue of dialect leveling that does not receive much attention is the measurable shift of Black English toward Standard English, through the ongoing process of decreolization. This shift is surprising because in many respects segregation—or, more accurately, self-segregation—in the late 1990s is stronger than at any time since the early 1950s.[1] Blacks and whites alike generally call bussing a failure; educators as well as parents are

---

[1]Some evidence of recreolization does exist. For example, young Black English speakers who want to emphasize an action will add a second participle to a verb to produce *walked-ed, talked-ed,* and *stopped-ed.*

reassessing the educational benefits to minority children of integrated class-rooms; and self-segregated schools, usually with an Afrocentric curriculum, are being hailed by many African Americans as the best answer to the persistent achievement problems black children experience in integrated schools. These factors should result in more separation between Standard English and Black English. However, they are mitigated by the fact that, at the same time, affirmative action has been successful in increasing the educational and economic opportunities among African Americans to such a degree that Black English speakers have more contact with standard speakers than in the past. In addition, Herrnstein and Murray (1994) reported that the black middle class has been growing steadily for about 25 years, providing a compelling incentive to shift toward Standard English as families move into middle- and upper-middle-class communities. The motivation to shift dialects is strongest among children of the growing black middle class, who must adjust their language to match the dialect of their socioeconomic peers if they hope to become insiders. Although the white middle class has been shrinking during this same period, there simply are no incentives to adopt a nonstandard dialect, to shift downward, among adults.

Nevertheless, there is cause for concern. The Usage Notes in the earlier chapters detailed many features of nonstandard English, and we saw that most of them are in the area of usage rather than grammar. For a growing number of young people who speak nonstandard English, the problems they face are more severe than any we have discussed. Their language exemplifies what linguists call *restricted code*, language that is impoverished with respect to syntax, vocabulary, meaning, and the ability to communicate beyond the most rudimentary level. Restricted codes today are unrelated to race or SES. Consider the following response, from a white, middle-class 10th-grade student in a history course who was asked to summarize how a congressional bill becomes a law: "Well, uhm, it's like, you know, the Congress, like, you know, uhm, they meet, right? And, uhm, they talk about stuff, you know, and uhm, like, the stuff gets written down, you know, and, well, like, that's how it happens."

This student clearly has a problem with logical thinking, but logical thinking is linked to language in important ways. The imprecision of the student's language, the absence of a vocabulary that allows him to convey what he knows, is characteristic of restricted code. Healy (1990) argued that nonstandard usage among our students "may account for many of the problems in logical thinking … that are becoming so evident in our high schools" (p. 110). She went on to note that "the most difficult aspect of writing clearly … is that it demands the ability to organize thought" (p. 111). In a similar vein, Orr (1987) suggested that many school problems are rooted in the fact that nonstandard speakers do not know what words mean. Reporting her experience as a teacher, Orr stated:

In a chemistry class a student stated that … the volume of a gas would be half more than it was. When I asked her if she meant that the volume would get larger, she said, "No, smaller." When I then explained that half more than would mean larger, indicating the increase with my hands, she said she meant twice and with her hands indicated a decrease. When I then said, "But twice means larger," … she said, "I guess I mean half less than." (p. 27)

A few studies and much anecdotal evidence suggest not only that the number of students who speak restricted-code nonstandard English is increasing, but also that their language is becoming ever more impoverished (Bohannon & Stanowicz, 1988; Healy, 1990; Vail, 1989). As nonstandard code seeps across socioeconomic lines and affects the language of students whose home dialect is Standard English, teachers must look even more closely at their goals and methods. Not all nonstandard speakers use a restricted code, but growing numbers of standard speakers do. For those who do not, instruction in the standard conventions can lead to measurable improvement in language skills, especially with respect to writing. For those who use a restricted code, like the two students just mentioned, their restricted code limits their ability to communicate beyond the most superficial level and raises serious obstacles to academic success.

DIALECTS AND EDUCATION

Because socioeconomic status is closely tied to level of education (Herrnstein & Murray, 1994), nonstandard speakers tend to be undereducated, and they also tend to be linked to the working-class poor. Education, however, is not an absolute indicator of dialect. The language skills of college graduates appear to have declined significantly over the last 25 years (Healy, 1990). Moreover, political agendas among highly educated people frequently militate against the use of Standard English, bringing them to use nonstandard language in an effort to achieve their goals, often with embarrassing results. White university presidents generally have a hard time "talkin' and testifyin'" in Black English Vernacular (BEV). The question of students' right to their own language has made schools, including colleges and universities, more tolerant of nonstandard English than they used to be, and it is fairly easy to observe college graduates—and, increasingly, college faculty—uttering nonstandard expressions such as "I ain't got no money," "The reason is because," and "Where's he at." Or consider the following quote, from a note that a teacher in Chicago sent home with a 3rd-grade boy: "Bobby was not allowed to go out for recess today becuz he had

to re-do his paper on dinosors, becuz I do not allow students to type there papers only to hand write them and Bobby's paper was typed or printed. Pleeze make sure that Bobby don't type his papers in the future."

Teacher complaints about the decline in student language skills over the last 2 decades therefore must be viewed in the context of a major shift toward nonstandard English among the well-educated nationwide.

The tensions faced by everyone who is reared in one language environment and schooled in another are very real and very compelling. It is hard to ignore the likelihood that the plunge in language skills among students is linked to a decline in skills among teachers. Approximately 60% of all university professors today are first-generation college graduates, and it is safe to assume that a large portion came from working-class backgrounds where nonstandard English was the norm and the Standard English of the schools the exception. Having established their careers and no longer facing the compulsion to be insiders, these teachers are in a position to abandon the Standard English that they mastered in order to succeed and to slip comfortably into the home dialects of their childhood. Large numbers of them have done so in an effort to return, figuratively, to the communities they left behind in their youth. Not surprisingly, several reports have shown that literacy levels in the public schools and in higher education have plummeted since the mid-1960s. Chall (1996) and Coulson (1996) reported serious declines in language and literacy levels for students in all age groups. Chall, for example, described her experience at a community college where the "freshmen tested, on the average, on an eighth-grade reading level. Thus, the average student in this community college was able to read only on a level expected of junior high school students" (p. 309). Findings like these are not limited to community colleges. Entering freshmen at a major research university in North Carolina, ranked among the top 25 schools in the nation, are tested each year for reading skill, and their average annual scores between 1987 and 1994 placed them at about the 10th-grade reading level.[2]

Efforts to explain the drop in language skills have focused on two factors: the high number of hours per week that children watch television (approximately 30) and the widespread shift from phonics as the basis for reading instruction to whole-language approaches. There is no question that television exerts an insidious influence on children's language development, if for no other reason than that it isolates young people from the social interactions with adults and peers that are crucial to good language skills. Instead of playing and having conversations with other children, too many young people are rooted in front of a TV set afternoons, evenings, and weekends.

---

[2]During this period, students took the Nelson-Denny reading test, which was administered by the university's learning skills center. I reviewed the data in my capacity as an administrator at the school.

Most of the programs children watch are cartoons, hardly a language-rich genre. Many parents justify the hours their children spend watching cartoons by believing that an hour or so of *Sesame Street* each day provides a restorative educational balance. The reasoning is similar to that displayed by the overweight person who orders a diet soda to wash down the cheese fries. Furthermore, the few studies that have examined the pedagogical foundations and benefits of *Sesame Street* suggested not only that the show did not employ sound pedagogical principles but also that it does more harm than good (Burns & Anderson, 1991; Meringoff, 1980; Singer, 1980).

Over the last several years, many educators have argued that the drop in language skills has been caused by the shift in many schools from phonics to whole-language approaches to reading instruction. Part of this argument is based on the understanding that reading leads to larger vocabularies and richer sentence structures, both of which have beneficial effects on language skills. If whole-language approaches lead to greater difficulty in reading, students will be less likely to become self-motivated pleasure readers. As a result, they will lack sufficient immersion in texts to develop vocabulary, rich sentence structure, and so forth. Whatever the cause, the amount of reading young people do today is significantly lower than it was just 30 years ago (Healy, 1990). Many young people today never do any pleasure reading.

As far as can be determined, no study has examined the role, if any, that nonstandard English among teachers plays in children's language and literacy development, even though the decline in students' language skills has occurred simultaneously with the increase in nonstandard English among teachers. Some teachers and social commentators have lauded the shift to nonstandard English as part of an effort to bridge the widening gap between the educated elite and the undereducated underclass, which is growing annually. This is misguided populism at its worst. Many educators speculate that we are witnessing the results of the precipitous decline in education and language skills that began in the 1960s and that has reached such a woeful state that the College Board, publisher of the Scholastic Aptitude Test (SAT), was forced to renorm the test in 1995, increasing scores by 150 points compared to the earlier version. When students with low skills become teachers with low skills, we can predict that they probably will produce students with low skills. The cycle becomes self-perpetuating.

Equally troubling is the observation that today's parents often do not engage children in activities that lead to the development of language skills and that lay the foundation for the mastery of Standard English in the event that the home language is a nonstandard dialect. Overextended parents commonly turn to TV as a reliable baby sitter, and they seldom have time for reading, telling stories, and engaging in conversations with their children—activities that build crucial language and cognitive abilities.

BLACK ENGLISH

The serious study of Black English was impeded for decades by myths and misconceptions, and it was not until the early 1970s that scholars began to move beyond the myths and examine Black English in a principled way. Dillard (1973) reported, for example, that until the 1960s it was often argued that Black English was a vestige of a British dialect with origins in East Anglia (also see McCrum, Cran, & MacNeil, 1986). According to this view, American blacks had somehow managed to avoid significant linguistic change for centuries, even though it was well known that all living languages are in a constant state of change. This romantic notion of a dialect somehow suspended in time is totally without substance. Dillard also described the "physiological theory," which held that Black English was the result of "thick lips" that rendered blacks incapable of producing Standard English. More imaginative and outrageous was Mencken's (1936) notion that Black English was the invention of playwrights: "The Negro dialect, as we know it today, seems to have been formulated by the songwriters for the minstrel shows; it did not appear in literature until the time of the Civil War; before that, as George P. Krappe shows … , it was a vague and artificial lingo which had little relation to the actual speech of Southern blacks (p. 71)."

Mencken didn't mention how blacks were supposed to have gone to the minstrel shows so that they might pick up the new "lingo," nor of why in the world they would be motivated to do so.

Pidgins

Linguists today support the view that Black English developed from the pidgin versions of English, Dutch, Spanish, and Portuguese used during the slave era. A pidgin is a contact vernacular, a form of language that arises spontaneously whenever two people lack a common language. It is a mixture of two (or possibly more) languages that has been modified to eliminate the more difficult features, such as irregular verb forms (Kay & Sankoff, 1974; Slobin, 1977). Function words like determiners (*the, a, an*) and prepositions (*in, on, across*) are commonly dropped. Function markers like case are eliminated, as are tense and plurals.[3]

---

[3]The broken English that Johnny Weismeuller used in the Tarzan movies from the 1930s and 1940s, which still air on TV, reflects fairly accurately the features of a pidgin.

European slavers came from England, France, Spain, Portugal, and Holland. Their human cargo came from a huge area of Western Africa, including what is now Gambia, the Ivory Coast, Ghana, Nigeria, and Zaire. These languages mixed together to serve as the basis for the early pidgins. McCrum et al. (1986) suggested that the pidgins began developing shortly after the slaves were captured, because the traders separated those who spoke the same language to prevent collaboration that might lead to rebellion. Chained in the holds of the slave ships, the captives had every incentive to continue using pidgin to establish a linguistic community. It is more likely, however, that the pidgins already were well established among the villages responsible for capturing and selling tribesmen and tribeswomen to the European slavers. Trade in humans as well as commodities had a long history in the region, and those who were captured may have grown up using one or more pidgins for trade in addition to their native languages. At the very least, they would have started using a pidgin almost immediately after capture. They would not have waited until they were placed on ships headed for the New World.

Creolization

Once in America, the slaves had to continue using pidgin English to communicate with their owners and with one another. Matters changed, however, when the slaves began having children. A fascinating phenomenon occurs when children are born into a community that uses a pidgin: They spontaneously regularize the language. They add function words, regularize verbs, and provide a grammar where none really existed before. When the children of the pidgin-speaking slaves began speaking, they spoke a Creole, not a pidgin. A Creole is a full language in the technical sense, with its own grammar, vocabulary, and pragmatic conventions.

Why, then, is Black English classified as a dialect of English rather than a Creole? The answer is that the Creole spoken in North America underwent a process of *decreolization*. True Creoles, like those spoken in the Caribbean, experienced reduced contact with the major contributory languages. Papiamento, the Creole spoken in the Dutch Antilles, offers a good example. This language is a mixture of Dutch, French, and English. Although Dutch has long been the official language of the Antilles, the linguistic influences of French and English disappeared about 200 years ago, and the influence of Dutch has waned significantly in this century. As a result, Papiamento continued to develop in its own way; it did not move closer to Standard Dutch. A different process occurred in the United States. The influence of Standard English on the slave Creole increased over the years, especially after the abolition of slavery. Thus, the Creole that was spoken by large numbers of slaves shifted closer and closer to Standard

English, until at some point it stopped being a Creole and became a dialect. It is closer to English than to any other language, which is why speakers of Standard English can understand Black English but not a Creole.

Although the process of decreolization was powerful, Black English preserved many features of its Creole and pidgin roots, which extend to the West African tribal languages as well as to Dutch, French, Portuguese, and Spanish. The most visible of these features are grammatical, and for generations these grammatical differences have led large numbers of Americans to assume that Black English was merely a degenerate version of Standard English. Speakers were believed to violate grammatical rules every time they used the language. Works like Dillard's, however, demonstrated that Black English has its own grammar, which is a blend of Standard English and a variety of West African languages seasoned with European languages.

Many people observe that there is a strong similarity between Black English and the English used by white Southerners, but the dialects are not the same, even though they are quite similar. Blacks and whites lived in close-knit communities in the South for generations. White children played with black children, who exerted a powerful influence on the white-minority dialect. As Slobin (1977) indicated, language change occurs primarily in the speech of children, and throughout the slave era white and black children were allowed to play together. Because whites were the minority, the various Southern dialects shifted toward Black English as Black English simultaneously shifted toward the various Southern dialects until they were closer to each other than to any other American dialect.

Socioeconomic status (SES) is often a more salient factor in dialect variation in the South than region, although region continues to play a major role owing to the tendency among Southerners to resist the increase in mobility that has characterized other parts of the nation. Anyone traveling from Virginia to South Carolina will recognize three distinct major dialects linked to region; however, within a given region there are additional dialectic variations linked to socioeconomic status. The Research Triangle area in North Carolina—composed of Raleigh, Durham, and Chapel Hill—has at least four distinct dialects, even though there are no geographical factors hindering travel or communication. These dialects are linked to SES and education.

Ebonics

The argument that students have a right to their own language has influenced discussions of dialect since the late 1960s. It emerged out of the Civil Rights Movement and concern that school policies that stress Standard English and disallow the use of Black English for recitation and writing are discriminatory and place an unfair burden on African-American children (see Robinson, 1990). From this perspective, Standard English is viewed as an obstacle to learning. The argument is that Black English Vernacular should be legitimized in the schools, which means that it would be deemed acceptable for recitation and writing assignments.[4] Some schools during the early 1970s embraced the notion of students' right to their own language with great enthusiasm and issued specially prepared textbooks written in Black English rather than Standard English. As the Civil Rights Movement dissolved, the issue of students' rights to their own language moved into the background for most teachers until the early 1990s, when postmodern pedagogical agendas tied to what is known as *radical pedagogy* made it a hot topic among educators once again.[5]

In 1996, the discussion entered the public arena when the superintendent of the Oakland, California, schools issued a policy statement declaring Black English—or, more accurately, *Ebonics*—to be a separate language.[6] The statement attributed the differences between Standard English and Ebonics to genetic factors and proposed that African-American students be taught Standard English as though it were a foreign language. Content courses were to be taught in Black English. The idea that Black English is a separate language flies in the face of the evidence that it is a dialect, but the teachers and administrators who issued the Oakland policy statement probably were well intentioned and motivated by the correct notion that the home dialect defines who each student is. Home language is at the heart of important bonds between children and their families. When the schools require students to master and ultimately use Standard English, they are subverting students' sense of personal identity and are weakening the home bond.

There is a powerful tension between the role language plays in students' personal identities and our schools' obligation to teach Standard English. Generally, those who embrace students' right to their own language deny this ob-

---

[4]Advocates of bilingualism have adopted this argument in an effort to provide better support of non-English-speaking students. The goal is to offer content-area instruction in the students' home language (L_1) while they study English as a second language (L_2).

[5]Although the details of radical pedagogy are far beyond the scope of this book, some discussion is necessary. Radical pedagogy is tied to Marxist ideology. It proposes that the nation's schools and colleges are instruments of some military-industrial complex that controls our lives; in this account, schools are places where young people are socially engineered to be docile, obedient servants of the ruling elite. The goal of radical pedagogy is "liberation," which is based on the principle of awakening students to their previous conditioning through shouting down ideas and views that mirror those of the status quo. From this perspective, Standard English is a tool of the ruling elite, whereas Black English is a dialect of the downtrodden, the oppressed. Thus, those who advocate Standard English in our schools, as opposed to those who advocate students' right to their own language, are supporters or dupes of the military-industrial complex.

[6]The origins of the term *Ebonics* is unclear. A neologism from the words *ebony* and *phonics,* it appears to have been first used in the early 1970s.

ligation, but their position is not taken seriously by many outside education. For example, in 1979, the question of this obligation entered the legal arena when a group of attorneys sued the Ann Arbor School District board on behalf of 11 children who spoke Black English and who were failing in school. The suit alleged that the district had not prepared teachers to instruct children whose home dialect was BEV. Although this case is perhaps best seen as yet another example of the appalling, unmitigated arrogance of judges, whose self-enhancing biases too commonly allow them to presume that they can understand and make judgments on complex topics after only a few hours of testimony, it nevertheless sets an inescapable precedent. Ruling for the plaintiffs, the court (Memorandum Opinion and Order, 1979) found that: "Black English is not a language used by the mainstream of society—black or white. It is not an acceptable method of communication in the educational world, in the commercial community, in the community of the arts and science, or among professionals (p. 1378).

The district was ordered to provide teachers with 20 hours of linguistic training that gave them insight into the structure of Black English. This training, however, did not include any instruction on how to utilize the new knowledge to teach better, nor did it provide any reduction in the underlying tension between home and school languages. If anything, the suit and the subsequent order exacerbated the overall problem by declaring, as a legal finding of fact, that Standard English is the language of schools and by simultaneously holding schools and teachers accountable for the failure of students whose home dialects cause difficulties when it comes to literacy. The ruling, in other words, is profoundly illogical—which is just what those familiar with the nations's legal system have come to expect.

Perhaps the biggest difficulty with the argument that students have the right to use their own language in school is that it oversimplifies a complex problem. Schools are obligated to provide students with the tools they need to realize their full potential, and they must do so within the framework of sociolinguistic realities. It is the case that people view certain dialects negatively; indeed, Wolfram et al. (1998) correctly noted that these negative views are held *even by those who speak these dialects*. Such views can hinder people's access to higher education and jobs. One can rail against the unfairness of this situation, but the reality remains unchanged, and efforts like the students' right to their own language movement do little more than provide some measure of political venting.

In some instances, they can be harmful. Students who in the late 1960s went through high school using texts written in Black English, for example, had an extremely difficult time when they enrolled in college. They discovered that they could not easily read their college texts, and many dropped out. It is worth asking how many of these students would have been able to complete college if they had not been caught up in an experiment. Equally important, there is no evidence to suggest that substituting Black English for Standard English improves academic performance one iota. Those who argue for students' right to their own language today have forgotten—or never learned—this lesson from the past. In addition, it is fairly easy to see that below the surface of the argument lies a disturbingly racist point of view: There is the undeniable—and unacceptable—hint that students who speak Black English are incapable of mastering Standard English. In addition, the suggestion that these students should learn Standard English in the way that English-speaking children currently learn, say, Spanish in our schools cannot be taken seriously for two reasons. Black English is not a foreign language, and even if it were, the awful state of foreign-language instruction in our schools does not bode well for a policy that intends to improve performance.

The situation that speakers of Black English face may be unfair. It may even be unjust. But it reflects the reality of language prejudice, which is extremely resistant to change because language is a central factor in how people identify themselves and others. Nonstandard dialects, because they are linked to SES and education levels, tend to be associated with negative traits. For this reason, many businesses may reject applicants for employment in certain positions if they speak nonstandard English. An African-American applicant for a position at a prestigious company may be rejected because he or she pronounces *ask* as *ax*. Efforts to change society such that people more readily accept Black English or any other nonstandard dialect reflect a lack of awareness of the dynamics of language. It simply is not possible to legislate language.[7]

In addition, efforts to validate the use of nonstandard English in education do little to modify the status of students from disadvantaged backgrounds. They do not expand students' language skills in any way that will help them overcome the very real obstacle to socioeconomic mobility that nonstandard English presents. As Williams (1992) noted, these efforts keep "these students ghettoized" (p. 836). Consequently, large numbers of educators believe that schools must adopt an *additive* stance with respect to dialects, and they view mastery and use of Standard English as complementing the home dialect, whatever it may be. This additive stance calls for legitimizing and valuing all dialects

---

[7]The French government has been trying to legislate language since the 1950s. Concerned that French is "debased" by Americanisms, the government regularly purges the language of English terms, such as *blue jeans*. Nevertheless, the terms remain a part of the French language and show no signs of disappearing. Likewise, recent reports indicate that the French government is concerned that English dominates the Internet. In 1997, it committed almost $30 million to study ways to make French a stronger presense—apparently without considering fundamental linguistic principles. Given the overwhelming dominance of the United States in the computer industry, and perhaps an even greater dominance on the Net, few users (including those who are French) have any motivation to use French when they are online. It simply is much more effective to use English. Those who do not—or cannot—are unable to join fully the group of people who use the Net regularly.

while simultaneously recognizing the appropriateness conditions that govern language use in specific situations. From this perspective, there are situations in which Black English is appropriate and Standard English is not; and there are situations in which Standard English is appropriate and Black English is not. The goals of schools, therefore, should include helping students recognize the different conditions and mastering the nuances of Standard English.

BLACK ENGLISH GRAMMAR

Black English grammar differs from Standard English grammar in several ways. For example, it normally omits the *s* suffix on present-tense verbs ("He talk pretty fast"), except in those instances where the speaker overcorrects in an effort to approximate standard patterns ("I goes to work"). It drops the *g* from participles ("He goin' now"), and it also uses four separate negators: *dit'n, not, don'* and *ain'*. Consider the following sentences:

1. Fred dit'n come yesterday.
2. Macarena not comin'.
3. Fritz don' eat them pies.
4. Fritz don' be goin' the the store.
5. Macarena ain' eat.
6. She ain' be eatin'.

One of the more significant differences between Standard English and Black English is that the two dialects treat tense and aspect differently. On page 24, we examined aspect as a feature of the English verb form, looking specifically at progressive and perfect forms. At that point, we considered the fact that Standard English marks verb tenses as past or present and that it provides the option of indicating the static or ongoing nature of an action (aspect) through the use of these two verb forms. Black English, in contrast, allows for optional tense marking but requires that the action be marked as momentary or continuous. Sentences 3 and 5 indicate a momentary action, whether or not it is in the past, whereas 4 and 6 indicate progressive action, whether or not it is in the past.

Aspect also allows speakers to stretch out the time of a verb, an important characteristic of Black English, which uses the verb form *be* to accomplish the task. Sentences 7 and 8, for example, have quite different meanings:

7. Macarena workin'.
8. Macarena be workin'.

In Sentence 7, Macarena may be working today, at this moment, but she normally doesn't. In Sentence 8, on the other hand, Macarena has been conscientiously working for a long time. We see similar examples in the following:

9. Fritz studyin' right now.
10. Fritz be studyin' every afternoon.

Studyin' agrees in aspect with *right now*, and *be studyin'* agrees in aspect with *every afternoon*. It therefore would be ungrammatical in Black English to say or write "Fritz studyin' every afternoon" or "Fritz be studyin' right now" (Baugh, 1983; Fasold, 1972; Wolfram, 1969).

Black English uses *been*, the participial form of *be*, as a past-perfect marker: *Been* signals that an action occurred in the distant past or that it was completed totally (Rickford, 1975). In this sense it is similar to the past-perfect form *have + verb* and *have + been* in Standard English as the following sentences illustrate:

11. They had told us to leave. (standard)
12. They been told us to leave. (black)
13. Kerri had eaten all the cake. (standard)
14. Kerri been eat all the cake. (black)
15. She had been hurt. (standard)
16. She been been hurt. (black)

Been is also used to assert that an action initiated in the past is still in effect, as in the following:

17. Macarena has known Fritz more than 3 months now. (standard)
18. Macarena been been knowin' Fritz more than 3 month now. (black)

Questions in Black English generally take two forms, depending on the aspect involved. Someone inquiring about a short-term state, for example, might ask:

19. Is you hungry?

The same question concerning a long-term state, however, would be structured as:

20. Do you be hungry?

We also see from Sentence 19 that *is* can function in two ways in Black English, as an emphasis marker and as a question marker. Thus, Sentence 21 is perfectly grammatical:

21. I is hungry.

A variant of 21 would be 22:

22. I'm is hungry.

As a question, 21 also would have two variants:

23. Is I hungry?
24. Is I'm hungry?

Other important features of Black English grammar are cited in the following list:

- The present tense is used in narratives to indicate past action, as in *They goes to the market.*
- When cardinal adjectives precede nouns, the noun is not pluralized, as in *The candy cost 1 dollar and 50 cent.*
- Relative pronouns in the subject position of a relative clause can be dropped, as in *Fritz like the woman has red hair.*
- The possessive marker is dropped, as in *He found Macarena coat.*
- Whereas Standard English alternates a negative and a positive in a sentence (*I never want to see you again*), Black English uses double negatives, as in *He don' never goin' call.*[8]

APPLYING KEY IDEAS

---

1. In addition to your own dialect, how many others are there in your community that you are aware of?
2. What may be some of the factors that inhibit the acquisition and use of Standard English among children?

---

[8]Criticism of the double negative is made on the grounds that two negatives make a positive. On this account, "I ain' got no money" means that the speaker actually has a great deal of money. Although two negatives make a positive in mathematics, they simply do not in language. No one ever, under any circumstances, would understand "I ain't got no money" to mean anything other than the fact that the speaker is broke. Furthermore, double negatives have a long history in English and are not peculiar to Black English.

3. Listen carefully to a dialect in your community and list the features that differ from your home dialect.
4. Television news anchors generally speak what is known as "broadcast standard," a hybrid dialect that is often identified as coming closest to spoken Standard English. What are some features of your home dialect that differ from broadcast standard?
5. What value is there in knowing that Black English Vernacular is well structured according to its own grammar?

CHICANO ENGLISH

The number of Spanish speakers in the United States has increased significantly over the last 40 years. Exact numbers are impossible to come by because so many Spanish speakers are illegal immigrants who avoid census takers; thus, census estimates vary a great deal. Conservatively, there are about 20 million Spanish speakers today; less conservatively, there are more than 40 million. In many parts of the Southwest, Spanish is the dominant language, and some demographers predict that it will be the dominant language throughout the Southwest early in the 21st century.

Chicano is a term that gained popularity in the 1960s to designate the children of Mexican immigrants. These young people sought their own identity distinct from Mexicans and Americans and recoiled from the appellation *Mexican Americans*. Since the 1960s, the number of Spanish-speaking immigrants from countries other than Mexico, which was very low prior to about 1970, has increased dramatically. Today, there are immigrants from Cuba, Nicaragua, Peru, Colombia, El Salvador, Costa Rica, and other Spanish-speaking countries. This situation makes it technically incorrect to use the term *Chicano English* to refer to the dialect that is spoken by large numbers of people with Mexican, Central American, and South American roots, but it nevertheless is used widely because it seems to be the most innocuous. *Mexican-American English Vernacular* clearly is unacceptable. *Hispanic English* is rejected by almost everyone from Mexico and South America, who argue that Hispanics are people from Spain. *Latino English* is resisted quite strongly by those of Mexican heritage, for they associate *Latino* with the white, Spanish ruling class, which is generally despised by those of mixed blood. As this book is being published, a popular T-shirt in cities like Chicago and Los Angeles, with large Spanish-speaking communities, depicts a group of dark-skinned farmers executing a group of white-skinned businessmen with the caption: "No soy latino. Soy Mexicano. Los latinos son la gente blanca de Sud America que los indios como yo queran matar. (I am not Latino. Latinos are the white people of South America who Indians like me want to kill.)"

Unlike Black English Vernacular, Chicano English has not been particularly well researched. One reason may be the complexity of studying a dialect that is influenced by a linguistic environment quite different from most others in the country. This environment includes many monolingual Spanish speakers, bilingual English–Spanish speakers, and monolingual English speakers. It also includes a variety of Spanish as well as English dialects. Chicano English blends all of these influences into its own unique sound.

Like all other dialects, Chicano English is closely linked to SES and education. Whereas there is evidence of dialect leveling in Black English, there is no evidence of a similar trend in Chicano English, probably because Mexican Americans have not benefited as extensively from affirmative-action programs as African Americans. The Mexican-American middle class has not grown appreciably during the last 30 years, and dropout rates have remained at about 50% before the end of the 10th grade for nearly two generations. The number of Mexican Americans attending university has increased only slightly since the mid-1970s.

Without the prospect of joining the middle class, there is little motivation to master Standard English and little motivation to excel in school. The situation is exacerbated by the widespread belief among Mexican Americans, even those whose families have been in the United States for generations, that they will return to Mexico one day. As is the case with many students who speak Black English Vernacular, large numbers of students who speak Chicano English have the perception that they are shut out of the socioeconomic mainstream, and this perception strengthens the bonding effect of the home dialect. Standard English represents the culture of otherness, perhaps even of repression, and it is difficult for many who speak Chicano English to see any value in that culture. The result is a culture clash that is evident not just in language but in dress, hairstyles, even posture.

The two most noticeable features of Chicano English are its grammar and pronunciation. It incorporates the double negative, for example, from Spanish, as in the following examples:

25. I didn't do nothing all day.
26. She couldn't dance or nothing.

Another influence involves possession, which in Spanish is designated using a prepositional phrase unless possession is marked by a pronoun, as in the following examples:

27. *El es mi novio.* (He is my boyfriend)
28. *Los ojos de Raul me hicieron enamorado.* (Raul's eyes made me fall in love)

Standard English allows both forms, but the preferred form involves the possessive marker rather than the prepositional phrase. Chicano English also allows both forms, but the possessive marker is not given preference:

29. This is the house of my mother (Chicano)
29a. This is my mother's house (standard)
30. The smile of Macarena lifted a thousand hearts. (Chicano)
30a. Macarena's smile lifted a thousand hearts.(standard)

Another grammatical feature involves the prepositions *in* and *on*. Spanish uses *en* for both, and Chicano English allows *in* to serve double duty, as in the following examples:

31. Macarena got in the bus before she realized that she had no change. (Chicano)
31a. Macarena go on the bus before she realized that she had no change. (standard)
32. We got in our bikes and rode down the hill. (Chicano)
32a. We got on our bikes and rode down the hill. (standard)

The final grammatical feature we examine here involves what is sometimes referred to as *topicalization*. Standard English has several mechanisms that allow us to focus on the topic of a sentence, as in Sentence 33:

33. *A complete fool* I was to believe her.

The italicized noun phrase has been fronted to put greater emphasis on it. Chicano English uses a variation of this mechanism, in which the topic is fronted but then is repeated as a pronoun. This structure has the effect of providing greater emphasis on the topic. Consider the following sentences:

34. My car, it was really fast.
35. Macarena, she liked to bake cookies on Sundays.
36. The party at Buggsy's, it got way out of control.

The phonological differences between Spanish and English cause students who speak Chicano English to have certain difficulties with spelling when they write. Students may hear the short /i/ sound in a word like *live* as a long /e/ sound. Consequently, they will write sentences such as the following:

37. I used to leave in Burbank, but now I leave in North Hollywood. (Chicano)
37a. I used to live in Burbank, but now I live in North Hollywood. (standard)
38. Seens I been in L.A. I ain' found no job. (Chicano)
38a. Since I have been in L.A. I haven't found a job. (standard)

In addition, Chicano English sometimes converts /v/ to /f/ when it appears between vowels, and it often replaces /t/ with /k/ at the end of words when it follows a consonant. It also commonly drops the *-ed* past-participle marker:

39. I try to safe as much money as I can. (Chicano)
39a. I try to save as much money as I can. (standard)
40. Buggsy watched the wafes at the beach. (Chicano)
40a. Buggy watched the waves at the beach. (standard)
41. My parents were raised old-fashion, and so they are really strick with me. (Chicano)
41a. My parents were raised old-fashioned, and so they are really strict with me. (standard)
42. We didn' like the Simpson verdick. (Chicano)
42a. We didn't like the Simpson verdict. (standard)

APPLYING KEY IDEAS

1. Chicano English gets much less attention than Black English. What might be some reasons?
2. Some teachers who work with students who speak Chicano English assume that the key to helping them move toward Standard English lies in eliminating the influence of Spanish. Why is this assumption incorrect?
3. Given the characteristics of Chicano English described previously, what kinds of activities could most benefit students who use this dialect?
4. Mainstream white teachers commonly find it difficult to avoid a negative reaction to the culture of their Chicano-English-speaking students. What might be some pedagogical consequences of this reaction, and what might be some ways to reduce its strength?
5. Some critics of the efforts to help students who speak Chicano English become bidialectical argue that our schools really should be helping students and teachers alike master Spanish because this will be the majority language in a large portion of the United States in just a few years. What are some weaknesses in this argument?

References

Baker, W., Prideaux, G., & Derwin, B. (1973). Grammatical properties of sentences as a basis for concept formation. *Journal of Psycholinguistic Research, 2*, 201–220.

Bateman, D., & Zidonis, F. (1966). *The effect of a study of transformational grammar on the writing of ninth and tenth graders.* Champaign, IL: National Council of Teachers of English.

Baugh, J. (1983). *Black street speech: Its history, structure, and survival.* Austin: University of Texas Press.

Berthoff, A. (1981). *The making of meaning: Metaphors, models, and maxims for writing teachers.* Montclair, NJ: Boynton/Cook.

Berthoff, A. (1983). A comment on inquiry and composing. *College English, 45*, 605–606.

Bever, T. (1970). The cognitive basis of linguistic structures. In J. Hayes (Ed.), *Cognition and the development of language.* New York: Wiley.

Bloomfield, L. (1933). *Language.* New York: Holt, Rinehart & Winston.

Boas, F. (1911). *Handbook of American Indian languages.* Washington, DC: Smithsonian Institution.

Bohannon, J., & Stanowicz, L. (1988). The issue of negative evidence: Adult responses to children's language errors. *Developmental Psychology, 24*, 98–117.

Braddock, R., Lloyd-Jones, R., & Schoer, L. (1963). *Research in written composition.* Champaign, IL: National Council of Teachers of English.

Burns, J., & Anderson, D. (1991). Cognition and watching television. In D. Tupper & K. Cicerone (Eds.), *Neuropsychology of everyday life.* Boston: Kluwer.

Chall, J. (1996). American reading achievement: Should we worry? *Research in the Teaching of English, 30*, 303–310.

Chomsky, N. (1955). *The logical structure of linguistic theory.* Mimeograph, MIT.

Chomsky, N. (1957). *Syntactic structures.* The Hague: Mouton.

Chomsky, N. (1965). *Aspects of the theory of syntax.* Cambridge, MA: MIT Press.

Coulson, A. (1996). Schooling and literacy over time: The rising cost of stagnation and decline. *Research in the Teaching of English, 30*, 311–327.

Crosby, A. (1997). *The measure of reality: Quantification and Western society, 1250–1600.* Cambridge, England: Cambridge University Press.

Dillard, J. (1973). *Black English: Its history and usage in the United States.* New York: Vintage.

Elbow, P. (1973). *Writing without teachers.* New York: Oxford University Press.

Elley, W., Barham, I., Lamb, H., & Wyllie, M. (1976). The role of grammar in a secondary school English curriculum. *New Zealand Journal of Educational Studies, 10*, 26–42. Reprinted in *Research in the Teaching of English, 10*, 5–21.

Elman, J., Bates, E., Johnson, H., Karmiloff-Smith, A., Parisi, D., & Plunkett, K. (1996). *Rethinking Innateness: A connectionist perspective on development.* Cambridge, MA: MIT Press.

Fasold, R. (1972). *Tense marking in Black English: A linguistic and social analysis.* Washington, DC: Center for Applied Linguistics.

Fodor, J. (1983). *The modularity of mind.* Cambridge, MA: MIT Press.

Fodor, J., Bever, T., & Garrett, M. (1974). *The psychology of language.* New York: McGraw-Hill.

Fodor, J., & Garrett, M. (1966). Some reflections on competence and performance. In J. Lyons & R. Wales (Eds.), *Psycholinguistics papers: Proceedings of the 1966 Edinburgh Conference.* Edinburgh: Edinburgh University Press.

Gale, L. (1968). An experimental study of two fifth-grade language-arts programs: An analysis of the writing of children taught linguistic grammar compared to those taught traditional grammar. *Dissertation Abstracts, 28,* 4156A.

Glucksberg, S., & Danks, J. (1969). Grammatical structure and recall: A function of the space in immediate memory or recall delay? *Perception and Psychophysics, 6,* 113–117.

Graves, D. (1981). The growth and development of first grade writers. In D. Graves (Ed.), *A case study observing the development of primary children's composing, spelling, and motor behaviors during the writing process. Final report.* Durham: University of New Hampshire Press.

Hall, M. (1972). *The language experience approach for the culturally disadvantaged.* Newark, DE: International Reading Association.

Harris, R. (1993). *The linguistics wars.* NY: Oxford University Press.

Haugen, E. (1966). *Language conflict and language planning: The case of modern Norwegian.* Cambridge, MA: Harvard University Press.

Healy, J. (1990). *Endangered minds: Why children don't think and what we can do about it.* New York: Simon & Schuster.

Herrnstein, R., & Murray, C. (1994). *The bell curve: Intelligence and class structure in American life.* New York: Free Press.

Hirsch, E. (1987). *Cultural literacy: What every American needs to know.* Boston: Houghton Mifflin.

Hudson, R. (1980). *Sociolinguistics.* Cambridge, England: Cambridge University Press.

Johnson-Laird, P. (1983). *Mental models.* Cambridge, MA: Harvard University Press.

Kalat, J. (1995). *Biological psychology,* (5th ed.). Pacific Grove, CA: Brooks/Cole.

Katz, L. (1989). *Engaging children's minds.* Norwood, NJ: Ablex.

Kay, P., & Sankoff, G. (1974). A language-universals approach to pidgins and Creoles. In D. DeCamp & I. Hancock (Eds.), *Pidgins and Creoles: Current trends and prospects.* Washington, DC: Georgetown University Press.

Kelso, J. (1995). *Dynamic patterns: The self-organization of brain and behavior.* Cambridge, MA: MIT Press.

Kilma, E. (1964). Negation in English. In J. Fodor & J. Katz (Eds.), *The structure of language.* Englewood Cliffs, NJ: Prentice Hall.

Langacker, R. (1987). *Foundations of cognitive grammar (Vol. 1): Theoretical prerequisites.* Stanford, CA: Stanford University Press.

Langacker, R. (1990). *Concept, image, and symbol: The cognitive basis of grammar.* New York: Mouton de Gruyter.

Lees, R. (1962). The grammatical basis of some semantic notions. In B. Choseed & A. Guss, *Report on the eleventh annual round table meeting on linguistics and language studies.* Washington, DC: Georgetown University Press.

Macaulay, R. (1973). Double standards. *American Anthropologist, 75,* 1324–1337.

McCrum, R., Cran, W., & MacNeil, R. (1986). *The story of English.* New York: Viking.

Mellon, J. (1969). *Transformational sentence-combining: A method for enhancing the development of syntactic fluency in English composition* (NCTE Research Rep. No. 10). Champaign, IL: National Council of Teachers of English.

Mencken, H. (1936). *The American language: An inquiry into the development of English in the United States.* New York: Knopf.

Meringoff, L. (1980). Influence of the medium on children's story apprehension. *Journal of Educational Psychology, 72,* 240–249.

Miller, G. (1962). Some psychological studies of grammar. *American Psychologist, 17,* 748–762.

Miller, G., & McKean, K. (1964). A chronometric study of some relations between sentences. *Quarterly Journal of Experimental Psychology, 16,* 297–308.

Murray, D. (1982). *Learning by teaching.* Montclair, NJ: Boynton/Cook.

National assessment of educational progress report. (1994). Washington, DC: U.S. Government Printing Office.

O'Hare, F. (1973). Sentence combining: Improving student writing without formal grammar instruction. *NCTE Committee on Research Report Series, Number 15.* Urbana, IL: National Council of Teachers of English.

Orr, E. (1987). *Twice as less.* New York: Norton.

Parker, R. (1979). From Sputnik to Dartmouth: Trends in the teaching of composition. *English Journal, 68*(6), 32–37.

Pinker, S. (1994). *The language instinct: How the mind creates language.* New York: Morrow.

Plato. (1937). Republic. In B. Jowett (Ed. & Trans.), *The dialogues of Plato* (Vol. I, pp. 773–776). New York: Random House.

Rickford, J. (1975). Carrying the new wave into syntax: The case of Black English *been.* In R. Fasgold & R. Shuy (Eds.), *Analyzing variation in language.* Washington, DC: Georgetown University Press.

Robinson, J. (1990). *Conversations on the written word: Essays on language and literacy.* Portsmouth, NH: Boynton/Cook.

Rose, M. (1984). *Writer's block: The cognitive dimension.* Carbondale, IL: Southern Illinois University Press.

Rumelhart, D., & McClelland, J. (1986). *Parallel distributed processing: Explorations in the microstructure of cognition* (Vols. 1 & 2). Cambridge, MA: MIT Press.

Searle, J. (1992). *The rediscovery of the mind.* Cambridge, MA: MIT Press.

Singer, J. (1980). The power and limitations of television: A cognitive-affective analysis. In P. Tannenbaum (Ed.), *The entertainment functions of television.* Hillsdale, NJ: Lawrence Erlbaum Associates.

Slobin, D. (1977). Language change in childhood and history. In J. Macnamara (Ed.), *Language, learning and thought.* New York: Academic.

Slobin, D., & Welsh, C. (1973). Elicited imitation as a research tool in developmental psycholinguistics. In C. Ferguson & D. Slobin (Eds.), *Studies of child language development.* New York: Holt, Rinehart and Winston.

Smolin, L. (1997). *Life of the cosmos.* New York: Oxford University Press.

Trudgill, P. (1974). *Sociolinguistics: An introduction.* New York: Penguin.

Vail, P. (1989). *Smart kids with school problems.* New York: Plume.

Vygotsky, L. (1978). *Mind in society.* Cambridge, MA: Harvard University Press.

Wanner, E. (1988). Psychology and linguistics in the sixties. In W. Hirst (Ed.), *The making of cognitive science: Essays in honor of George A. Miller.* Cambridge, England: Cambridge University Press.

White, R. (1965). The effect of structural linguistics on improving English composition compared to that of prescriptive grammar or the absence of grammar instruction. *Dissertation Abstracts, 25,* 5032.

Whitehead, C. (1966). The effect of grammar diagramming on student writing skills. *Dissertation Abstracts, 26,* 3710.

Williams, J. (1992). Politicizing literacy. *College English, 54,* 833–842.

Williams, J. (1985). Coherence and cognitive style. *Written Communication, 2,* 473–491.

Williams, J. (1987). Covert linguistic behavior during writing tasks: Psychophysiological differences between above-average and below-average writers. *Written Communication, 4,* 310–328.

Williams, J. (1993). Rule-governed approaches to language and composition. *Written Communication, 10,* 542–568.

Williams, J. (1998). *Preparing to teach writing: Research, theory, and practice* (2nd ed.). Mahwah, NJ: Lawrence Erlbaum Associates.

Williams, R., & Herrup, K. (1988). The control of neuron number. *Annual Review of Neuroscience, 11,* 423-453.

Wolfram, W. (1969). *A sociolinguistic description of Detroit Negro speech.* Washington, DC: Center for Applied Linguistics.

Wolfram, W., Christan, A., & Adger, L. (1998). *Dialects in schools and communities.* Mahwah, NJ: Lawrence Erlbaum Associates.

Author Index

Subject Index

A

Acquired language, 256
  language usage and, 6–7, 149–150
Active constructions, 143–144,
     154–155, 171, 200, 227–228,
     235
Adjectivals, 29t–33, 57, 67, 80
Adjective complements, 29, 106
Adjective phrases, 57–58
Adjectives, 9, 29t, 34, 48, 155, *see also*
     Predicate adjectives
Adverbials, 28–33, 30, 42, 67, 101, 126,
     129–130, 143, 206, *see also*
     Transformation rules
  movement of, 209–221
  prepositional phrases and, 39, 80,
     210
  subordinate clauses and, 37–38, 100,
     106
Adverbs, 41, 80, 146, 206, 209
Ambiguity, 71, 79
Antecedents, 19, 20, 173
Articles
  definite, 34
  indefinite, 34, 48
  phrase-structure rules and, 95, 97

Aspect, 24, 90, 256–257

B

Black English, 260, *see also*
     Creolization; Ebonics; Pidgins
  grammar, 256–258

C

Case, 250, *see also* Pronouns
  language usage and, 17–18, 22
  relative clauses and, 121–122
Chicano English, 259–261
Chomsky, Noam (Syntactic Structures),
     see also Language Acquisition
     Device;
     Transformational-generative
     grammar
  theory of mind and, 141, 144,
     230–231
Classification
  nouns/verbs and, 11–12
  traditional grammar and, 7–8
Clauses, 11, 22–23t, 30, 35, 84,
     129–130, 219, *see also* Com-
     plement clauses; Dependent